baker

the best of international baking

from Australian and New Zealand professionals

Dean Brettschneider and
Lauraine Jacobs

Photographs by
Kieran Scott

TANDEM PRESS

First published in New Zealand in 2001 by

Tandem Press

2 Rugby Road

Birkenhead, Auckland 10

New Zealand

ISBN 1 877178 79 9

Cover and text design by Christine Hansen

Photograph of Kingsley Sullivan on page 138 by Adrian Lander

Produced by *Book* NZ

Printed in Hong Kong by South China Printing Co.

CONTENTS

PROFILES

DEAN BRETTSCHNEIDER is a professional baker and patissier. He began his career at the age of 16 as an apprentice at the award-winning Rangiora Bakery, in a small rural North Canterbury township in New Zealand. In 1988 he won the New Zealand Apprentice of the Year for Baking and Pastry Cooking and captained the victorious New Zealand Baking Training Centre Apprentice Baking Team in the Trans Tasman Baking Competitions in Melbourne.

He worked in the USA, Britain and Europe after completing his apprenticeship, gaining experience in all areas of the baking and patisserie trade, including work in exclusive hotels, supermarket in-store bakeries and alongside some of Europe's leading bakers and pastry chefs. On his return to New Zealand, he was employed on Ernest Adams' research and development team, and attended the American Institute of Baking in Kansas, USA. He then moved on to teach at the New Zealand Baking Training Centre in Christchurch, and two years later bought a small craft bakery, Windsor Cakes, in Dunedin.

Always the competitor, Dean entered and won many awards at the annual New Zealand Baking Society competitions and joined the executive of the society as their youngest member. After three years of running his own business, Dean moved to Auckland to join Goodman Fielder, heading up their technical support department, where he assists customers with problem solving, and supplies staff training and product development. He travels to major bakery expositions throughout the world to ensure he is up to date with all the latest innovations and bakery trends.

Dean regularly writes articles for the *New Zealand Bakers Journal*; gives presentations and demonstrations in New Zealand, Australia and the USA; judges the New Zealand Baker of the Year Competition; and moderates all bakery Trade Certificate Examinations in New Zealand. His philosophy for successful baking is 'commitment, dedication and passion combined with a little fun'.

He lives in Auckland with his wife Susan and their young son, Jason. This is his second book, the first being the award-winning *New Zealand Baker*.

LAURAINE JACOBS is an award-winning senior feature writer and restaurant reviewer for *Cuisine* magazine. She trained at the London Cordon Bleu School of Cookery where she passed the Advanced Certificate of Cookery and is one of only four New Zealanders to have been awarded the prestigious Certified Culinary Professional designation from the International Association of Culinary Professionals.

Lauraine was a principal of Austin's Cooking School and regularly gives cooking classes at Auckland's Epicurean Workshop and other cooking schools in New Zealand. She travels frequently to the USA where she is the President of the IACP, and has spoken at workshops at several international conferences.

She lives in Auckland with her husband Murray and their university student son Scott, and lists her hobbies as golf, food and wine, and e-mailing daughter Katie who has flown the coop to New York. This is her third book for Tandem Press, the first being the award-winning *New Taste, New Zealand*, and most recently the award-winning *New Zealand Baker*.

ACKNOWLEDGEMENTS

We would like to thank all the professional bakers and chefs from around Australia and New Zealand for their generosity in sharing their recipes, and for the time spent with us as we gathered information and asked endless questions.

Susan Brettschneider has been very supportive, proofing Dean's writing, and understanding the late nights and early starts, and holding the home together through frequent absences. Thanks also to Dave Ramsey for his assistance in test baking these recipes.

We are indebted to Tandem Press and all the team who have been associated with the book and its production: Kieran Scott for his brilliant photography, Bob Ross and Helen Benton for their guidance, Jane Hingston for production, Alison Mudford for editing, and designer Christine Hansen for her excellent, appealing layout and design.

—Dean Brettschneider and Lauraine Jacobs, 2001

INTRODUCTION

'BREAD IS THE STAFF OF LIFE.'

Australians and New Zealanders have always been champions of baking – whether in large commercial bakeries churning out loaves by the thousands, the small village bakery turning out just enough bread and cakes for the local community, or the keen housewife baking to fill empty tins and empty tummies. There's nothing more satisfying than the aroma of freshly baked bread, or the knowledge that there is a rich, moist cake waiting to be cut into.

Right from the days of the first settlers, bread has been a very important, indeed staple item, in the national diet. Australia and New Zealand, like most of the western world, has been heavily influenced by the traditional European baker, with his flair for producing a variety of breads, wholesome cakes and dainty pastries. The professional baking industry has relied on a continual influx of mainly French, Dutch and German bakers to lead the way, and right up to the end of the past century it has been these people who have dominated professional baking.

Great baking requires painstaking care, knowledge of technique and procedures, and a great deal of passion and commitment. Recent directions in baking around the world are leading bakers everywhere back to their baking roots. The artisan style of baking, reflecting passion and interest inspired by the feel of the dough, has sparked a return to the smaller, more personal bakery with a highly individual touch.

Another big influence on Antipodean baking has been the shift from tea to coffee in our diet and the rise of the café culture. Social gatherings over a cup of coffee, accompanied by a baking 'treat' have become a daily ritual in our lives. Bakeries, recognising this trend, have met the market by installing comfortable seating, coffee machines and producing tasty cakes and pastries to accompany the coffee they serve.

This book was inspired by such bakers – true professionals who produce top quality baking for an appreciative audience. We sought the classical, the innovative and the passionate bakers who could share their recipes with other professional bakers and the sophisticated home baker. A real cross-section of regional bakers, leaders in the industry, and influences from the great bakers of Europe are included, along with some of the smart new business-driven and artisan-style bakers. We are very grateful to them for generously sharing these recipes and their time. Dean Brettschneider, co-author, has meticulously tested and adapted these professionals' recipes, and shares his vast knowledge and understanding of baking in the book's comprehensive reference section. Dean currently holds the position of technical support manager for the baking industry at Goodman Fielder. In this capacity he assists, advises and counsels bakers and is frequently invited to speak at conferences throughout the world.

HOW TO USE THIS BOOK

The reference section of this book has been carefully written with information on every aspect of baking. There are several comprehensive sections: All About Bread, All About Cakes, All About Pastries, and lots of information about ingredients, measurements and much more. Before attempting the recipes in this book, take the time to read through these notes. In order to be a successful baker it is important to understand and appreciate the background information, the processes and the reasons for following baking formulas. Baking, although a real art, is an exact science with no room for improvisation and error.

The recipes are all set out in metric, imperial and volume (standard American cups and spoons) measurements and should be measured in the exact quantities given, or can be scaled up in direct proportion. If using scales, seek out a set that has increments of one gram or two grams for accuracy. There are charts included that identify faults that commonly occur, and we hope that bakers will find these useful, if anything seems imperfect.

These recipes have all been adapted from the bakeries who supplied them. We hope that bakers will use and enjoy this professional fare, and spend many long, satisfying hours baking.

THE INGREDIENTS

WHEAT FLOUR

Wheat flour is the most important ingredient in the bakery. It provides bulk and structure to most of the baker's products, including breads, cakes, biscuits and pastries. There are many different types and each has been designed for a specific reason or with a finished end product in mind.

Flour is obtained from the cereal wheat. A grain of wheat consists of six main parts, but the endosperm, bran and the germ are the most important:

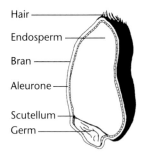

Hair
Endosperm
Bran
Aleurone
Scutellum
Germ

1. Endosperm, 85 percent: is the white part of the wheat grain from which white flour is milled once the bran and germ have been removed.

    It largely consists of:

    *   tightly packed starch granules
    *   soluble proteins (albumens)
    *   insoluble gluten forming proteins (glutenin and gliadin)
    *   oil
    *   moisture
    *   mineral matter

2. Bran, 13 percent: is the outside skin of the wheat grain and consists of six different principal layers, ranging from protective layers to colouring and enzyme active layers. During the milling of white flour the bran layers are mostly removed. The bran is blended back in with the finely ground endosperm (white flour) to produce wheatmeal or brown flour.

3. Germ, 2 percent: is located inside the wheat grain and is the embryo from which wheat can reproduce itself. It is mostly removed in the milling of white flour because the oil soon becomes rancid and the enzymes have a detrimental influence on the fermentation process in bread making. The germ is rich in:

    *   oil
    *   calcium
    *   vitamin B (thiamine, riboflavine and nicotinic acid)
    *   enzymes (diastatic and proteolytic)

The germ is blended back into the endosperm and bran to produce wholemeal flour.

Milling Wheat

There are two styles of flour milling still being done in Australia and New Zealand: stone milling and roller milling, the latter being the most popular for flour quality and profitability.

The stone milling method was used in the Middle Ages to produce a meal from which a loaf of bread could be made. The system consisted of two large grooved stones placed one on top of the other. The bottom one remained stationary while the top one revolved. Grain was fed into the centre of the two stones and gradually crushed to a coarse meal. Generally this mechanism was powered by man, donkey, or in latter years, by water wheel or windmill. Today, authentic stone milled flour is produced by mechanised methods.

Roller milling is more specialised and sophisticated and involves gradual reduction. The wheat grain goes through many different processes to achieve top quality flour, for example:

- cleaning – the grains are checked for foreign matter and screened
- conditioning – this softens the endosperm and toughens the bran layers
- break rolls – fluted rollers fracture and split apart the grain (many times)
- sifters – sieve and separate the bran, endosperm (semolina) and germ
- reduction rolls – smooth rollers crush the endosperm further to finally produce flour
- packaging – flour placed into bag or bulk tankers
- flour testing – flour undergoes many analytical tests to ensure quality
- test baking – flour undergoes test baking

Composition of Flour

The composition of flour will naturally be similar to that of the wheat from which it is milled. An average composition would be:

STRONG FLOUR %	CONSTITUENTS	SOFT FLOUR %
70	Starch	72
11–13	Insoluble gluten forming proteins	7–8
13–15	Moisture	13–15
2.5	Sugar	2.5
1–1.5	Fat	1–1.5
1	Soluble proteins	1
0.5	Mineral salts	0.5

Extraction Rate

This term refers to the amount of flour that is obtained from the wheat after milling, for example, if the flour miller obtains 78 kg of white flour from 100 kg of wheat, the extraction rate equals 78 percent. The extraction rate for wholemeal flour is 100 percent and for pastry flours it is between 55 percent and 65 percent (given that you require a cleaner, whiter speck-free flour for the manufacture of pastry products).

Insoluble Gluten-Forming Proteins

The insoluble proteins present in flour are known as gluten. Gluten is made up of two proteins called glutenin and gliadin, both having different characteristics: glutenin producing elastic properties and gliadin producing extensible properties. Gluten is produced in a bread dough, for example, when water has been added and the dough has been mixed sufficiently to develop the gluten. The suitability of a flour for bakery products is determined by the quality of the gluten and in some cases the quantity it contains. Flour that contains good quality gluten is known as strong flour; flour that contains low quality gluten is known as soft flour.

Storage of Flour

Flour and meals should be stored under the following conditions to prevent deterioration:

- Temperature: 10–16°C (50–60°F)
- Environment: dry conditions
- Time:

White flours	3–6 months
Wholemeal and brown flours	3–4 months
Meals and grains	2–3 months

Always ensure that stock rotation is adhered to: F.I.F.O. (first in, first out).

Hand Test for Flour Strength

The strength of the flour can be identified by squeezing it in the hand. A weak/soft flour will cling and clump together and feels very smooth when the hand is opened, whereas a strong flour will crumble again to a powder and feel slightly coarse when rubbed between the fingers.

Types of Flour

A wide variety of flour is milled from wheat and other grains.

Strong flour contains a high level of protein (gluten) which is beneficial for the manufacture of bread, yeast-raised varieties and puff pastry. Heavy fruit cakes are sometimes made using strong flours.

Plain or Medium flour has been milled to provide medium strength for use in such goods as short pastry products, powder aerated goods (scones, light fruit cakes, muffins, biscuits and slices).

Soft flour has a low protein (gluten) content and is ideal for making cakes, sponges and some biscuits.

Pastry flour has been milled from the centre of the wheat, giving a cleaner, whiter speck-free flour which is ideal for the manufacture of pastry products that require refrigeration or freezing in their raw state. The protein (gluten) level is of medium quality; however, since it is milled from the centre of the wheat grain it is of very good quality with excellent extensibility properties. This flour is mainly used by commercial pastry manufacturers for top quality pies, pastries, sausage rolls, etc.

High ratio flour (special cake flour) is milled to a very fine particle size and heavily bleached, a treatment that increases its moisture absorbing properties and makes it an ideal flour for cakes and sponges that contain a high level of sugar and liquids to the quantity of flour, thus increasing the shelf life. This flour is mainly used in commercial bakeries.

Self rising flour is usually a medium strength flour into which has been blended a proportion of baking powder at the rate of approximately two percent of the flour. It is used for batters, scones, pikelets, etc. This product is mainly used when the weighing of baking powder is difficult due to the small amount required. A simple recipe for self rising flour is 16 parts flour to 1 part baking powder. Sieve several times to achieve an even distribution of flour and baking powder.

Wholemeal flour is milled from the whole wheat grain and therefore contains the bran and germ. It is suitable for all bread and yeast-raised products, pastries, cakes and biscuits. When using wholemeal flour in a recipe, consideration should be given to the obviously high amount of bran the flour contains. Bran acts like tiny pieces of glass within an unbaked product, cutting and damaging the gluten (protein) network that has been developed in order to give strength, structure and volume to the finished baked product. In most cases the addition of extra dried gluten or strong flour is necessary to compensate.

Semolina flour is simply coarsely ground endosperm and can be used for thickening pie fillings, dusting the baker's peel for ease of transferring the breads onto the oven's hearth, and as an ingredient in crusty bread formulations.

Rye flour is the next most popular flour for bread making, after white and wholemeal, and is milled from the cereal rye. Milling of the rye grain is done in the same manner as for the wheat grain. Although rye flour contains some flour proteins, they do not form gluten. Therefore, breads made with 100 percent rye flour will be sticky at the dough stage and heavy and dense after baking. It is common practice to use a percentage of white strong flour when making rye breads, at a ratio of 25–40 percent rye flour and 60–75 percent white strong flour. Rye flour is available as either light rye or dark rye and is commonly used for dusting breads prior to baking.

Rye meal is produced by grinding the entire rye grain. It is coarse and dark and mainly used for pumpernickel bread and rolls.

Gluten flour is simply dried protein (gluten) from within wheat flour. Flour milled in Australia and New Zealand is of excellent quality and the addition of dried gluten is only necessary when excessive amounts of enriching and softening products (fats, sugar, grains and excessive liquids) are used within a recipe.

Cornflour is obtained from the cereal maize. It is almost 100 percent starch and does not contain any insoluble gluten-forming proteins. Cornflour is mainly used as a thickening agent for custards, sauces and fillings. It can also be used to dilute strong flours when short, tender eating qualities are required, for example, in shortbread.

Rice flour is obtained from the cereal rice. It is almost 100 percent starch and does not contain any insoluble gluten-forming proteins. Rice flour is added to cake recipes and biscuits to assist with absorbing the liquids for either keeping qualities or crispness properties, for example, in shortbread.

Soya flour is obtained from the soya bean and is very rich in protein but does not contain any insoluble gluten-forming proteins. It is very high in fat, making it an excellent ingredient for any bread recipe that requires keeping qualities, even texture and increased volume.

Malt flour and malt products are obtained from barley and wheat that have undergone a controlled process known as malting. This begins after the grains have been cleaned.

Germination then takes place in an environment that has been controlled by temperature and humidity. During this period, the starch within the grain is converted into simple sugars. This is then halted when the grains are subjected to heat during the drying stages. Malt products are an important food source for yeast in yeast-raised doughs and the following improvements are to be expected if used:

- volume
- texture
- colour
- flavour
- eating qualities
- increased shelf life

Organic flour is milled from organically grown wheat. This wheat is grown by selected farmers and not cross-contaminated with wheat that is treated with chemical sprays, etc. Commercial flour mills are unable to process organic grains in conjunction with other grains, therefore organic flour is produced in dedicated mills. Most baked products can be made using organic flours. Quality is sometimes variable and yields are usually lower, therefore a premium price is charged.

SALT

Salt is a natural mineral. It comes in many different forms: table salt, sea salt, iodised salt, vacuum salt and rock salt (the latter mainly used for decoration due to its large crystal size). The chemical name is *sodium chloride*.

Salt plays a very important role in baking. More than just a flavour or seasoning enhancer, it also has these functions:

- strengthens the gluten structure and makes it more stretchable
- controls the rate of fermentation within yeast-raised doughs
- enhances the flavour and eating qualities
- improves the crust and crumb colour and stability
- increases the shelf life

Salt is hygroscopic and should be stored away from moisture.

SUGAR

By the term 'sugar' we mean sucrose which is obtained from two sources: cane and beet sugar. They are natural substances and belong to the chemical group of carbohydrates. Once refining of sugar has been completed, it can be categorised into two divisions: grains and syrups.

Grains

- caster sugar – fine crystals
- granulated sugar – coarse crystals
- nib sugar – large crystals (similar to rock salt in size)
- cube sugar
- brown sugar – soft and coarse
- raw sugar
- icing sugar – granulated sugar crushed to a powder, with starch added

Syrups

- golden syrup
- treacle
- honey
- glucose
- molasses

Sugar and syrups possess the following properties:

- sweetness and flavour
- creates tenderness and fineness of texture by weakening the gluten structure (shortens)
- caramelises during baking and gives crust colour
- acts as source of food for yeast during fermentation
- improves shelf life by retaining moisture
- acts as a creaming agent with fats, and as a foaming agent with eggs

Sugar is also hygroscopic and should be stored away from any moisture.

EGGS

An average fresh egg composition is as follows:

	WHOLE EGGS %	WHITES %	YOLKS %
Water	73	86	49
Protein	13	12	17
Fat	12	–	32
Minerals	2	2	2

The types of eggs used in bakeries include:

- shell eggs
- chilled liquid egg pulp
- frozen liquid pulp
- frozen egg white
- dried egg white

Note: egg whites are known as albumen.

Eggs possess the following properties when used in bakery products.

(i)   Moisturising: eggs contain 73 percent water and have the ability to moisturise their own weight in flour.

(ii) Aeration: whisked eggs can incorporate air and increase volume in such products as meringues and sponges.

(iii) Structural: when eggs are subjected to heat during the baking process, they expand, the proteins coagulate (set) and the structure is established.

(iv) Emulsifying: the egg yolk contains a natural emulsifying agent known as lecithin. The lecithin assists in combining two substances or ingredients that normally do not mix well – water and fat.

(v)   Enriching: eggs contain high levels of protein and fat which add to the nutritional value of the baked product.

(vi)   Flavouring: eggs have their own distinctive flavour.

(vii) Colouring: eggs give bakery products a yellow tinge.

(viii) Glazing: when eggs are mixed with the appropriate amount of water or milk, they can be used to glaze the surface of many bakery products.

(ix)   Eating quality: eggs give lightness, moistness and flavour to baked products.

(x)   Keeping qualities: the moisturising, emulsifying, enriching and general softening properties of the egg will assist in extending the shelf life of baked products.

All fresh eggs should be stored in a cool place (preferably in a refrigerator) and be used within three to four weeks of purchase.

The average weight (excluding the shell) of a:

small egg   is 45–50 g
medium egg is 50–55 g
large egg   is 55–60 g

Weighing eggs is not difficult. Lightly beat eggs in a cup or small bowl, then pour into your weighing container. Any left over egg can be stored in the freezer in an air tight container until needed.

MILK AND MILK PRODUCTS

Whole milk is fresh milk as it comes from the cow, with nothing added or removed. It contains 3.5 percent fat (known as milk fat), 8.5 percent nonfat milk solids and 88 percent water. Milk adds the following characteristics to bakery products:

- moistness
- texture
- colour
- eating qualities
- shelf life
- nutrition

Milk also comes in other forms:

Milk powder is whole or skim milk that has been dried to a powder. Both can be reconstituted with water. Milk powders are often used in bread recipes to add richness and assist as a food source for yeast. It will also add crust colour. Store in a cool dry place.

Condensed milk is whole milk that has been heat treated and has had approximately 60 percent of its water removed before adding sugar at a concentration of 42–45 percent. It is then packed into sterile containers. Condensed milk is used as an enriching or sweetening agent, for example, in caramel filling. Once opened, cover and store in a cool place. The high sugar content acts as a preservative.

Evaporated milk is milk, either whole or skim, with approximately 60 percent of the water removed. It is then sterilised and canned. It is not that commonly used in bakeries. Once opened, store in the refrigerator.

Fresh Cream

Fresh cream is not often used as a liquid in doughs or batters, except in a few speciality products. This is mainly due to the high fat content which would act as a shortening agent rather than a moisturising agent.

Cream is more important in the production of fillings, toppings, dessert sauces, and cold desserts such as mousses and bavarois. It can also be flavoured and sweetened; however, care should be taken when doing this as an excess can cause problems like curdling and splitting during processing.

If whipping fresh cream, care should be taken; once overwhipped the only thing to do is to continue whipping it to produce butter. Whipped cream should double in volume.

Fresh cream must always be kept in the refrigerator at 0–4°C (32–40°F) and once used in a bakery product it must be refrigerated.

Imitation Cream

Australians and New Zealanders are not familiar with imitation cream, because we have been brought up on fresh dairy cream.

Nowadays this provides an alternative to fresh cream (useful for people who cannot eat dairy products). Imitation cream is an emulsion which includes water, vegetable oils, sugar and stabilisers. Unopened imitation creams have a very long shelf life, but once opened they must be used as soon as possible.

FATS AND OILS

Fats and oils are obtained from the following sources:

- vegetables
- animals
- milks
- marine

The most common types of fats and oils are:

- butter
- cake and pastry margarine
- shortening
- lard
- high ratio shortening
- vegetable oil

Fats and oils possess the following properties in the production of bakery products:

	VOLUME	SHORTENING	LAYERING	EMULSIFYING	FRYING	FLAVOUR	EATING QUALITIES	NUTRITIONAL VALUE	KEEPING QUALITIES
Butter	•	•	•	•		•	•	•	•
Cake margarine	•	•		•			•	•	•
Pastry margarine	•	•	•				•	•	•
Shortening	•	•		•			•	•	•
Lard		•				•	•	•	•
High ratio shortening	•	•		•			•	•	•
Vegetable oil		•			•		•	•	•

Suitability of fats and oils for bakery products:

	BREAD	FERMENTED PRODUCTS	SWEET PASTRIES	SAVOURY PASTRIES	PUFF PASTRIES	POWDER AERATED PRODUCTS	CAKES	ALMOND PRODUCTS	CHOUX PASTRY
Butter		•	•		•	•	•	•	•
Cake margarine		•	•			•	•	•	•
Pastry margarine		•		•	•				
Shortening	•	•	•	•		•	•		
Lard	•	•		•					
High ratio shortening							•		
Vegetable oil	•	•				•	•		

All fats and oils should be stored in a cool place, 16–21°C (60–70°F), away from direct sunlight, to reduce rancidity (butter must be stored in the refrigerator before use). In some cases fats and oils must be conditioned before use (for example, for croissants the layering butter must be stored at 4°C (40°F), and when fat is required for creaming, as for cake batters, it is advisable to condition the fat to 16–21°C/60–70°F).

BAKING POWDER

Baking powder is a mixture of acid and alkali. The acid content is cream of tartar and the alkali content is bicarbonate of soda. They are mixed together in the ratio of two parts of cream of tartar with one part bicarbonate of soda. Preparation involves sieving the two chemicals several times to ensure even dispersal. However, it is common practice nowadays to purchase blended baking powders.

Baking powder is responsible for the aeration, final volume and often crumb structure of a product. When baking powder becomes moist during the mixing process and is heated in the oven, the reaction between the acid and alkali produces carbon dioxide. The gas lifts and pushes up the final product until the proteins from the eggs and flour have coagulated (set) during baking.

All batters and doughs containing baking powder should be kept cool (21°C/70°F or below) to prevent the gas from working on the table and not in the oven. Hence the products should not sit for too long before baking.

Baking powder should be kept in a cool, dry environment.

CREAM OF TARTAR

Cream of tartar is used in the following ways:
* added to fruit cake batters to help prevent the fruit from sinking
* sometimes added to puff pastry to mellow the flour proteins (gluten), allowing it to become more extensible

BICARBONATE OF SODA

Bicarbonate of soda is used as an aerating agent in ginger goods and also improves the colour of chocolate cake when cocoa powder is used.

NUTS

All nuts have a limited shelf life because of their high fat content. Rancidity occurs quickly if they are incorrectly stored. All nuts should be kept in a cool place, with larger quantities stored in the freezer.

The following are the most commonly used nuts.

- Almonds: available in whole natural, blanched, split, flaked, nibbed and ground.
- Walnuts: used either as pieces or whole for decoration.
- Pecans: expensive and should be used in premium goods.
- Peanuts: are the only nuts to be grown in the ground.
- Coconut: unsweetened is the most used variety. Can be used in cakes or biscuits and is often used as a coating or decoration.
- Hazelnuts: have a distinctive flavour and are best if roasted first.

Nuts are used extensively as an ingredient in many bakery products, including macaroons, almond pastes, frangipane filling, biscotti and walnut bread. However, it is becoming increasingly popular to use a variety of nuts for garnishing, and in the decoration of, rich deluxe fruit cakes.

FRUITS

Dried fruits include currants, sultanas, raisins, mixed peel, figs, dates, apricots, peaches, apples and bananas. All are suitable in unbaked mixtures and fillings.

Preparation may involve:

- washing
- drying
- cleaning – removing stones, stalks
- soaking (often termed as conditioning of the fruit)

The storage of most dried fruits is between four to six months in a cool dry place.

Fresh, tinned and frozen fruit give excellent visual appeal and a fresh look to many bakery products.

Fresh fruit should be used as soon as possible, but frozen and tinned fruit can be used when required.

In general, dried, fresh, tinned and frozen fruits are added towards the end of the mixing process, thus avoiding crushing and destroying the fruits' structure.

COCOA

Cocoa is the dry powder that remains after part of the cocoa butter is removed from chocolate liquor. Cocoa contains starch, which tends to absorb moisture in a cake batter; therefore, when cocoa powder is added to a batter, the amount of flour is reduced to keep the recipe balanced.

A standard rule of thumb is: for every 100 g of cocoa added to a recipe, reduce the flour by .0375 g (37.5 percent of the weight of cocoa).

CHOCOLATE COVERTURE AND CHOCOLATE COMPOUNDS

Chocolate coverture is prepared from the following ingredients: cocoa butter, cocoa and sugar which have been milled together. Chocolate coverture is expensive and is usually used when producing high class chocolate products. It also requires a process called tempering (see page 186) to ensure that the chocolate coverture sets.

Chocolate coverture is available in dark, milk and white.

Chocolate compounds are also known as chocolate coating and are prepared from the following ingredients: vegetable fats, cocoa powder, sugar, milk solids and emulsifiers. This product is much easier to use and does not require any special treatment before using. It is available in dark, milk and white chocolate compound.

White chocolate compound is very similar to chocolate compound, but the cocoa powder is replaced with milk powder.

Melting chocolate using a bain-marie (a bowl over a pot half-filled with water), gently melt the chocolate until a temperature of 37–45°C (98–110°F) is obtained.

Caution: water or steam must not come into contact with the chocolate because it will thicken and become unusable.

To thin chocolate, use a hard vegetable fat, such as Kremelta.

SPICES

Spices are aromatic or pungent vegetable substances used to flavour food. They are obtained from various parts of different plants, including barks, buds, flowers, fruits, leaves, roots, seeds and stems.

Spices are generally whole or ground, but the latter loses its flavour rapidly, so it is important to replace spices after six months. All spices should be kept in airtight containers in a cool environment.

Spices can also be obtained in more concentrated and convenient forms, such as essential oils, extracts or essences.

Spices should be used in moderation, as too much can make the product inedible. Spices also have a retarding effect on yeast, so when using them in yeast-raised products (hot-cross buns, etc.) it is advisable to increase the yeast level.

YEAST

Yeast is a species of the fungi family of plants. The strain used by commercial bakers is called *Saccharomyces cerevisiae*. Yeast is a living single cell organism, oval in shape and can only be seen under a microscope.

Yeast is responsible for the volume in bread, buns, rolls, croissants, Danish pastries and similar products. The activity of yeast within a dough is called fermentation, which is the process by which yeast acts on sugars and changes them into carbon dioxide and alcohol. This release of gas produces the rising (often called leavening) action in yeast-raised products. The alcohol evaporates completely during, and immediately after, baking.

Yeast Requirements for Fermentation

In order for yeast to produce carbon dioxide and alcohol four conditions are required:

- time – to ferment and produce carbon dioxide
- moisture – to survive and grow

- warmth – ideal temperature is between 28–32°C (82–89°F)
- food – food source (sugar, etc.) to feed upon and produce carbon dioxide

Without the above conditions the yeast cell will die and result in an inferior product.

Effects of Ingredients and Temperature on Yeast

- Salt slows down the activity of yeast, controlling fermentation when used at a responsible level. Excessive salt levels will retard or kill the yeast cell. You should never allow yeast to come into direct contact with salt, due to salt's hygroscopic properties (i.e., withdrawing moisture from the yeast cell).
- Sugar is a food source for yeast, but if used at too high a concentration will slow down (retard) the activity of yeast, therefore, in some cases, an increase in yeast is required to compensate (for example, for sweet doughs, Danish pastries, brioches, etc.).
- Fats used at high levels have a retarding effect upon the activity of yeast.
- Temperatures: 0°C (32°F) and below – will cause some yeast cells to die
- Temperatures: 0–10°C (32–50°F) – cause yeast activity to become slow and halted
- Temperatures: 28–32°C (82–89°F) – yeast activity is at its optimum
- Temperatures: 32–45°C (89–113°F) – yeast activity excessive and uncontrollable
- Temperatures: 45–55°C (113–131°F) – yeast activity stopped and the yeast cell is destroyed

Types of Yeast

- Compressed yeast – most commonly used in commercial bakeries, can be purchased from local bakeries. Limited shelf life. Do not freeze.
- Active dried yeast – used within commercial and domestic home bakeries, can be purchased from your local supermarket. Excellent shelf life unopened.
- Wild yeasts – these are living organisms and are found floating in the air. See more on wild yeast throughout the book.

WATER

Water is obviously an essential ingredient in bread making but it has various roles in a dough.

- Water hydrates the flour proteins to produce the elastic and extensible substance called gluten which forms the dough skeleton and holds the gas produced by the yeast (often called gas retention).
- Part of the water is absorbed by the starch present in the flour.
- When the dough is mixed, some of the water is absorbed by the flour proteins and by the starch. The rest stays as free water which helps the dispersion of such ingredients as salt, sugar, etc. Yeast can only absorb food which is in a solution.
- Water plays an important part in the final finished temperature of a dough (which should be between 28–32°C (82–89°F) for optimum yeast activity). This is controlled by the baker with experience and with a simple calculation, so the finished dough temperature should always remain consistent.
- Without the correct amount of water, the shelf life of the dough would be reduced, so it is important that the dough has the correct amount of water added. Approximately 12 percent water is evaporated during baking.

FOOD FLAVOURS

Food flavours are obtained from natural and artificial sources, for example, fruits, plants, herbs, spices and organic acids combined with alcohol and chemicals.

They are available in liquid, paste and powder form.

ASCORBIC ACID (NATURAL BREAD IMPROVER)

Ascorbic acid is an oxidising agent that stabilises the gas cell in a yeast dough and results in a baked crumb with uniform cell size. It is largely destroyed during baking. It is not common to use it in home baking.

DOUGH CONDITIONERS

Dough conditioners contain a mixture of natural and chemical substances which assist and condition the dough throughout the whole bread making process (mixing, final shaping, proofing, baking shelf life, etc.). These substances include:

- L-Cysteine
- soya flour
- emulsifiers
- specialised fats
- mould inhibitors

Dough conditioners have a beneficial effect on the following characteristics of a yeast-raised product:

- volume
- texture
- crumb and crust colour
- eating qualities
- shelf life

THE EQUIPMENT

YOUR HANDS

The most important tools are your hands. Without these you cannot feel the texture or the warmth (temperature) of your dough or batter, nor will you know the precise moment to proceed to the next delicate stage of preparing your irresistible breads, pastries and the lightest of sponges.

The more direct contact you have with your doughs or batters, the better you will get to know their idiosyncrasies.

SCALES

Scales are one of the most important pieces of equipment when weighing individual ingredients for a recipe.

Flour and other dry ingredients are difficult to weigh in measuring cups, as dry ingredients settle and compact during movement and weighing, making it difficult to get an accurate measurement or reading (a kilogram of flour, for instance, may measure 7 cups one day and 6¼ cups another day).

Several types of scales are available, but digital scales, in increments of one or two grams, are recommended for accuracy and can be purchased at most specialist kitchen stores for a reasonable price (see Sources section).

THERMOMETER

Using a thermometer allows accurate temperature readings of both your ingredients and your environment. This is particularly important when dealing with yeast-related products, given that yeast is a living organism and requires a consistent temperature to produce carbon dioxide and alcohol.

A long-stemmed digital thermometer works well for reading dough and ingredient temperatures. You should also give some consideration to having an oven thermometer, because most ovens (particularly domestic ones) can be inconsistent and have a temperature variation as much as 20°C (68°F). These can be purchased from specialist kitchen stores (see Sources section).

DOUGH SCRAPER OR CUTTER

This is simply a rectangular piece of stainless steel with a rolled or wooden handle and a sharp edge. The dough scraper can be used for everything from cutting or dividing the dough to scraping off excess flour that clings to your work surface and proofing cloths. A flexible plastic scraper can be used to scrape down the sides of the mixing bowl.

MIXER

Most yeast doughs in this book can be mixed by hand or made in a domestic bread maker. If you are using a standard electric mixer, ensure that it is heavy duty and capable of generating a lot of work input (dough development/kneading). For the serious home baker, small commercial mixers can be purchased from specialist kitchen stores (see Sources section).

From a commercial point of view there are many types of mixers, ranging from spiral and hi-speed mixers for yeast doughs and pastry to planetary (standard) mixers for cakes, biscuits, icing and cream fillings (the latter usually having a dough hook, paddle and whisk attachment).

DOMESTIC BREAD MAKER

There are several types of bread maker available on the Australian and New Zealand market which produce very good quality bread. However, when selecting your model, ensure that you select one with a 'mixing only' function, as this will allow you to develop your dough within the bread maker and finish it off by hand on the bench (for pizza bases, focaccia and croissants, etc.).

MIXING BOWL

It is important to have a good set of mixing bowls, ranging from 500 ml to five-litre (2 cups to 1.5 gallon) capacity. They can be plastic, earthenware, stainless steel, glass or ceramic.

PROOFING BASKET

These are baskets made from coiled cane or plastic and are round or oval in shape (called *banneton* in France) which turn out rustic-looking loaves with a beehive pattern of flour etched on to the surface. They can be either cloth-lined or unlined naked cane and are always heavily dusted with rye flour before having the dough placed inside to proof. Once the loaf has reached its required proof size, simply turn it upside down directly on the baking stone or hearth of the oven, taking care when removing it from the proofing basket. Without a proofing basket, dough spreads too much on the tray and has trouble rising properly in the oven. A basket is better than a bowl because it allows the dough to breathe during proofing.

If you are unable to obtain specialised proofing baskets, it is simple to improvise. Buy some heavy linen (calico) from a fabric store and line or drape it over a cane or wicker basket before dusting it with rye flour. The basket should be high enough to allow the dough to double in volume. Proofing baskets can be purchased from specialist kitchen stores (see Sources section).

PROOFING CLOTH

Some breads – baguettes, rolls, braids or Vienna rolls – never see a proofing basket or even a bread tin. They are proofed instead in what the French call a *couche* (which is simply a large piece of heavy linen or canvas) that has been dusted with rye flour, then gathered around the shaped dough piece to help hold the shape of the loaves and protect the bottom and sides from drying out. Another proofing cloth is then placed on top of the dough.

Never place *couches* into a washing machine: simply scrape off the excess flour using your dough scraper and allow them to dry completely before putting away. If this is not done, the *couches* will become mouldy.

Proofing cloths can be made from heavy calico purchased from any fabric shop. Remember to overlock the edges to prevent them from fraying.

BAKING TRAYS/TINS AND MOULDS

Most breads are baked on the oven hearth or in bread tins, but there are some breads and other bakery products that require baking on trays/tins or specialised moulds (fougasse, fancy bread rolls, Danish pastries, croissants, apple strudel, biscuits, muffins, sponges, pies and tarts, etc.).

There are many different shapes and types of baking mould, including tart and quiche tins with removable bases, kugelhopf mould, panettone and pandoro moulds, baguette trays, brioche tins, fruit cake tins, hamburger trays, cake hoops and rings, tuiles trays – all of which should be kept in peak condition.

Most baking trays/tins and moulds require cleaning and greasing before each use – more usually the latter – otherwise you wash off the grease from the previous bake which can help prevent your product sticking.

Silicone and baking paper can be used instead of placing your products directly onto the baking tray, thus keeping your tray in excellent condition and ensuring your product does not stick. Silicone and baking paper can be used several times over.

An alternative is a Teflon-coated baking mat, which fits inside your baking tray and lasts for many years. All tins, trays and specialised baking moulds can be purchased from specialist kitchen stores (see Sources section).

PROOFING CABINET

This is where you place your dough to rise or ferment. Within a basic proofing cabinet (known as a prover in a commercial bakery) there are two specific functions: one to supply heat (never above 40°C/105°F) and the other to supply humidity (60–80 percent relative humidity). Generally, the two functions work together.

However, in some cases more of one or less of the other is required, for example, croissants require a lower heat (28–30°C/82–86°F) so the butter layers do not melt, but also require a relative humidity of 60–75 percent to prevent the surface drying out.

Placing your dough in the proofing cabinet prior to baking is known as 'final proof'. In many bread recipes you are not required to place your dough in a proofing cabinet for final proofing – you simply allow the dough to rise in a warm, humid environment, often covered with a proofing cloth to prevent the dough forming a skin and drying out. This is often the case with breads from Europe.

In the domestic environment it is common practice to leave your yeasted doughs to rise or final proof in a warm draught-free place such as the hot water cupboard or even on top of your refrigerator, remembering to cover the dough lightly with a clean tea towel or a piece of plastic to prevent a crust from forming.

REFRIGERATOR

Often, bread doughs are kept in the refrigerator to slow down the action of yeast (referred to as retarding). This enables the dough to develop the flavour and texture that is often seen in European breads, especially sourdough, which require a long and cool fermentation process. At home you can place your yeasted dough in the refrigerator after it has had its first rise, then scale and final mould it many hours later (in much the same way as brioche is made).

FREEZER

Can be used for storage of unbaked and baked products. In general, the faster you freeze, the better your product will be once it has been through its freeze-thaw cycle.

FINE MESH SIEVE

A fine mesh sieve is used to sift or dust rye flour over your proofing cloths and baskets. You may also dust rye flour over your dough prior to baking so that you can slash the dough and give it your artistic signature.

When dusting with icing sugar, tap the sieve lightly to ensure even dusting.

Larger sieves can be used for incorporating several dry ingredients together before being combined into a cake batter.

RAZOR BLADE OR DOUGH SLASHING KNIFE

The artistic signature of each baker is slashed or cut into the loaf just before the loaf is placed in the oven (at 75 percent of final proof to avoid the dough piece collapsing). This artistic signature is simply done with a double-edged razor blade threaded onto a piece of steel or bamboo skewer or a special small serrated knife. To give an attractive appearance, each loaf is cut so that it has a planned and predictable place at which to burst and achieve the oven spring it needs to develop to its full potential. The cut is as important as any other process in bread making. It must be done at the correct time and at the correct angle to prevent the dough from collapsing before being placed into the oven. Practice makes perfect!

SCISSORS

If you are baking rolls, instead of slashing them you can snip the tops with scissors and create peaks that toast nicely in the oven, giving a little extra crunch when eating. However, this must be done at 75 percent of final proof to avoid the dough piece collapsing.

BAKER'S PEEL

Baker's peels are used at the critical moment in the baking process when you transfer the dough from its proofing place to the oven. At this stage, if you are not careful you can deflate the dough, preventing it from acquiring its correct shape. If using a baker's peel to transfer your dough piece, lightly dust your peel's head with semolina flour and gently place or roll your dough piece onto it. Open your oven door and with a quick forward and backwards jerk, slide your dough piece on to the oven's hearth or baking stone. Again, practice makes perfect!

Commercial bakeries also use baker's peels for loading and unloading the oven filled with trays of cakes, biscuits and pastries. Peels are usually made from wood and have very long handles, enabling the baker to reach to the back of the oven. When using a domestic oven, use a thin wooden board (in the shape of a peel, with a short handle) that has been sharpened at the end.

Peels can be purchased at most specialist kitchen stores for a reasonable price (see Sources section).

BAKING STONE

It is best to bake bread on the oven hearth or on baking stones. They provide insulated and solid heat, which helps the bread bake more evenly than it would on a metal baking tray. The hearth or oven stones absorb the moisture from the dough as it bakes, which gives the loaf a crispier bottom and chewier crust.

For a domestic oven, baking stones can be purchased from specialist kitchen stores (see Sources section) or you could even get your local ceramic tile specialist to cut one to suit your oven tray size. When you first receive your baking stone, condition it in the oven at a low temperature for several hours or overnight so it will not crack when you turn the heat up high to bake your bread.

SPRAY BOTTLE OR PLANT MISTER

Within the first few minutes of baking bread, you want to create a moist, hot environment. Most commercial bakeries have steam-injected ovens, but to simulate this in your domestic oven, spray hot water directly onto the sides and hearth or baking stone just before placing your dough piece in. Lightly spray the inside of the oven two or three times within the first five minutes of baking. Ensure that you use hot water because spraying with cold water will lower the oven temperature too drastically. Another way to create steam is to place a tray full of water in the bottom of your oven.

A spray bottle can also be useful when applying seeds, cheese, etc., to your dough piece prior to baking. Simply spray the dough piece and apply seeds or cheese, etc.

If you notice that during the final proofing stage your dough piece is skinning and crusting over, you must ensure that the crusting is removed as quickly as possible because it prevents the dough from rising and achieving its correct volume. Lightly spray the surface with warm water.

OVEN

There is no need for the home baker to invest thousands of dollars in a 'state of the art' commercial oven – just make a few adjustments to your domestic oven. Spray your oven with hot water or place a tray full of water in the oven to create a steamy, humid atmosphere, and place a baking stone at the bottom of your oven to simulate a traditional friendly bread-baking oven. The same oven will produce excellent pastry and cake products.

Before placing your products into the oven always check that the oven is:
* set at the correct temperature for the product
* is up to that correct temperature (usually assessed by checking whether the thermostat light has switched off)

COOLING RACK

Always place your baked loaf directly onto a cooling rack. This enables air circulation around the whole loaf and prevents the bottom from sweating and going soggy.

When cooling cake-related products, it is better to leave the cake in the tin for 5–10 minutes to allow the cake to settle before turning out onto a cooling rack or wire to cool.

SERRATED KNIFE

When cutting any bakery product use the correct knife. For baked bread and cakes use a sharp, serrated knife; use dry when cutting bread, and dip in hot water when cutting cakes such as gateaux and torten to ensure a clean and crumb-free cut.

ROLLING PIN AND PASTRY SHEETER

Very few breads require the use of a rolling pin for final shaping. The exceptions are croissants, Danish pastries, hamburgers, focaccia, panini and chelsea buns. Therefore, the rolling pin or pastry sheeter is best suited to pastry products.

Select either the French variety of rolling pin, which is a thin solid cylinder of wood, or the thicker American/English kind, which has handles that are mounted on ball bearings. Whichever you choose, make sure it is at least 35–40 cm (13–15 inches) in length.

Pastry sheeters are found in almost every commercial bakery, usually having one canvas conveyor belt either side of two automatic revolving rollers set on top of each other. The rollers can be opened and closed to reduce the thickness of the pastry.

PASTRY DOCKER

A spiked mini rolling pin set on a handle is the best way to describe this piece of baking equipment. It is used to dock or puncture puff pastry to stop it from rising, allowing the steam to escape during baking (often called docking).

A pastry docker can also be used to dock the top of dough pieces to give a decorative effect.

PASTRY BRUSH

The ever versatile pastry brush has many uses, for instance, brushing olive oil on focaccia and panini after baking, dusting flour off the surface of dough or pastry, glazing the tops of pies, tarts, pastries, biscuits and even bread with egg wash, washing interior edges of pastry turnovers or calzone with water so they stick together during baking, and cleaning the sides of a copper pot during the boiling of sugar for sugar decorating.

PASTRY BAG AND PIPING TUBE

Pastry bags (also called savoys or piping bags) and piping tubes (also called piping nozzles) are used for making borders, inscriptions, designs, flowers and many other decorations out of icing and cream fillings. The basic tubes are as follows: plain, star, rose, leaf, and ribbon or basket-weave. Many other specialised tubes are available for unusual shapes, however, the plain and star tubes are by far the most important.

The easiest way to use a pastry bag and piping tube is to fit the tube inside the pastry bag, then push the bag into the tube to prevent the icing from flowing straight out during filling. Turn back the top of the bag and then fill the bag no more than two-thirds full. Gather the top of the bag with one hand and twist it securely. Place the other hand just above the tube and apply even pressure at the top of the bag so that the filling flows smoothly and evenly from the tube.

PASTRY/BISCUIT CUTTER

There are many different shapes and sizes of pastry or biscuit cutter, ranging from plain, crinkled, round, square and oblong, to gingerbread people and teddy bears, etc. Generally, the round cutters are the most popular and are used for cutting discs of pastry so they can line pastry cases, tart and flan rings. After washing your cutters, dry them well to prevent any rusting or metal deterioration, then store in a container to protect them from damage.

PASTRY WHEEL

Imagine 8–10 pizza cutters (the wheel type) joined together on an adjustable concertina-type brace which can be enlarged or retracted. Pastry wheels are used when you require many items of the same shape to be cut from one large sheet of pastry (usually square, rectangle, triangle or diamond) or when you require the top of your cakes or slices to be marked to achieve a consistent yield time after time.

PALETTE KNIFE

The palette knife is to a baker what a trowel is to a brick layer. These are thin, flexible, round-ended, blunt-edged knives that are used for spreading creams, jams, icing and royal icing, etc., onto slices, sponges, cakes and gateaux.

Palette knives come in various sizes and are either straight or trowel-shaped (the latter is often referred to as a crank-handled palette knife).

MEASURING CUPS AND SPOONS

Some measurements given in this book are given in spoons and cups as well as metric measurements. (In any case, we recommend that all ingredients are weighed on a set of accurate scales.) If you decide to measure your ingredients with spoons and cups ensure that you have purchased your measuring implements from a specialist kitchen shop. The standard domestic teaspoon, tablespoon and cup will vary from kitchen to kitchen and even country to country, and if used will result in an inferior finished baked product.

FORMULAS AND MEASUREMENTS

SCALING INGREDIENTS

All ingredients must be measured accurately. Water, liquid milk and beaten eggs (commonly called egg pulp) may be measured by volume. They are scaled at one kilogram per litre i.e., 1.000 kg of water = 1.000 litre of water. However, if quantities are large, it is advisable to weigh these ingredients on an accurate set of scales.

Volume measurements have been calculated using the dip-and-sweep measuring technique. To dip-and-sweep, scoop up the ingredient with your measuring cup or spoon. Heap up more than you need, then level off the excess with the back of a knife.

RECIPE BALANCE

Recipes are balanced formulations, therefore if you add too much of one ingredient this will, in turn, upset another ingredient and unbalance the recipe. Special care must be taken when measuring salt, baking powder, spices, sugar and other ingredients used in small amounts, as it is often the case that the smaller the amount the more effect it has on the finished baked product.

BAKER'S PERCENTAGES

Bakers use a simple but versatile system of percentages for expressing their formulas or recipes. Baker's percentages indicate the quantities of each item that would be required if 100 kg of flour were used. In other words, each ingredient is expressed as a percentage of the total flour weight. To put it differently, the percentage of each ingredient is its total weight divided by the weight of the flour, multiplied by 100. For example:

$$\frac{\text{Total weight of ingredient}}{\text{Total weight of flour}} \times 100 = \% \text{ of ingredient}$$

The flour is always expressed as 100 percent. If two kinds of flour are used, their total is still 100 percent. Any ingredient that weighs the same as the flour is also expressed as 100 percent. See the formulations below to understand how these percentages are used. Check the figures with the above equation to make sure you understand them.

WHITE BREAD FORMULATION

INGREDIENT	WEIGHT	%
Bread flour	1000 g (5 kg)	100
Salt	20 g (0.1 kg)	2
Sugar	10 g (0.05 kg)	1
Fat	30 g (0.15 kg)	3
Yeast	30 g (0.15 kg)	3
Water	560 ml (2.8 lt)	56
Total weight	1090 g (8.250 kg)	
Yield @ .550 kg	15	

CAKE FORMULATION

INGREDIENT	WEIGHT	%
Ingredient	Weight	%
Cake flour	2.5 kg	100
Sugar	2.5 kg	100
Baking powder	0.125 kg	5
Salt	0.063 kg	2.5
Shortening	1.25 kg	50
Milk	1.5 lt	60
Egg whites	1.5 lt	60
Total weight	9.438 kg	
Yield @ .500 kg	18.8	

Advantages of using baker's percentages The formulations or recipes are easy to adapt for any yield, and single ingredients may be varied and other ingredients added without changing the whole formulation. For example, you can add blueberries to your muffin formulation and the percentages of all the other ingredients will stay the same.

METRIC CONVERSIONS

All recipes in this book are in the metric system. This system has one basic unit for each type of measurement:

- the gram and kilogram are the basic units of weight
- the litre is the basic unit for volume
- the centimetre and metre are the basic units of length
- the degree celsius is the basic unit of temperature

To convert Fahrenheit (F) to Celsius (C):
Formula: F – 32 ÷ 9 x 5 = C
Example: 425°F – 32 ÷ 9 x 5 = 218°C

To convert Celsius (C) to Fahrenheit (F):
Formula: C ÷ 5 x 9 + 32 = F
Example: 218°C ÷ 5 x 9 + 32 = 424°F

To convert ounces (oz) to grams (g):
Conversion: 1 ounce = 28.4 grams
Example: 16 oz x 28.4 g = 454.4 grams

To convert pounds (lb) to kilograms (kg):
Conversion: 1 lb = 0.454 grams (1 lb = 16oz)
Example: 1 lb 3 oz = 19 oz x 28.4 g = 0.539 kilograms

Calculating the required water temperature to achieve a finished dough temperature It is important when working with yeast doughs that you understand that for the yeast to produce carbon dioxide it must have favourable conditions to work in. One of the most important conditions is temperature (refer to Yeast in the Ingredients section).

All yeast-raised recipes have a finished dough temperature figure. This tells you the best temperature for the yeast to operate in once the dough has completed mixing. The following calculation best explains the method that should be used with all yeast-raised recipes in this book (Note: this is the calculation used for mixing yeast-raised doughs by hand).

- Required finished dough temperature x 2
- Subtract the flour temperature
- Add adjustment for hand mixing
- Equals required water temperature

Example: **Finished dough temperature**   **29°C (84°F)**
Finished dough temperature x 2 =   58°C (168°F)
Subtract flour temperature (68°C)   −20°C (−68°F)
_____
38°C (100°F)
Add adjustment for hand mixing   +3°C (+ 37°F)
_____
Equals required water temperature   **41°C (137°F)**

In the domestic environment, when mixing your dough by hand, a general rule of thumb for the required water temperature is:
- body or blood temperature (approximately 37°C/98°F)

ALL ABOUT BREAD

BASIC INGREDIENTS

There are four main ingredients required to make successful bread:

- strong, good quality bread flour
- salt
- yeast (commercial or natural)
- water

All other ingredients used to make bread are often called enriching agents or bread improvers, for example, sugar, fats or oils, eggs, milk, dried fruits, etc.

Basic ingredient functions

Strong flour is the most important ingredient in bread. Without the protein (gluten) present in the flour there could not be bread as we know it; therefore, the protein content must be of excellent quality and quantity. During the baking process the starch gelatinises and protein coagulates to provide the structure and framework of the baked loaf or roll. Of course, this goes hand in hand with correct mixing or kneading, which is explained in further detail later in this section.

Salt provides flavour to bread, along with strengthening the gluten. Used at its recommended usage rate, salt controls the fermentation of yeast. If used in excessive amounts, salt retards or kills the yeast cells.

Yeast is used as the aerating agent in bread doughs. Without yeast the loaf or roll would be small in volume and very dense in texture.

The main functions of yeast in the production of bread are:

- production of carbon dioxide for aeration
- development of the gluten network through the action of fermentation
- development of the bread flavour and aroma

Water levels provide the dough consistency; however, this level can be quite variable depending on the quality of flour and other ingredients used. Adjustments may be necessary to produce good quality bread. The water also controls the dough temperature which has an influence on the speed of fermentation, that is, the colder the water, the colder the dough, the slower the yeast produces carbon dioxide.

BREAD MAKING PROCESSES

There are four commonly used bread making processes:

Bulk fermentation is used to achieve full-flavoured bread. It requires no special ingredient consideration but needs time to produce from start to finished baked loaf. This process is the most commonly used in the domestic environment.

No-time is for breads requiring only a short time from the raw ingredient stage to the finished baked loaf (often only one-and-a-half hours). Commonly used in supermarket in-store bakeries and many hot bread shops. This process requires special oxidising ingredients and dough conditioners such as ascorbic acid, emulsifiers, enzymes, L-Cysteine, etc. This process is not commonly used in the domestic environment.

Sponge and dough is the oldest method of making bread, often using a starter dough which may contain either commercial baker's yeast or wild natural yeasts. Bread produced using this method has a wonderful texture, flavour and aroma, for example, traditional sourdough and many other European breads. Producing bread using this method requires experience, knowledge, passion, understanding and plenty of tender loving care. This process is commonly used in the domestic environment.

Mechanical dough development (MDD) was developed in the 1970s for the large commercial plant bakeries that required a fast mixing and processing bread to maximise their production. This process is largely the same as the no-time process with a shorter mixing time operated under vacuum to achieve a fine cell structure that is required for sliced sandwich breads, etc. This process is not commonly used in the domestic environment.

STEPS IN YEAST-RAISED PRODUCTION

There are 12 basic steps that are used in the production of yeast-raised products. These steps are generally applied to all yeast products, with some variations depending on the required finished product.

STEPS	BULK FERMENTATION	NO-TIME	SPONGE & DOUGH	MECHANICAL DOUGH DEVELOPMENT
Scaling ingredients	•	•	•	•
Preparation of sponge or starter			•	
Mixing or kneading	•	•	•	•
Bulk fermentation	•		•	
Knocking back	•		•	
Dividing or scaling	•	•	•	•
Rounding	•	•	•	•
Intermediate proof	•	•	•	•
Final make up & placing on trays	•	•	•	•
Final proof	•	•	•	•
Cutting, seeding, dusting, etc.	•	•	•	•
Baking	•	•	•	•
Cooling	•	•	•	•
Storing	•	•	•	•

Scaling ingredients Special care must be taken when measuring salt, sugar and spices, as these ingredients will have an effect on the fermentation process.

Preparation of a sponge or starter Some yeast-raised doughs require a sponge or starter dough. This step requires forward planning and consists of a two-stage process. A sponge is a basic dough made from the four main ingredients: flour, salt, yeast and water. The sponge is then allowed to ferment for 18 hours in bulk or in some cases until the sponge falls back onto itself. The speed of fermentation can be controlled by the levels of salt and yeast and also by the temperature of the water used.

A starter dough is commonly used in the production of sourdough-type breads that require a crisp crust, irregular crumb and a wonderful tarty fermented flavour and aroma. The starter can take 14 days to raise from scratch: nine to grow the culture and five to build the starter to the strength you require to bake a loaf of bread. The starter culture consists of only flour and water, which attract wild natural yeasts and bacteria.

Don't be put off by the length of time it takes to grow the starter, as you only have to grow it once. After that, as long as you feed and maintain it, your starter will be ready to use over and over again. See the recipe and instructions in this section for preparing a sourdough starter, or leaven as it is commonly known in France.

Mixing or kneading This is one of the most important steps and should not be taken for granted, especially when kneading your dough by hand, as one of the most common faults in bread is under mixing, resulting in a poor volume loaf. There are two purposes of mixing:

(i)   combining the ingredients into a dough, hydrating the gluten and distributing the yeast are accomplished during the first stage of mixing

(ii)   the remaining time is required for developing the gluten network and allowing air and gases to be trapped within the dough (see Understanding Dough Development)

All mixing times that relate to yeast-raised products are guidelines only. You must learn by feel and sight when your dough has been fully developed. A correctly developed dough should be smooth, elastic and silky.

IMPORTANCE OF DOUGH TEMPERATURE

During any type of mixing, whether in a mixer or by hand, the dough will increase in temperature, caused by friction. It is important that you achieve the correct finished dough temperature so that your dough is not going to ferment too fast or in some cases too slowly, resulting in poor quality baked products (see the Formulas and Measurements section on how to calculate the required water temperature to achieve the desired finished dough temperature).

Achieving the correct finished dough temperature lets you know what your dough is doing and how it will react within the conditions and environment, for example, during winter or summer. You should always take and record your dough temperature once you have developed your dough.

Most doughs within this book require a finished dough temperature between 27–32°C (80–89°F) unless specified in the recipe.

STEPS IN MIXING AND KNEADING BY HAND

Mixing or kneading should be fun and enjoyable. Ensure that you knead on a solid surface with plenty of space and that the bench is of a suitable height.

The first four steps can be done in a large bowl if you prefer.

Make a well with the flour in the middle of the bench. Sprinkle the other dry ingredients around the edge.

Slowly add the water, taking care not to overflow the well. Keep a small amount of water back to adjust the dough to the correct consistency. The yeast or starter must be added at this stage.

Using your fingertips, slowly mix in a circular motion, picking up the dry ingredients from around the outside. Be careful not to break the well and cause the liquids to flow out.

At this stage, you should have a porridge-like consistency. Continue to mix but now gather the flour from the outside, using your scraper, to form a firm dough. Keep one hand clean at this stage.

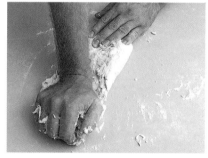

Clean the bench and your hands with your scraper. At this stage, begin to knead your dough by the traditional method of turning, folding and pushing with the heel of your hand repeatedly. Adjust your dough consistency by adding water or liquid at this early stage of kneading.

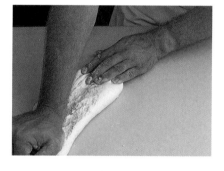

Continue to knead the dough using the method described. This should take anywhere from 10–15 minutes, and your dough should become smooth, silky and elastic. See Understanding Dough Development below.

UNDERSTANDING DOUGH DEVELOPMENT

This is one of the most important steps in successful bread making. Good bread flour contains a protein called gluten which gives structure and strength to all yeast-raised goods.

In order for gluten to be developed, the proteins (glutenin and gliadin) must first absorb water or liquids, then, as the dough is mixed or kneaded, the gluten forms long, elastic and rubbery strands, known as the gluten network.

As the dough begins to rise the gluten network captures the gases (produced by the yeast) in tiny pockets or cells and allows the dough to rise and expand. If the gluten network within the dough has not been correctly developed, these gases will escape, resulting in a collapsed small volume loaf.

There are many factors that determine when a dough is developed:

- temperature of water
- speed of mixing or kneading
- selection and amounts of raw ingredients; high fat and sugar doughs take less time to develop due to the 'shortening' effect these ingredients have on the gluten network

The dough is developed when:

(i)   the dough clears from the sides of the mixing bowl in a smooth silky mass, assuming that the correct liquid amounts have been used

(ii)   the dough has a smooth, silky and elastic texture

(iii) a small piece of dough can be stretched to achieve a smooth satiny sheen which is elastic and extensible (often called the 'stretch test' – see below)

An under-developed dough. Notice the rough and easily broken texture of the dough when stretched out.

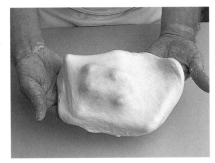

A correctly developed dough: smooth, elastic and extensible when stretched.

Bulk fermentation, or first rising as it is sometimes called. This term is used to describe the length of time that the dough is allowed to ferment in bulk. The bulk fermentation period is measured from the end of mixing to the beginning of scaling or dividing the dough. This period can be from 1–18 hours depending on the levels of salt and yeast in the recipe, as well as the dough temperature, which should be between 25–27°C (77–80°F).

During bulk fermentation the following conditions must be observed:

(i)   place the dough into a lightly oiled container large enough to allow the dough to double in size

(ii)   the dough must be covered to prevent the dough surface from skinning

(iii) place the dough in an environment where the temperature will remain constant (for example, the hot water cupboard)

Knocking back During the bulk fermentation period the dough increases in volume (often double), due to the gases given off by the yeast. To prevent the gases from escaping prematurely the dough is gently 'knocked back' or 'punched down', generally three-quarters of the way through the bulk fermentation period. This is done by hand, by gently pushing, punching and folding the dough. Knocking back is done for the following reasons:

* to expel the gases and revitalise the yeast's activity
* to even out the dough temperature because the outside of the dough will be colder than the inside
* to stimulate and help develop the gluten network
* to even out the cell structure

Once the knocking back stage has been completed, the dough is returned to the container and covered until it is required for scaling. Bulk fermentation and knocking back times are included in the relevant recipes within this book.

Dividing or scaling This takes place directly when the dough has either completed its mixing or bulk fermentation period. Using your scales and dough scraper, gently divide your dough into the required sizes and weights. This should be done as quickly as possible to avoid excessive fermentation.

Rounding After scaling, the dough pieces are shaped into smooth, round balls. This assists the gases within the fermenting dough to remain. Another important reason why this stage is included is to pre-shape the dough before it undergoes its final shaping. To achieve this, cup your hand or hands over the dough piece, and with a little pressure begin to move your dough in a circular motion making sure that the dough is in contact with the bench all the time. Avoid rounding on a floured surface, as you want the dough to grip the bench. This movement stretches the surface of the dough so that it is completely smooth except for a seam at the bottom where the dough has gripped the bench (see photograph to the right).

Intermediate proof This is sometimes referred to as 'first proof', 'recovery time' or 'bench time'. This is a resting period of 10–15 minutes that takes place between rounding and final make up or shaping, allowing the gluten network to relax. If insufficient intermediate proof time is given, the dough piece will tear and become misshapen during final make up or shaping. During the intermediate proof you must cover your dough piece with a sheet of plastic, dough cloth, or a clean tea towel to stop the dough surface from skinning.

Final make up and placing on trays Once the dough piece has had its intermediate proof, mould it into its final shape before placing into bread tins, proofing baskets or onto baking trays. Correct make up or moulding is critical to the finished baked loaf or roll. All moulded bread doughs have a seam and the seam should always be placed bottom side down (with the exception of cane proofing baskets where the smooth surface should be placed at the bottom). This avoids splitting during the baking process.

Once the final shaping has taken place, toppings can be put onto the dough piece before it enters the final proof stage, for example, sesame and poppy seeds, cheese, flour, etc.

There are many great, effective shapes that breads, rolls and buns can take. These techniques will be explained and shown in the recipe section of this book.

Final proof Often known as 'proofing'. This is critical for product quality and should be monitored closely. Once the dough is ready to enter the prover there are three main areas that require attention:

(i) temperature – proofing temperatures should be higher than the dough temperature, as this prevents the dough from chilling and allows the yeast to function effectively. The ideal temperature should be 35–40°C (95–104°F).

(ii) humidity – moisture in the air. The requirement for humidity in final proofing is to prevent drying of the dough piece. Skinning prevents a glossy crust forming during steaming and baking. Lack of humidity will slow proofing. Higher humidity will result in undesirably fast proofing and an inferior product. In the domestic environment a spray bottle can be used to prevent skinning during proofing.

(iii) time – proof times depend upon dough size, final dough temperature, yeast levels and even ingredients used; 45–90 minutes are common proof times.

If a prover is not available, come as close to the above conditions as possible by covering the products loosely to retain the moisture and setting them in a warm place (hot water cupboard or similar).

How do we determine when a dough piece is under- or over-proofed or proofed to its correct size when using the indentation test?

Under-proofed This is when you lightly press your finger into the side of the dough and the indentation 'springs' out quickly to its original shape. More proof time is required.

Correct proof When you lightly press your finger into the side of the dough, the indentation slowly springs back, but does not obtain its original shape. It leaves a small indentation mark. At this stage, the dough piece is ready to enter the oven.

Over-proofed When lightly pressed, the dough piece will collapse and the indentation mark will not spring back. Place the dough piece into the oven as soon as possible at the correct oven temperature. The product, however, will be of poor quality.

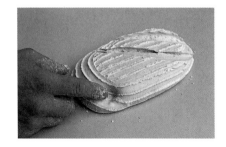

Cutting, seeding and dusting This is done for the decorative appearance of the finished baked loaf or roll.

- Cutting or slashing: see the Equipment section under Razor Blade or Slashing Knife for detailed information.
- Seeding is done either after the final shape or just before the fully proofed loaf or rolls enter the oven. If the latter is done then the loaf or rolls need to be lightly sprayed with water before the seeds are sprinkled on. Grated cheese can also be applied at this stage.
- Dusting the loaf or rolls with flour at full proof allows the flour to bake onto the product. Dusting and cutting are normally done hand in hand with each other to achieve a decorative pattern.

Cutting or slashing a boule – notice the angle of the blade.

Baking Proofed doughs are fragile until the flour proteins have been coagulated (set) by baking. The dough should be handled with care when being loaded into the preheated oven. The heat causes the yeast, in the last stages of life, to lift the dough one more time before it is killed by the excessive heat; this is called 'oven spring'. For this to happen the oven must be hot and moist. Professional bakers use steam-injected ovens which prevent the crust from drying out and being dull in colour. (The gelatinisation that occurs between the steam in the oven and the starch in the dough gives the loaf or roll its characteristic 'bloom'.) In the domestic oven, spray the sides and baking stone of the oven with warm water one minute before putting the dough piece into the oven. Repeat this two to three times within the first five minutes of baking. Ensure that you only open the door narrowly to avoid excessive steam and heat loss each time you spray. Once your dough piece is in the oven, avoid spraying it directly with the water, as this will cause an inferior finished product.

Baking on baking stones or the hearth of the oven To load the oven, place the proofed dough piece or pieces onto peels that have been well-dusted with semolina or cornmeal. Slide the peel into the oven; then, with a quick forward and backward jerk, slide the dough piece onto the baking stone or hearth of the oven.

Baking on trays or in tins Many products, such as rolls, buns and tin breads, are baked on trays or in tins which are directly placed onto the baking stones or the hearth of the oven. However, these are not known as traditional hearth breads.

Baking the ideal product is dependent on time, temperature and dough weight.

- Large dough pieces (400–500 g/1 lb) require high temperatures and longer baking periods, i.e., 220–230°C (430–445°F) for 30–40 minutes.
- Small dough pieces (100–200g/3½–7 oz) require significantly less time and lower baking temperatures, i.e., 200–210°C (390–410°F) for 12–18 minutes.

BAKING GUIDELINES

The longer the baking time:
- the thicker the crust
- the greater the moisture loss
- the darker the crust colour

The higher the baking temperature:
- the shorter the baking time
- the thinner the product crust
- the more risk the larger dough pieces will be underbaked and may collapse

The lower the baking temperature:
- the longer the total baking time
- the thicker the product crust
- the more oven spring

To tell if a loaf of bread is correctly baked, tap the bottom, and if it sounds hollow, the loaf is correctly baked.

Cooling The flavour and aroma do not fully develop until the loaf has cooled completely. Always place your baked breads directly onto a cooling rack or wire to prevent sweating.

Storing Breads to be served within eight hours may be left in the open air or in a paper bag. Breads that are to retain a crust must not be packaged, as this will cause the crust to soften and become leathery. If storing your bread in the freezer, place it into a plastic bag to extend its shelf life. Never place bread into the refrigerator as this speeds up the staling process.

FAULTS IN BREAD & YEAST-RAISED PRODUCTS

FAULTS \ CAUSES	Overmature dough	Tight dough	Slack dough	Underproof	Overproof	Baking time too long	Baking temp too low	Baking temp too high	Insufficient steam in oven	Flour used too weak	Poor final moulding	Lack of salt	Dough temp too high	Undermixing of dough	Excessive steam in prover	Excessive steam in oven	Excessive salt	Insufficient yeast	Excessive sugar
Poor volume & oven spring		•		•	•		•	•		•		•		•	•			•	
Flat appearance	•		•		•		•			•		•		•			•	•	
Pale crust colour	•						•					•					•	•	
Excessive crust colour								•	•									•	•
Thick crust						•		•	•										
Unstable internal open crumb	•	•			•					•	•		•					•	•
Poor crumb colour	•		•	•	•					•	•		•					•	
Poor shape	•	•	•	•	•				•			•							
Wrinkled crust					•											•			
Poor shelf life	•	•		•	•	•				•			•						

ALL ABOUT CAKES, SPONGES & BISCUITS

BASIC INGREDIENTS

Cakes There are four main ingredients that are required to make successful cakes:

- soft flour
- fresh eggs
- sugar
- butter

A cake baked with equal parts of each of the above ingredients is often referred to as a pound cake:

> 1 lb soft flour
>
> 1 lb fresh eggs
>
> 1 lb sugar
>
> 1 lb butter

The pound has now been replaced with grams and kilograms, but the principle remains the same.

Many other ingredients are added to further enrich the cake and aid its keeping qualities, for example, liquid milk, water, special emulsifiers, dried fruit, chocolate and flavours, baking powders, etc.

Sponges The basic ingredients required to make a light textured sponge are:

- soft flour
- sugar
- fresh eggs

Again, many other ingredients can be added to increase its keeping qualities and also add texture and flavour, for example, melted butter, special emulsifiers, water, baking powders, etc.

Biscuits The basic ingredients required to make biscuits vary depending on size, texture, flavour, etc. However, the following can be used as a base, with many other ingredients being added to obtain a desired texture, flavour or eye appeal, for example, chocolate chips, peanuts, cocoa, baking powder, dried fruit, etc.

- soft flour
- sugar
- butter
- fresh eggs

BASIC INGREDIENT FUNCTIONS

Flour and eggs These two ingredients alone have the ability to form a structure which will expand during baking and coagulate (set) when a high enough temperature has been reached. Remember that both contain protein, flour (gluten) and eggs (albumin).

Eggs contain a natural emulsifier called lecithin, which assists in combining two substances or ingredients which do not normally go together: fats and water. This is known as an emulsion.

Butter or fats are added to cake batters to assist in aeration, to supply flavour and to make the cakes more tender to eat. They also play an important part in shortening the flour proteins, which allow the cake to expand during the baking process. Fats also assist in the keeping quality of the cake.

Sugar is used to produce tenderness, sweetness and crust colour. Sugar also assists in aeration and can be regarded as an 'opening agent', opening the structure of the cake which increases the volume in the finished baked product. This is only true if the butter and sugar are beaten until light and fluffy.

Milk is sometimes substituted for egg in a recipe and acts as a moistening agent. Milk, or any liquid, is generally regarded as a 'closing agent', closing the structure of the cake which reduces the volume in the finished baked product.

Baking powder is used to aerate the cake during the baking process by producing carbon dioxide in the presence of moisture and heat. Baking powder is regarded as an 'opening agent'. Too little baking powder will result in a dense, poor volume cake, while excessive baking powder will result in an open texture with a darkened crumb, and often the cake will sink in the middle.

MIXING METHODS

In order for cakes and sponges to be light and airy in texture this requires beating or whipping air into the batter. This is known as aeration. Aeration can be achieved through many different methods for cakes, sponges and biscuits. Let's take a closer look at the mixing methods required for each.

All cake and sponge batters should have a final batter temperature of 18–24°C (65–75°F); therefore, it may be necessary to warm the eggs and other liquids to room temperature (21°C/70°F) before adding to the batter.

Cakes

Sugar Batter or Creaming Method
1.   Cream together the sugar and softened fat until light, creamy and fluffy.
2.   Add warmed eggs in 4–5 additions. Incorporate each addition thoroughly.
3.   Sieve together the dry ingredients, add to the above and mix until a smooth clear batter is obtained. Do not overmix as this will result in a tough cake with small volume.

Note: if milk or other liquids are to be incorporated, this should be done when the batter is half mixed, thus avoiding overmixing.

Flour Batter or Blending Method
1.   Mix the sugar with the warmed eggs and whisk until a thick spongelike consistency is achieved, commonly know as the ribbon stage (see photograph).
2.   Cream the fat with an equal amount of flour.
3.   Add (1) to (2) in four additions, blending each addition of sponge in well to the fat/flour mixture.

Eggs and sugar that have been whipped to the ribbon stage. Ribbon stage is when a mixture can hold its own weight for 10 seconds or more. Notice the thick sponge-like consistency.

4. Blend in the remainder of the flour, so that a smooth lump-free mixture is formed.

5. Lastly, add any other ingredients, such as milk, dried fruits, etc., blending in carefully to ensure even distribution.

Sponges

Traditional Method

1. Whisk together the warmed eggs and sugar to the ribbon stage (see photograph on opposite page).

2. Sieve the flour and carefully fold through the sponge. Avoid overmixing.

3. Once deposited into tins you must bake immediately.

Emulsified or All-in Method

1. Mix together the egg, water and sponge emulsifier.

2. Sieve together the dry ingredients, add to the above and blend to form a pastelike consistency.

3. Whisk on top speed for 5 minutes or until a thick sponge is reached (ribbon stage).

4. Once deposited in the tin this sponge can stand for 30–60 minutes before entering the oven.

Note: this method is used in commercial bakeries due to the special sponge emulsifiers which produce an excellent quality sponge.

Viennese biscuits being piped onto a baking tray.

Biscuits

Creaming Method

1. Beat together the sugar and softened fat until light and creamy.

2. Add the egg in 4–5 additions, beating well during each addition.

3. Sieve the dry ingredients and blend in on low speed until the batter is smooth and clear.

Note: this method is best suited to piped biscuits, for example, Viennese, Melting Moments, Toffee Biscuits, etc.

Blending Method

1. Blend together the sugar and softened fat until the two are well combined and soft. Do not cream or aerate this mixture.

2. Add the eggs all at once (if required) and slowly blend in. Do not cream or aerate the mixture at this stage.

3. Sieve the dry ingredients and blend in until the dough has cleared the sides of the mixing bowl and formed a solid mass.

Note: this method is best suited to rolled, refrigerated, cut and pressed biscuits, for example, Speculaas, Shortbread, Chocolate Chip, etc.

POINTS TO CONSIDER WHEN PROCESSING CAKES AND SPONGES

Cakes

1. Prepare all ingredients correctly and measure your ingredients accurately.
2. Always adhere to the procedures and mixing times stated in the recipe.
3. Scrape down the sides of the bowl frequently to ensure an even mixture is achieved.
4. Once the flour has been added avoid overmixing the batter.
5. Always check that the oven is preheated and set on the correct baking temperature required for the product.
6. Place the cakes into the oven as soon as possible to avoid the loss of aeration.

Sponges

1. Always ensure that your equipment is free from grease.
2. Prepare all ingredients correctly and measure your ingredients accurately.
3. Always adhere to the procedures and mixing times stated in the recipe.
4. If using the traditional method, avoid overmixing when folding in the flour, as this will result in a loss of volume in the finished baked product. Bake immediately.
5. Always check that the oven is preheated and set on the correct baking temperature required for the product.

WHAT HAPPENS DURING THE BAKING PROCESS?

When a cake or sponge batter goes into the oven many things happen:

1. The fat melts, causing the batter to flow level.
2. As the temperature rises, the batter becomes quite fluid and if knocked at this stage the cake could lose volume.
3. The air trapped during the creaming stage begins to expand and, as carbon dioxide is given off by the baking powder (if used), the bubbles become larger and join together.
4. The volume of the batter increases and the proteins of the flour and egg stretch to accommodate the expanding gases.
5. Steam is also produced as boiling point is reached, which assists in aeration.
6. As the heat increases, the starch of the flour begins to gelatinise and takes up much of the moisture present.
7. The expanding proteins begin to coagulate (set).
8. The centre of the cake is the last to be baked.
9. The sugar near the crust caramelises to give a golden brown colour.
10. The cake is baked when it springs back after being lightly pressed with your fingertips.

BAKING GUIDELINES

This is a general guide to the baking of cakes and sponges. All times and temperatures are guides only and will vary from oven to oven.

PRODUCT	TEMPERATURE	TIME (VARIABLE)
Fruit Cakes	160–170°C (320–340°F)	2–4 hours
Madeira-style Cakes	170–180°C (340–355°F)	20–30 minutes
Muffins	180–190°C (355–375°F)	15–18 minutes
Sponge Cakes	180–200°C (375–390°F)	20–30 minutes
Swiss Rolls	220–230°C (430–445°F)	5–7 minutes
Biscuits	170–180°C (340–355°F)	12–18 minutes

COOLING

Once the cake or sponge leaves the oven you should allow it to stand in its tin or tray for 5–10 minutes to allow it to settle and become firm. This will avoid it becoming damaged.

If you do not require the cake or sponge straight away, cool then wrap and freeze until required.

BASIC CAKE DECORATING TECHNIQUES

Enrobing is the term used to cover a cake or sponge base with a coating, for example, ganache or fondant.

The cake base is placed on a wire cooling rack which is placed over a dip tray. The coating is poured over the cake base and quickly spread with a palette knife to allow the coating to flow all down the sides; the excess will run directly onto the dip tray. The coating is allowed to set slightly before removing to be finished further. It is important to get the consistency of the coating right. It should evenly coat the back of a wooden spoon when poured over the spoon.

Making and using a paper piping bag This is one of the most difficult tasks of cake decorating to learn, but it can allow you to add those finishing touches to your cake to impress even the most skilled professional baker.

Hold the paper triangle as shown, grasping the centre of the long side between the thumb and forefinger of the left hand.

While still holding the paper, using the right hand, roll the top corner down to the centre of the triangle. Hold the paper in this position with the right hand.

With the left hand, roll the bottom corner up to complete the cone.

Adjust the cone so that the point is completely closed and the point is sharp. Fold the loose edges of the open end of the cone so that it will not unroll.

Fill the cone and fold the open end several times so that the filling doesn't come out. Hold the cone between the thumb and forefinger as shown. Cut off the tip to produce a fine hole.

Apply pressure from the top of the cone and pipe or decorate.

Using a pastry bag and piping tubes allows you to add those finishing touches to that perfect gateau or can be used to fill those light, crisp choux pastry eclairs with freshly whipped cream. There are many designs, borders and inscriptions that can be achieved using a pastry bag fitted with different piping tubes, however, there is one common mistake that many good home bakers make – that is not knowing when to stop decorating. The end result is a heavy, unattractive mess! The message when it comes to finishing is: 'Unless you are very experienced and skilled, keep it simple!'

For those needing to practise filling and using the pastry bag and piping tubes, refer to the Equipment section in this book, under Pastry Bag and Piping Tube, for more details.

CAKE PRODUCT FAULTS

FAULTS / CAUSES	Underbaked	Overbaked	Oven temp too low	Oven temp too high	Excessive sugar	Excessive fat	Excessive baking powder	Excessive flour	Too little baking powder	Knocked entering the oven	Flour too weak	Flour too strong	Batter overmixed	Fruit too wet	Lack of steam in oven	Insufficient sugar	Overcreaming batter	Insufficient liquids
Sunken fruit														•			•	
Cake sinking in the middle	•				•	•	•			•							•	
Peaked tops				•				•			•	•		•		•		•
Poor volume	•		•	•	•	•	•	•	•	•	•	•	•	•	•	•		•
Spots on crust				•			•											
Dense texture		•	•			•			•	•							•	•
Open texture					•		•										•	
Coarse dry texture		•	•	•					•	•								•
Poor keeping properties		•	•	•				•			•		•			•	•	•
Excessive crust colour		•		•	•		•									•		

ALL ABOUT PASTRIES

Pastry making is a real art. In most recipes the pastry is the vehicle that carries the other flavours and it should have a presence but not be the dominant component.

For bakers in a hurry or for those who have not perfected their pastry skills, there is a range of pastries in the supermarket. Frozen pastries include sweet short pastry, puff pastry, flaky pastry and phyllo pastry in convenient size packs. Some pastry can be bought ready rolled, which is very easy and convenient to use. If thawing pastry, take care to thaw it slowly. The best way is to place it in the refrigerator overnight. If in a real hurry, the pre-rolled sheets will thaw at room temperature in under half-an-hour.

BASIC INGREDIENTS

Puff Pastry
There are four basic ingredients used in the manufacture of puff pastry:
- medium or strong flour
- butter or special pastry margarine
- salt
- water

Often the only other ingredients used are lemon juice or cream of tartar.

Short and Sweet Pastry
Short and sweet pastries are made using a completely different manufacturing procedure and this is reflected in the ingredients used:
- standard baker's flour
- butter or margarine
- salt
- sugar (for sweet pastry)
- egg and/or water

Other ingredients used can be cocoa for chocolate sweet pastry, baking powder, lemon zest or vanilla essence for flavour.

Choux Pastry
In the make up stages of choux pastry it is more like a batter than a traditional pastry; however, once cooked, it has all the characteristics of a pastry – light and delicate. Choix pastry contains:
- strong flour
- water
- butter or margarine
- eggs

Choux pastry is the most difficult to make, as it requires skill, experience and understanding to achieve the desired finished product.

BASIC INGREDIENT FUNCTIONS
Listed overleaf are the ingredient functions for all pastry types.

Flour is important because its protein- (gluten) forming potential can dictate the lift that will be obtained, and because it forms the final structure of the pastry. For both puff and choux pastry strong flour should be used, as you require the strength and good quality protein (gluten). In the case of short and sweet pastry a medium or strong flour is suitable due to the high percentage of fat or butter used, which softens and weakens the protein (gluten), allowing the pastry to be more biscuit-like.

Salt improves the flavour and has a strengthening effect upon the protein (gluten) which is required for puff and choux pastry.

Butter or special pastry margarine has different functions in all three pastries.

Puff Pastry: Butter or special pastry margarines are used in the dough stage to make the dough softer and easier to handle. It also makes the finished pastry more tender and shorter to eat. Butter or special pastry margarines are used to separate the layers of dough which influence the degree of lift of the pastry and also have an effect on the eating quality of the baked pastry (this butter or special pastry margarine is often referred to as the layering fat). The amount of layering fat can vary between 50–100 percent based on the flour weight.

In commercial terms we usually define the type of pastry made by the amount of layering fat used:

- Half puff pastry: 50 percent of layering fat based on flour weight
- Three-quarter puff pastry: 75 percent of layering fat based on flour weight
- Full puff pastry: 100 percent of layering fat based on flour weight

Short and sweet pastry Butter or special pastry margarines are used to shorten and weaken the protein (gluten), allowing the pastry to be more biscuit-like (shortbread).

Choux Pastry Butter or special pastry margarines are used to allow the extensible protein (gliadin) to stretch without snapping or breaking when the choux pastry rises in the oven.

Water is largely required to obtain the correct consistency of the dough. Water also hydrates the protein (gluten) and allows it to become elastic and extensible. The amount used depends upon the absorption rate of the flour, the amount of fat used in the dough and the process used.

Sugar is mainly used in the manufacture of sweet pastry, which requires a sweeter tasting finished product. Sugar in conjunction with butter has a softening and shortening effect on the protein (gluten). The higher the sugar percentage, the crispier and more biscuit-like the sweet pastry will be. Caster sugar is always used to ensure the sugar crystals dissolve.

Eggs are generally not used in the manufacture of puff pastry but are essential in choux pastry.

Choux Pastry: Eggs make up the highest percentage in the recipe, approximately 200 percent based on flour weight. It is important that fresh good quality eggs are used as, unlike most recipes where the flour protein (gluten) supplies the structure, in choux pastry the egg protein (albumin) supplies the structure.

Sweet Pastry: Eggs are mainly used to enrich the dough for top quality sweet pastry goods. Eggs also improve the handling qualities of sweet pastry when rolling the pastry thin and pressing into tart moulds, etc.

Baking powder adds lightness and apparent shortness to sweet pastry. In top quality sweet pastry this is not necessary.

Cream of tartar and lemon juice are both acids which have a toughening but mellowing (allowing extensibility) effect on the protein (gluten), resulting in improved volume. If using either one of these acids always ensure you do not use an excessive amount, as this will turn your puff pastry sour and result in a low volume puff pastry. If using good quality flour, the addition of acid is not required.

MIXING AND PROCESSING METHODS

PUFF PASTRY

Once the initial dough has been formed by mixing the flour, chilled water, salt and the dough fat together to achieve a three-quarter developed dough, there are three methods of incorporating the layering fat.

Scotch Method (also known as the blitz, rough puff or all-in method)
1. The layering fat is cut into small cubes and incorporated during the formation of the dough made from flour, chilled water, salt and dough fat.
2. It is essential that the dough is not overmixed at this stage, as the layering fat needs to remain intact.
3. Allow this dough to rest for 5–10 minutes to allow the protein (gluten) to relax.
4. The pastry is now ready to be given its layers (known as the lamination stage).

English Method
1. Once the basic dough of flour, chilled water, salt and dough fat has been made, allow the dough to rest for 5–10 minutes to enable the protein (gluten) to relax.
2. Roll out the dough to a large rectangle approximately 1.5 cm ($^1/_2$ inch) thick.
3. Condition the layering fat so that it is of the same consistency as the dough. Then shape it to cover three-quarters of the rolled out dough. This is often the success or failure of the puff pastry. Ensure the layering fat is not too hard or too soft.
4. Place the conditioned layering fat over three-quarters of the rolled out dough.
5. Fold the uncovered third of dough over the layering fat.
6. Fold the remaining third back over to obtain three layers of dough and two layers of layering fat.
7. The pastry is now ready to be given its layers (known as the lamination stage).

French Method (often known as the envelope method)
1. Once the basic dough of flour, chilled water, salt and dough fat has been made, allow the dough to rest for 5–10 minutes to enable the protein (gluten) to relax.
2. Roll out the dough to a large rectangle approximately 2 cm ($^3/_4$ inch) thick.
3. Condition the layering fat so that it is of the same consistency as the dough. Then shape it to fit inside the rolled out dough. This is often the success or failure of the puff pastry. Ensure the layering fat is not too hard or too soft.

Scotch puff pastry at the completion of mixing ready for the lamination stage to take place. Note the layering fat still intact.

English method, step 4

English method, step 5

English method, step 6

4. Place the conditioned layering fat in the centre of the rolled out dough.
5. Fold each corner of the dough into the centre to encase the layering fat in an envelope, obtaining two layers of dough and one layer of layering fat.
6. The pastry is now ready to be given its layers (known as the lamination stage).

French method, step 4

The Lamination Process

The method used to incorporate the layering fat into the dough is irrelevant to the lamination process. There are two methods of layering the dough and fat that have been formed. These are commonly referred to as turns or folds. In this procedure we are trying to achieve hundreds of thin layers of fat and dough – in most cases up to 400 layers are formed.

French method, step 5

Half Fold: (also known as a 3-fold or half turn)
1. Roll out the pastry to a rectangle 1.25 cm (¹/₂ inch) thick.
2. By eye mentally divide the rectangle into thirds.
3. Fold A to C and then D to B to complete three layers of pastry. Rest for 15–20 minutes, covered with a plastic bag to prevent the pastry drying out and skinning.
4. Repeat this process three times.
5. The pastry is either ready to be rolled out to its final thickness for product make-up or to be kept in the refrigerator or freezer until required.

Book Fold: (also known as a 4-fold or full turn)
1. Roll out the pastry to a rectangle 1.25 cm (¹/₂ inch) thick.
2. By eye mentally divide the rectangle into half.
3. Fold A to B and then C to B. Then fold the whole pastry in half again to complete four layers of pastry. Rest for 15–20 minutes, covered with a plastic bag to prevent the pastry drying out and skinning
4. Repeat this process twice more.
5. The pastry is either ready to be rolled out to its final thickness for product make-up or to be kept in the refrigerator or freezer until required.

Rolling and folding to achieve a half fold.

Points to consider when processing puff pastry
1. Always adhere to the resting times stated to avoid shrinkage in the finished baked product.
2. When rolling and folding your puff pastry, use as little dusting flour as possible, brushing away any excess flour before completing each fold.
3. When making puff pastry ensure that all your ingredients are kept cool.
4. During resting periods keep the pastry covered with plastic and keep cool in the refrigerator.
5. Always rest your puff pastry products before baking – the longer the better (anywhere from 2–12 hours in the refrigerator). Allow to warm up before baking.
6. When rolling out for each fold, ensure that the open ends are folded back into the dough.
7. Always ensure that your dough and layering fat are the same consistency when incorporating the layering fat.

Rolling and folding to achieve a book fold.

8. Always use chilled water. In the summer you need to use iced chilled water (do not put the ice cubes in the dough, as they will not dissolve during mixing).

How does puff pastry rise?

1. Once the hundreds of layers of dough and layering fat enter the oven (the oven must be at the correct temperature) the fat melts and the moisture within the dough begins to produce steam.
2. The protein (gluten) in the dough layers begins to expand.
3. The steam pushes the dough layers upwards.
4. Once the puff pastry has reached its maximum volume and all the moisture within has escaped, the protein (gluten) begins to coagulate (set), giving it its structure.
5. If the puff pastry is taken out of the oven before complete coagulation (setting), the structure will collapse.

Storage of puff pastry

Unbaked puff pastry can be stored in the refrigerator or freezer in block or rolled form. Thaw your puff pastry in the refrigerator overnight, then let it stand at room temperature for approximately 30 minutes.

Baking guidelines

This is a general guide to baking puff pastry. All times and temperatures are guides only and will vary from oven to oven.

PRODUCT	TEMPERATURE	TIME (VARIABLE)
Unfilled puff pastry	220–230°C (430–445°F)	18–20 minutes
Filled puff pastry (sweet)	215–220°C (420–430°F)	20–25 minutes
Filled puff pastry (savoury)	220–225°C (430–437°F)	25–30 minutes
Reheating puff pastry products	190–200°C (375–390°F)	15–25 minutes

Cooling

Puff pastry should be cooled on a cooling rack to avoid sweating. Pies should be allowed to cool slightly before being removed from their tins. This will stop the pie from collapsing.

SHORT AND SWEET PASTRY

The main difference between short and sweet pastry is the amount of sugar used. There are four methods of making short and sweet pastry, but the two most common methods are the creaming and blending.

Creaming Method

1. Beat the butter, salt and sugar until light, creamy and fluffy.

2. Continue beating on low speed while adding the liquid or egg.
3. Slowly mix in the dry ingredients and mix until a clear, smooth paste is formed. Do not overmix.
4. The pastry is ready for processing.

Blending Method
1. Mix the butter and flour together until no lumps are left and the mix resembles ground almonds or a crumble.
2. Mix liquid or eggs with the sugar and salt, then slowly add to the dry mixture while mixing on a slow speed.
3. Mix until a clear, smooth paste is formed. Do not overmix.
4. The pastry is ready for processing.

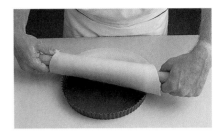

A flan tin being lined with sweet pastry before being filled.

Creating shortness in short and sweet pastry
The mixing methods that are used in making short and sweet pastry are designed to coat the flour particles with fat, thus protecting the development of the protein (gluten) network when the liquids are added. Mixing this way will always ensure that a short, tender pastry is obtained. Of course this is only achieved in conjunction with the correct mixing time.

Points to consider when processing short and sweet pastry
1. Do not overmix.
2. Avoid excessive handling of the pastry.
3. Work in a cool environment.

Storage of short and sweet pastry
Unbaked short and sweet pastry can be stored in the refrigerator and freezer, unfilled or filled. It is advisable to thaw your short or sweet pastry out in the refrigerator overnight, then let it stand at room temperature for approximately 30 minutes.

Baking guidelines
This is a general guide to baking short and sweet pastry. All times and temperatures are guides only and will vary from oven to oven.

PRODUCT	TEMPERATURE	TIME (VARIABLE)
Unfilled short pastry	200–220°C (390–430°F)	18–20 minutes
Filled short pastry	215–220°C (420–430°F)	20–25 minutes
Unfilled sweet pastry	180–190°C (355–375°F)	18–20 minutes
Filled sweet pastry	180–190°C (355–375°F)	25–30 minutes
Reheating short and sweet pastry products	180–190°C (355–375°F)	15–25 minutes

Cooling
Baked short or sweet pastry should be cooled on a cooling rack to avoid sweating. Pies

should be allowed to cool slightly before being removed from their tins. This will stop the pie collapsing.

CHOUX PASTRY

One of the secrets to top quality choux pastries is cooking the roux or base and knowing how much egg to add. There is only one method of producing choux pastry.

General Method

1. Boil the water and butter, then remove from the heat.
2. Add the strong flour and return to a medium heat. Cook this basic roux for 4–5 minutes, stirring all the time. Avoid overcooking the roux as this will dry it out.
3. Allow the roux to cool slightly before adding the eggs in small additions. Beat well between each addition.
4. Add enough egg to hold 'soft peaks'.
5. Place into a piping bag with a tube attached and pipe onto a greased tray.
6. Bake in a hot oven (210–225°C/410–435°F). Do not open the door for the first 15–20 minutes.

Choux pastry ready to be piped. Notice the consistency of the batter.

Points to consider when processing choux pastry

1. Always use strong flour.
2. Do not leave the water and butter boiling too long, as some of the water will evaporate.
3. Always use fresh eggs.
4. Do not overcook the roux.
5. Ensure you add the correct amount of egg, beating well between each small addition. The egg amounts will always be variable.
6. Always bake in a hot oven.
7. Never open the oven door too early, as this will allow the steam to escape.

What causes choux pastry to rise?

1. The choux pastry enters the oven as a thick, shiny mass.
2. Once steam is produced from the water within the batter, it pushes upwards causing the choux pastry to 'balloon' and rise.
3. Once the pastry has risen to its maximum height and the moisture from the batter has escaped, the protein (albumin) present within the eggs will coagulate (set), giving the choux pastry strength and structure.
4. At this stage, the choux pastry must be given time to dry out, otherwise the proteins inside will not support the outer shell, and it will collapse upon cooling.

Baking guidelines

This is a general guide to baking choux pastry. All times and temperatures are guides only and will vary from oven to oven.

PRODUCT	TEMPERATURE	TIME (VARIABLE)
Choux pastry	220–225°C (430–435°F)	20–25 minutes (drying time 5 minutes)

Storage of choux pastry

Unbaked choux pastry should be baked fresh straight away. It is common practice to freeze baked choux pastry, which only requires thawing before use. Some bakers place the thawed choux pastry in a warm oven for a few minutes to dry any moisture collected during freezing.

Cooling

Once the choux pastry has been baked, place directly onto cooling wire. This will allow air circulation and prevent the product sweating.

FAULTS IN PUFF PASTRY

FAULTS \ CAUSES	Incorrect rolling technique	Fat too hard	Too short rest before baking	Uneven oven heat	Too many turns/folds	Rolled out too thin	Flour used was too weak	Layering fat too soft	Room temp too warm	Too much fat used	Not enough fat used	Oven temp too low	Incorrect cutting out	Tough layering fat used	Too strong flour used	Dough made too tight	Dough made too slack	Skinning of pastry	Poor sealing	Insufficient turns/folds	Pastry left uncovered
Uneven lift	•	•	•	•									•					•	•	•	
Poor volume	•				•	•	•	•	•	•	•	•	•			•	•	•			
Distorted shape	•		•	•									•					•		•	
Shrinkage			•												•	•	•				
Fat seepage during baking		•						•		•										•	
Tough eating					•						•			•	•	•	•	•			
Filling spilling out			•										•					•			
Skinning																					•

FAULTS IN SHORT AND SWEET PASTRY PRODUCTS

FAULTS \ CAUSES	Not enough fat, egg, sugar	Too strong flour used	Too little egg/liquid used	Too much egg/liquid used	Not rested before baking	Too much aeration	Too much sugar	Oven temp too high	Oven temp too low	Too much fat used	Overmixed	Undermixed	Too much filling
Tough pastry	•	•	•	•							•		
Shrinkage	•	•		•	•						•		
Distort shape	•	•		•	•						•		
Dense texture	•	•	•								•		
Dark in colour							•	•					
Lack of colour	•								•				
Pastry breaking, too short						•	•			•		•	
Brown spot on the crust							•						
Filling boiling out during baking													•

ALASYA

Cemal Bekir arrived in Melbourne from Cyprus in 1977 and within six months had set up a tiny family restaurant and bakery, Alasya, in Brunswick. From the beginning it was busy with a steady stream of customers arriving to eat the delicious, genuine Turkish fare he offered. His vision was to expand, opening another restaurant every two years. But he found the need to increase his original site to cope with the numbers (now up to 500 people daily), and has gradually taken over adjacent stores for his extensive premises.

One of the real successes of Alasya is the traditional Turkish pide bread, baked in a huge authentic purpose-built Turkish wood-fired oven. Cemal remains active in the restaurant, putting in 14-hour days, overseeing the baking, and is assisted by Fatma (below), one of his three daughters. The soft, chewy bread is in great demand – it is supplied to over 120 restaurants and stores around Melbourne and also served, accompanied by dips, to Alaysa's diners.

Plans are on the drawing board to expand the bakery and to build another even larger oven to keep up with the growing number of daily orders for pide.

Turkish Pide

To achieve the right result with this bread it is important that the dough is almost fluid. It requires careful handling and the shape largely takes place as it is handled into the oven. The bakers coax and stretch it into position, working quickly to place it on a very hot oven floor or baking tray and do not let it completely dry out. Serve fresh or toasted with Mediterranean dips, as the bread does not keep well.

1. Sieve the flour onto your work surface. Make a well and add the sugar, salt, yeast and olive oil.
2. While mixing by hand, slowly add the water to the well.
3. Mix or knead the dough by hand using the technique shown in the All About Bread Section. Every couple of minutes you should stop and check the gluten development and temperature of the dough (and take a quick breather!). This final kneading should take about 15 minutes (check if you have fully developed the dough by using the stretch test). It is important to ensure that the dough is fully developed. The dough will be slightly slack and a little sticky. Do not be tempted to add more flour, as this is how the dough should be after mixing.
4. Lightly oil a bowl large enough to allow the dough to double in bulk. Put the dough in the bowl and cover with plastic. Leave in a warmish place (23–25°C/ 73–77°F) for 1½ hours. By this time the dough should be nearly double in size.
5. Gently tip the dough out onto a lightly floured bench and, using a dough scraper, cut the dough into 3 pieces of approximately 300 g (10½ oz) each. Be gentle with the dough, do not aggressively punch it down, or squeeze all the gas from within. Pick each piece up and gently tuck the edges underneath, pulling the surface tight around the mass to form an oblong shape. Lay the pieces back on the floured bench and cover with a proofing cloth or plastic. Give an intermediate proof of 20 minutes.
6. Uncover the dough and then on a floured bench, using both hands, very gently stretch the dough piece to an oblong shape almost to the full length of a baking tray (280 mm long). Place onto a baking tray lined with baking paper. Repeat for the second and third dough piece. Allow about 40 mm (2 inches) between each piece of dough.
7. Using a pastry brush, brush each oblong dough piece well with egg wash.
8. Using your fingers (spread apart) dock each dough piece 5-6 times down the length of the dough. Very lightly sprinkle with sesame or cumin seeds.
9. Allow to stand in a warm place for 15 minutes.
10. With a baking stone in place, gently slide the dough pieces directly into a preheated oven set at 250°C (480°F) (with the baking paper still underneath the dough) and bake for 8–9 minutes only. Alternatively, place the baking tray directly into the oven. Do not overbake the Turkish bread as it will ruin the effect of soft eating flat bread.
11. Cool on a wire rack.

500 g (4 cups) strong flour
10 g (2 teaspoons) sugar
10 g (2 teaspoons) salt
5 g (1¼ teaspoons) dried active yeast
15 g (1¼ tablespoons) olive oil
360 ml (1½ cups + 1 tablespoon) water
egg wash (made with 1 egg and
*   50 ml/3½ tablespoons water,*
*   whisked together)*

3 tablespoons sesame or cumin seeds
*   for topping*

Finished Dough Temperature:
*   27°C (80°F)*

NIKO AND SASHA LEWIS

BABKA BAKERY CAFÉ

Regulars cram this tiny café and the queue for the jam-packed tables stretches out the door into Brunswick Street. Meanwhile the kitchen is chaotic as simple delicious meals are prepared amongst the racks of breads and pastries that appear from the steamy commercial ovens. Babka, a genuine European-style bakery and café in the heart of Melbourne's Fitzroy, is overseen by Sasha Lewis, who started this popular venture eight years ago after being involved with several other cafés in the city.

Her son Niko had grown up in the restaurant environment and always had a creative streak that saw him drawing, illustrating and clay modelling tiny food objects into earrings for his schoolmates as a boy. At age 15 he took a part-time job in a bakery, awakening his passion for better bread without additives. He has never looked back and although he missed out on the big overseas experience that is so much part of an Antipodean youth, Niko had his dream of running a bakery fulfilled when he joined Sasha to open Babka.

The excellent breads and pastries Niko produces are snapped up by many local customers and several fine Melbourne restaurants. He has personally developed his own style of sourdough breads and many other superb bakery items.

Wholemeal Vegetable and Sesame Seed Loaf

This loaf, chock-full of vegetables, is moist and tasty. It keeps well for several days and when toasted develops even more flavour. Niko suggests that the perfect way to enjoy it is to toast slices and spread with peanut butter. It is very popular with Babka's customers.

1. In a large bowl, toss the vegetables and salt.
2. Cover and leave to stand for 1 hour. This will draw the moisture out of the vegetables, which is required for the dough later on.
3. Place onto your work surface all the flours and vegetable mix. Make a well and add the yeast and water.
4. Mix or knead the dough by hand using the technique shown in the All About Bread Section. Continue kneading until the ingredients are well combined. This final kneading should take about 10–15 minutes (check if you have fully developed the dough by using the stretch test). Check the dough throughout kneading for stickiness (due to the moisture coming out of the vegetables), adding more water or flour if necessary to achieve a soft but not too firm dough.
5. Place the dough into a lightly oiled bowl large enough to allow the dough to double in bulk. Cover with plastic and leave in a warmish place (23–25°C/73–77°F) until the dough has doubled in size – approximately 1½ hours.
6. Gently knock back the dough in the bowl. This will deflate it slightly, but it will develop more strength. Cover again and leave for 30 minutes. Take care in doing this as the dough is very fragile at this stage.
7. Tip the dough out onto a lightly floured bench and, using a dough scraper, cut the dough into 2 pieces (approximately 570 g (20 oz) each). Be gentle with the dough, do not aggressively punch it down, or squeeze all the gas from within. Pick each piece up and gently tuck the edges underneath, pulling the surface tight around the mass. Lay the pieces back on the floured bench and cover with a proofing cloth (or tea-towel). Give an intermediate proof of 10 minutes. While you wait, lightly grease 2 medium size bread tins.
8. Uncover the dough pieces and mould them into oblong shapes (much like a vienna loaf but not with tapered ends. To achieve this, flatten the dough piece out as for rolling up a swiss roll, then tightly roll the dough towards you. Apply pressure with your hands as you roll – the tighter the roll the better.
9. Lightly roll each loaf on a wet clean cloth or tea-towel and then roll in sesame seeds. Wetting the surface of your dough piece will allow the sesame seeds to adhere evenly.
10. Lay each dough piece seam-side down in the prepared bread tins.
11. Final proof for approximately 1 hour or until almost doubled in size. Cover with plastic to prevent skinning and chilling of the dough. Use the indentation test to tell when the dough is fully proofed.
12. Just before you load the bread into the oven, spray water into the oven cavity with a spray gun. Close the door quickly so you don't lose any of the steam.

VEGETABLE PREPARATION

165 g (1¾ packed cup) grated carrot

165 g (1 heaped cup) finely chopped onion

85 g (½ heaped cup) mixture of finely sliced and roughly chopped zucchini

85 g (½ cup) diced red peppers

10 g (2 teaspoons) salt

DOUGH

335 g (2¼ cups) wholemeal flour

170 g (1⅓ cups) strong flour

15 g (1½ tablespoons) gluten flour

salted vegetables from above

5 g (1¼ teaspoons) dried instant yeast

100 ml (½ cup + 2 tablespoons) water (variable depending on the amount of moisture drawn out of the vegetable)

100 g (½ cup) sesame seeds for rolling the dough in

Finished Dough Temperature: 26°C (80°F)

13. Quickly place the loaves into a preheated oven set at 220°C (430°F), bake for 20 minutes then turn the oven down to 200°C (390°F) and bake for a further 10–15 minutes. Check the loaf for readiness by tapping the bottom and listening for a hollow sound.

14. Tip the loaves out onto a wire cooling rack.

Photo of recipe on back cover.

Shoo Fly Buns

Shoo Fly Buns

When Niko was learning his craft, he adapted this bun from a recipe given to him at trade school, and Sasha immediately gave them their quaint name. The orange purée in the buns gives a lovely zesty flavour and they are best served warm with fresh butter melting into them.

1. Place the sugar, water and orange zest into a saucepan and bring to the boil to dissolve the sugar. Do not boil too long otherwise the water will evaporate.

2. Place into a container and cover until required.

3. Wash and dry the oranges.

4. Leaving the skins on the oranges, cut into quarters and remove any pips.

5. Purée orange quarters in a food processor.

6. Place into a bowl and cover until required.

7. Place onto your work surface the flour, salt, sugar, milk powder, and butter. Make a well and add the yeast, water and puréed oranges.

8. Mix or knead the dough by hand using the technique shown in the All About Bread Section. Continue kneading until the ingredients are well combined. This final kneading should take about 10–15 minutes (check if you have fully developed the dough by using the stretch test). Check the dough throughout kneading for stickiness, adding more water or flour if necessary to achieve a soft, but not too firm dough.

9. Add the currants and gently incorporate into the dough, taking care not to damage the fruit too much.

10. Place the dough into a lightly oiled bowl large enough to allow the dough to double in bulk. Cover with plastic and leave in a warmish place (23–25°C/ 73–77°F) until the dough has doubled in size – approximately 1½ hours.

11. Gently knock back the dough in the bowl. This will deflate it slightly, but it will develop more strength. Cover again and leave for 30 minutes.

12. Tip the dough out onto a lightly floured bench and, using a dough scraper, cut the dough into 12 pieces (approximately 100 g (3½ oz) each).

13. Mould each piece of dough into a round ball. This is done by cupping your hand over the dough piece on a flourless bench, applying downwards pressure and moving your hand around in circular motions.

14. Place the buns onto a baking tray, lightly greased or lined with baking paper, 12 per tray, 4 across and 3 down. Ensure the buns are not too close together – they should be individual buns once baked.

15. Final proof for approximately 1 hour or until almost doubled in size. Cover with plastic to prevent skinning and chilling of the dough. Use the indentation test to tell when the buns are fully proofed.

16. Place the baking tray into a preheated oven set at 200°C (390°F) and bake for 15–20 minutes. Turn the oven tray around halfway through baking if needed. The buns should be lightly coloured on the sides and slightly darker on the tops.

17. Remove from the oven and immediately brush each bun all over with the prepared glaze.

18. Cool on a wire rack.

STICKY BUN GLAZE
100 g (½ cup) sugar
60 ml (4 tablespoons) water
zest of ½ orange

DOUGH
500 g (4 cups) strong flour
10 g (2 teaspoons) salt
50 g (¼ cup) sugar
25 g (3 tablespoons) milk powder
50 g (3 tablespoons + 1 teaspoon) unsalted butter, softened
8 g (1½ teaspoons) dried yeast
150 g (½ cup + 2 tablespoons) water (variable depending on how much juice the oranges have)
250 g (1½) medium oranges – puréed (see steps 3 to 6)
250 g (2 cups) currants

Finished Dough Temperature:
26°C (80°F)

Apple Tarte Tatin

A real favourite at Babka, the pastry literally melts in your mouth, and the dark rich caramel combines with the apples to make a luscious dessert. Serve this warm with softly whipped cream.

PUFF PASTRY

250 g (1³/₄ cups + 2 tablespoons) strong flour

40 g (3 tablespoons) chilled butter

pinch of salt

130 ml (¹/₂ cup + 1 tablespoon) water, chilled (place in the refrigerator overnight)

150 g (³/₄ cup) butter, chilled, for layering

CARAMEL AND APPLE FILLING

5–6 small to medium sized dessert apples (granny smith, etc.). The number of apples depends on the size of the pan used.

100 g (¹/₂ cup) unsalted butter (softened)

220 g (1 cup + 2 tablespoons) caster sugar

1. Choose the method of making puff pastry from the All About Pastry Section.
2. Once you have incorporated the layering fat give the pastry either 4 'half folds' or 3 'book folds' (see the All About Pastry Section).
3. It is best if the pastry is made 1 day in advance.
4. Remove the pastry from the refrigerator and leave for 20 minutes at room temperature.
5. On a lightly floured surface roll out half the puff pastry to a thickness 4–5 mm (¹/₄ inch).
6. Then using a sharp pointed knife cut out a circle 200 mm (8 inches) in diameter (the size will depend on the diameter of your ovenproof frying pan). Fold the pastry in half and then in half again to make a quarter and keep for later.
7. Gently press the pastry scraps and remaining pastry together and wrap in plastic wrap. Place in the refrigerator or freezer until required.
8. Peel and core apples, then cut in half.
9. Evenly coat the bottom of a 200 mm (8 inch) diameter ovenproof frying pan or large, thick-bottomed, round baking dish with the softened butter and sugar.
10. Place the apples round-side down in a circular pattern in the pan. Ensure you start from the outside first and work your way into the middle. For a 200 mm (8 inch) frying pan you should have 7 halves around the outside and 4–5 quarters in the inner circle.
11. Place the frying pan on a stove element and cook on a slow heat. Allow the sugar and butter to dissolve and start to bubble. Shake the pan gently to ensure even cooking.
12. When the caramel syrup is simmering evenly, turn the heat up to medium, cover with a lid and cook for approximately 10–15 minutes or until the apples are tender and the caramel syrup has thickened and turned golden brown. Occasionally shake the pan gently to ensure even cooking.
13. Remove from the direct heat and allow to cool for 5 minutes.
14. Place the pre-rolled puff pastry circle on top of the apples, tucking the edges of the pastry inside the rim of the frying pan.
15. Prick with a fork or knife several times to allow the steam to escape and prevent the pastry from doming.
16. Place the frying pan into a preheated oven set at 220°C (430°F) and bake for 10 minutes, then reduce the heat to 200°C (390°F) and bake for a further 10–12 minutes or until the pastry is golden brown and cooked through.
17. Remove the tart from the oven and cool for a few minutes. Gently shake to ensure the apples are not stuck.
18. Place a large, flat serving plate on top of the pastry and then, holding the plate and the pan firmly together, invert so the plate is now on the bottom. Take extreme care when doing this, as the caramel syrup is still runny and very hot.
19. Serve warm or cool.

JEAN LOUIS MACADRÉ

BORDEAUX BAKERY

Genuine French breads and pastries are baked by this passionate, authentic French baker in his busy bakery and café on bustling Thorndon Quay in the heart of Wellington. Out the back, the bakery is filled with linen baskets, enormous ovens and mixers, and shelves are crammed with special sugars, fruit purées and special patisserie moulds. Jean Louis hails from Bordeaux and is genuinely pleased with the success he has found in New Zealand.

'Customers drive from the Wairarapa and all over the Wellington region to buy my bread,' he boasts, 'but it would have taken two generations in France to have built a business to this size!'

The shelves of his shop are filled with a full range of such specialities as baguettes, boules, rustic breads, couronne, and such delicate patisserie as canèles, the tiny treats from Bordeaux that are almost custard-like in their interior. Jean Louis remains French in his loyalty, and sources baking equipment, machinery, ingredients and, above all, authentic recipes directly from France. His love for the art of baking is evident as he explains that he makes bread with his heart, and that a baker must have total 'feel' for his dough, adding something of his passion to every loaf.

Brioches

A classic French bread, brioche is a light yeast-baked sweet bread that is perfect for toasting or simply buttering when fresh, soft and airy. Brioche is also the base for many French desserts and it is the most perfect bread to use in a good old-fashioned bread and butter pudding.

1. Sieve the flour onto your work surface. Make a well and add the salt, sugar and yeast.
2. Slowly add the water and three-quarters of the egg, knead the dough for 6–7 minutes or until the dough is almost fully developed (it is important to develop the gluten structure before all the egg is added).
3. Continue to add the balance of the egg slowly while the dough is still being kneaded. Add sufficient egg to achieve a very soft, elastic, very smooth and shiny dough.
4. While kneading, slowly add the softened butter in small amounts. Knead in all the butter to achieve a smooth, elastic, silky dough. Do not overmix the dough as this will cause overheating and the dough will become oily and greasy.
5. Transfer the dough into a lightly oiled container covered with plastic wrap; give a bulk fermentation time of one hour in a warm draught-free place. The dough should double in size.
6. Gently knock back the dough to expel all the gases, reactivate the yeast and strengthen the gluten structure. Finally, push the dough out to a thickness of 5 cm, place into a shallow container, then cover with plastic wrap.
7. Place in the refrigerator overnight (12 hours). This makes the dough easier to mould since the dough will be cold and firm.
8. The following day, scale off into 300 g (10½ oz) and 50 g (1½ oz) pieces for large brioches or 50 g (1½ oz) and 10 g (½ oz) pieces for small brioches. Mould both pieces into round shapes, flatten the larger ball slightly and make a hole in the middle with your finger; then place it into a greased brioche mould. (This recipe makes approximately 4 large brioches or 20 small brioches.)
9. Mould the smaller ball into a tear drop and push it into the hole of the larger ball firmly with your fingers. Alternatively, place six 70 g (2½ oz) round balls inside a greased bread tin (three each side).
10. Cover and prove in a warm, draught-free place until double in size (2–3 hours).
11. Using a pastry brush, gently glaze with egg wash.
12. Place directly into a preheated oven at 210°C (410°F) for 12–15 minutes or until golden brown.
13. Remove from the moulds after 10 minutes and place on a wire cooling rack.

500 g (4 cups) strong flour
10 g (2 teaspoons) salt
50 g (¼ cup) granulated sugar
8 g (1 tablespoon) dried active yeast
50 ml (¼ cup) water
350 g (7) eggs (variable)
250 g (1 cup + 3 tablespoons) softened butter

Finished Dough Temperature:
  27°C (80°F)

Variations
You can roll chocolate pieces or fruit fillings into the centre of the brioche at step 8, if desired. Process as for standard brioche.

Croissants

An infinite amount of care and patience is needed to achieve the perfect croissant. There is nothing quite like a warm croissant, flaky and light and served with a steaming bowl of milky coffee.

DOUGH

500 g (4 cups) strong flour (chilled in the refrigerator overnight)

15 g (1½ tablespoons) gluten flour

10 g (2 teaspoons) salt

50 g (¼ cup) sugar

8 g (1 tablespoon) dried active yeast

egg wash for finishing

140 ml (1 cup + 2 tablespoons) chilled water (placed in the refrigerator overnight)

130 ml (1 cup + 1 tablespoon) chilled milk

Finished Dough Temperature:
15°C (60°F)

LAYERING FAT

280 g (1 cup + 4 tablespoons) butter (if using special butter sheets delete the flour below)

50 g (⅓ cup) strong flour

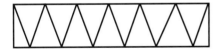

1. Sieve the flour and gluten onto your work surface. Make a well and add the salt, sugar, yeast, milk and water.

2. Mix or knead the dough by hand using the technique shown in the All About Bread section. Continue to knead the dough by hand. Every couple of minutes stop and check the gluten development and temperature of the dough. Only half develop your dough. This should take 5–7 minutes. At this stage the dough should be firm and cold.

3. Place the dough in a floured bowl. Cover with plastic and rest for 45 minutes in a warm, draught-free place. While the dough is resting prepare the layering fat by placing the butter and flour into a mixing bowl fitted with a beater. Mix together on a low speed until it forms a solid mass. Don't overmix or soften the butter too much. Place the layering fat between two layers of plastic and roll out to a flat square 17 cm x 17 cm (7 inches x 7 inches). Place in the refrigerator to firm up.

4. Gently knock back the dough, place back into the bowl and cover. Rest in the refrigerator for 3 hours.

5. Incorporate the layering fat into the dough using the French Method (see Mixing and Processing in the All About Pastries section). Ensure the dough is kept cool during the make up of croissants.

6. You should now have an envelope of dough with the layering fat inside. Carefully roll out the dough on a lightly floured board lengthways to achieve a rectangle 10–15 mm (½ inch) in thickness. Give a half fold (see the Laminating Process in the All About Pastries section). Place on a floured tray, wrap in plastic and place in the freezer for 5 minutes.

7. Remove from the freezer and repeat the above process.

8. You should have now given the croissant dough three half folds. Rest the dough for 15 minutes in the freezer.

9. Remove from the freezer and gradually roll the dough out on a floured surface to a rectangle shape of 80 cm (31 inches) wide x 20 cm (8 inches) long and 4 mm (¼ inch) thick, ensuring that the pastry is freely moving during the rolling process. Keep the pastry as rectangular and as even as possible. Trim the outside edges.

10. Using a large chef's knife cut the rectangle into even triangles (see diagram, left). Average triangle size is 8 cm (3 inches) wide x 15 cm (6 inches) long.

11. Roll each triangle up starting at the base and rolling and stretching to the bottom, bend and pinch the ends on each other to form a crescent shape.

12. Place onto a greased or baking paper lined baking tray.

13. Cover with plastic and place in a warm place to proof for 45 minutes or until almost double in size.

14. After proofing, very gently brush the croissants with egg wash (two parts egg to one part milk or water).

15. Place directly into a preheated oven set at 220°C (430°F) and bake for 15–18 minutes until golden brown.

16. Place onto a wire cooling rack.

Paris Brest

Filled with a rich, creamy French custard, this delicate choux pastry ring is a classic gateau found throughout France. Take care to read the notes on choux pastry in the All About Pastries section before commencing. Paris Brest makes a stunning dessert or can be an excellent accompaniment to coffee.

PASTRY

125 ml (¹/₂ cup) cold water

pinch of salt

75 g (¹/₂ cup) butter

105 g (³/₄ cup + 1 tablespoon) strong flour

175 g (3¹/₂) eggs (variable)

40 g (¹/₂ cup) flaked almond

icing sugar to dust

FILLING

250 ml (1 cup) milk

2–3 drops vanilla essence

65 g (¹/₄ cup + 1 tablespoon) granulated sugar

75 g (1¹/₂) eggs

35 g (¹/₄ cup) plain flour

5 g (2¹/₄ teaspoons) cornflour

20 g (1¹/₂ tablespoons) butter

300 g (3 cups) whipped cream (sweetened)

Side view

1. Place the water, salt and butter in a saucepan and bring to the boil. Remove from the heat.
2. Add the flour and mix in using a wooden spoon until well combined.
3. Return to a low heat and cook the basic roux for 2 minutes, stirring all the time to avoid the mixture sticking to the bottom. This will slightly dry the mixture out.
4. Place in a mixing bowl, and beat to cool the mixture.
5. Slowly add the eggs (almost one by one) beating well between each addition (all of the eggs may not be required).
6. The mixture should not be runny; it should hold soft peaks or when the spoon is run through the mixture the trench walls will remain standing for approximately 10 seconds before collapsing in on themselves.
7. Place the mixture in a piping bag fitted with a 1 cm (³/₈ inch) piping tube.
8. On a lightly greased and floured baking tray, trace a 10 cm (4 inch) round circle. This choux pastry is enough to do two 10 cm (4 inch) Paris Brest.
9. Pipe a ring of choux paste around the circle.
10. Pipe another circle inside the first one so that it is just touching the side.
11. Finally pipe a third circle on top and in the middle of the two bottom circles (see diagram).
12. Using a pastry brush, lightly egg wash the choux paste, then very lightly scrape the top with a fork to give a decorative pattern.
13. Sprinkle the top with flaked almonds.
14. Place into a preheated oven set at 230°C (445°F) and bake for 20 minutes before checking. Ensure that you do not open the oven door during this first 20 minutes, as this will cause the choux paste to collapse.
15. Reduce the heat to 200°C (390°F) and open the oven door. Continue to bake the choux for another 15–20 minutes or until the choux paste has dried out.
16. Place directly onto a wire cooling rack and cool completely.
17. To assemble, slice the choux paste ring in half horizontally, and carefully remove the top half. Using a piping bag fitted with a star piping tube, pipe the crème diplomat filling (see recipe below) around the ring.
18. Replace the top half of the choux paste ring and place onto a serving plate.
19. Dust lightly with icing sugar before serving.

Crème Diplomat Filling

1. Place the milk, vanilla essence and half the sugar in a saucepan. Stir and bring to the boil.
2. Meanwhile in a bowl whisk the egg and the remaining sugar until the mixture becomes pale yellow and thick.
3. Sieve the flour and cornflour together and slowly add this to the egg and sugar mixture while still whisking to avoid any lumps. Do not overmix.
4. Once the milk and sugar mixture has come to the boil, add half of this to the

Durum Semolina Rolls

Ideal for restaurants, these neat little bread rolls reheat beautifully so that they can be served crisp. The starter is a sourdough style, but the end product is sweet and smooth.

1. Place onto your work surface the flour, durum semolina, and yeast. Make a well and add the water and sourdough starter.
2. Mix or knead the dough by hand using the technique shown in the All About Bread Section. Continue kneading until the ingredients are well combined – this should take approximately 5 minutes.
3. Add the salt and continue to knead for a further 10–15 minutes or until the dough is fully developed (check if you have fully developed the dough by using the stretch test).
4. Place the dough into a lightly oiled bowl large enough to allow the dough to double in bulk. Cover with plastic and leave in a warmish place (23–25°C/ 73–77°F) until the dough has doubled in size – approximately 2 hours.
5. Gently knock back the dough in the bowl. This will deflate it slightly, but it will develop more strength. Cover again and leave for 45 minutes.
6. Tip the dough out onto a lightly floured bench and, using a dough scraper, cut the dough into 12 pieces (approximately 100 g (3½ oz) each).
7. Mould each piece of dough into a round ball. This is done by cupping your hand over the dough piece on a flourless bench, applying downwards pressure and moving your hand around in circular motions.
8. Place the buns onto a baking tray, lightly greased or lined with baking paper, 12 per tray, 4 across and 3 down. Ensure they are not placed too close together – they should be individual buns once baked.
9. Final proof for approximately 1 hour or until almost doubled in size. Cover with plastic to prevent skinning and chilling of the dough. Use the indentation test to tell when the buns are three-quarters to almost fully proofed.
10. Using a sharp knife or razor blade cut a criss-cross on top of each roll, then sprinkle liberally with the sea salt.
11. Just before you load the tray of rolls into the oven, spray water into the oven cavity with a spray gun. Close the oven door quickly so you don't lose any of the steam.
12. Quickly place the baking tray into a preheated oven set at 220°C (430°F) and bake for approximately 20 minutes. Turn the oven tray around halfway through baking if needed. For the last 5–8 minutes of baking, open the oven door slightly to assist in creating a crisp roll.
13. Cool on a wire rack. The rolls should be golden brown and crisp and are best eaten warm.

380 g (2³/₄ cups + 2 tablespoons) strong flour

285 g (2 cups + 2 tablespoons) durum semolina

¹/₄ teaspoon dried active yeast

380 ml (1¹/₂ cups + 2 tablespoons) water (variable depending on how liquid the starter is)

130 g (¹/₂ cup) sourdough starter (see Pane Acido recipe)

15 g (3 teaspoons) salt

2 tablespoons Sel de Gris sea salt for topping

Finished Dough Temperature: 26°C (78°F)

Walnut Sourdough

Full of nuts and figs, this is an ideal bread for serving with cheese, or simply enjoying with butter. Be sure to buy walnuts that are fresh and sweet for the best result. The process for making this bread stretches over two days, but it is well worth the effort.

SPONGE

150 g (1 cup + 1¹/₂ tablespoons) wholemeal flour

100 g (³/₄ cup) rye flour

3 pinches of sea salt

20 g (2 tablespoons) liquid malt extract

10 g (1¹/₂ tablespoons) milk powder

225 ml (1 cup + 1¹/₂ teaspoons) water (25°C/77°F)

75 g (¹/₄ cup + 1 tablespoon) rye or white sourdough (see Pane Acido recipe)

DOUGH

sponge from day one

350 g (2¹/₂ cups) strong flour

¹/₄ teaspoon dried active yeast

185 ml (³/₄ + 1 tablespoon) water

¹/₂ teaspoon sugar

10 g (2 teaspoons) sea salt

10 g (1 tablespoon) walnut oil

200 g (2 cups) roasted walnut pieces, lightly roasted in an oven and cooled before use

200 g (2 cups) dried figs, stems removed and cut into small pieces

Finished Dough Temperature:
26°C (78°F)

Day one: the sponge

1. Mix all ingredients in a bowl with a wooden spoon until well combined and then cover with plastic wrap.
2. Leave in a warm place (23–25°C/73–77°F) for 12–15 hours.

Day two: the dough

1. Place the sponge, flour, yeast, water, sugar and salt into a mixing bowl. Mix together for approximately 5 minutes until a thick creamy dough is formed – this can be done either by hand or by using a wooden spoon. The dough will be sticky in texture, similar to that of a stiff biscuit dough. You will not achieve a smooth elastic developed dough, as rye flour does not contain any elastic and extensible gluten-forming proteins.
2. Add the walnut oil, walnuts and figs then mix for a further 2-3 minutes until well combined.
3. Place the dough into a lightly oiled bowl large enough for the dough to double in size. Cover with plastic wrap and leave in a warm place (23–25°C/73–77°F) to ferment – this should take 3¹/₂–4 hours.
4. Gently knock back the dough, then tip onto a floured work surface and, using a scraper, divide the dough into 2 pieces (approximately 750 g (1 lb 10 oz) each).
5. On a lightly floured bench, shape each dough piece into an oblong roll (much like a vienna loaf but not with tapered ends). To achieve this, flatten the dough piece out then tightly roll the dough towards you as you would when rolling a swiss roll. Apply pressure with your hands as you roll – the tighter the roll the better. The dough will be slightly sticky, this is normal.
6. Place into greased bread tins, ensuring the smooth-side is at the top and the seam is at the bottom. The bread tins should be approximately 230 mm (9 inches) in length x 80 mm (3 inches) in width x 75 mm (3 inches) in height.
7. Cover the tins with plastic and proof in a warm place approximately 1¹/₂–2 hours. Use the indentation test to tell when the dough is fully proofed.
8. Place the proved loaves directly into a preheated oven set at 175–180°C (355°F) and bake for 40 minutes, then remove the loaves from their tins and bake for a further 5 minutes, or until a hollow sound is heard when the bottom is tapped.
9. Cool on a wire rack.

CITY CAKE COMPANY

With a clean, slick New York feel to its two retail outlets, the City Cake Company has very quickly found a niche market in Auckland for specialty individualised cakes. There are three partners in this thriving business: Maureen Keene, her daughter Tracy Baird, and Susanna Pattisson. Surprisingly none are involved in hands-on baking but all definitely have a hand in product conception and development, and provide a strong business base.

The main focus is superbly presented cakes that taste as good as they look. Baking is done in a busy factory in an Auckland suburb by a team of bakers who produce cakes for the retail shops and for customers who seek specially designed wedding and occasion cakes. The team is totally committed to cakes baked with the best ingredients, and the business was founded on Maureen Keene's desire to bake cakes 'that tasted fabulous'.

It can take weeks to develop a new idea to the point where a cake is ready for marketing, and it is then showcased through the retail shops. City Cake Company offers a constantly changing 'menu' of cakes to be eaten by the slice with coffee, or taken home to be savoured at smart dinner parties and special events.

Greek Coconut Cake

With a wonderful lemony syrup and almost crunchy coconut topping, this cake is particularly moreish and decidedly moist.

1. Place the butter and sugar in a mixing bowl fitted with a beater.
2. Beat until the butter and sugar just begin to change colour (do not cream).
3. Add the eggs, coconut and flour in five additions: starting with the egg, then the coconut and lastly the flour, repeating until each is mixed in. Beat well between each addition to ensure the mixture does not curdle.
4. Place the batter into a 23 cm (9 inches) round, loose bottomed spring release cake tin that has been prepared lightly greased and lined on the bottom and sides with greaseproof paper. This is necessary to avoid overbaking due to the long baking time required.
5. Place directly into a preheated oven set at 150°C (300°F) and bake for 2–2 ½ hours. Insert a cake skewer in the centre of the cake, and if it comes out clean then the cake is baked.
6. Allow to cool in the tin for 30–40 minutes, then using a cake skewer prick 60–70 holes in the top of the cake and evenly pour over the syrup (see recipe below).
7. Immediately spread the coconut topping (see recipe below) evenly over the top.
8. Preheat the oven to 190°C (375°F) and place the cake back into the oven to bake the coconut topping. Bake until golden brown.
9. Allow the cake to cool in the tin for 20–30 minutes then carefully remove the cake from the tin. Carefully remove the greaseproof paper while still warm.

Syrup
1. Place the sugar, water and lemon or orange quarters in a saucepan.
2. Bring to the boil, stirring occasionally to ensure the sugar is dissolved.
3. Remove from the heat and pass through a sieve.
4. Cool for 30–45 minutes before use.

Coconut Topping
1. Place the brown sugar and cream in a saucepan.
2. Bring to the boil, stirring to dissolve the sugar and avoiding burning.
3. Remove from the heat and stir in the coconut. Use while still warm.

CAKE
240 g (1 cup + 2½ tablespoons) softened butter
460 g (2⅓ cups) granulated sugar
450 g (9) eggs
345 g (4½ cups + 2 tablespoons) fine coconut
315 g (2½ cups + 1 tablespoon) self rising flour

SYRUP
275 g (1⅓ cup + 1¼ tablespoons) granulated sugar
300 ml (1⅓ cup) water
½ lemon or orange (cut in half again)

TOPPING
165 g (1 packed cup) soft brown sugar
240 ml (1 cup + 3 tablepoons) fresh cream
165 g (2¼ cups) shredded coconut (thread)

Carrot Cake

Moist, delicious carrot cake is a favourite with young and old. This is especially good for those who have allergies to dairy products as the cake is kept moist with oil. Be sure to use a fresh, light oil such as grapeseed or light olive oil.

CAKE

250 g (1³/₄ cup + 4 tablespoons)
   plain flour

10 g (2 teaspoons) baking soda

5 g (1 teaspoon) salt

5 g (2 teaspoons) mixed spice

5 g (2 teaspoons) cinnamon

200 g (4) eggs

165 g (1 cup + 3 tablespoons)
   soft brown sugar

290 g (1¹/₂ cups) granulated sugar

370 g (2¹/₄ cups) oil

200 g (1¹/₂ cups) grated carrot

120 g (1 cup) walnut pieces

135 g (¹/₂ cup) crushed pineapple
   (well-drained)

ICING

105 g (¹/₂ cup) cream cheese

90 g (6 tablespoons) softened butter

190 g (1¹/₄ cups) icing sugar (sieved)

1 tablespoon lemon zest

1. Sieve the flour, baking soda, salt, mixed spice and cinnamon into a mixing bowl fitted with a beater.
2. Add the eggs, brown sugar, granulated sugar, oil, carrot, walnut pieces and pineapple to the mixing bowl.
3. Beat on a slow speed for 1 minute then scrape down the sides of the bowl. Beat for a further 2 minutes on a medium speed.
4. Pour the batter into a 23 cm (9 inch) round, loose bottomed spring release cake tin that has been prepared lightly greased and lined on the bottom and sides with greaseproof paper. This is necessary to avoid overbaking due to the long baking time required.
5. Place directly into a preheated oven set at 150°C (300°F) and bake for 1¹/₂–2 hours. Insert a cake skewer in the centre of the cake, and if it comes out clean the cake is baked.
6. Allow to cool in the tin for 30 minutes, then remove from the tin and allow to cool completely. Remove the greaseproof paper.
7. Once the cake is cold, spread the cream cheese icing (see recipe below) on the top using a palette knife. Ensure the icing is smooth and evenly spread.
8. Sprinkle a ring of whole or pecan pieces on top of the icing approximately 2 cm (1 inch) from the edge of the cake.

Cream Cheese Icing

1. Place the cream cheese, butter, icing sugar and lemon zest in a mixing bowl fitted with a beater.
2. Beat on medium speed until the icing is white and fluffy.
3. Use immediately or store in a covered bowl until required. Keeps for 2–3 days.

Summer Fruit Tart with Lemon Cream

This is quite spectacular when made at the height of the summer berry season, using the colourful combination of as many berries as possible. If you wish to make it in the winter, you could always try topping it with freshly sliced oranges.

PASTRY

170 g (³/₄ cup) salted butter
85 g (¹/₃ cup + 2 teaspoons) sugar
50 g (1) egg
260 g (1³/₄ cups + 5 tablespoons)
   plain flour

FILLING

500 g (2¹/₂ cups) granulated sugar
1 heaped tablespoon lemon zest
250 ml (1 cup) fresh lemon juice
450 g (9) eggs
2 egg yolks
330 g (1³/₄ cups + 1¹/₂ tablespoons)
   softened butter

TOPPING

fresh, seasonal fruits, e.g., raspberries,
   blackberries, cherries, gooseberries,
   strawberries (glazed), grapes,
   blueberries, etc.

clotted cream to serve

Sweet Pastry Base

1. Lightly cream the butter and sugar in a mixing bowl fitted with a beater or beat in a bowl with a wooden spoon.
2. Add the egg and mix until combined.
3. Lastly add the flour and mix to a paste. Only mix until the paste comes clean off the bowl. Be careful not to overmix or the pastry will become too elastic and doughy.
4. Transfer to a bowl. Cover and refrigerate for 30 minutes or overnight.
5. On a lightly floured workbench roll the pastry out into a sheet about 5 mm (¹/₄ inch) thick, and big enough to cover a 23 cm (9 inch) greased fluted loose bottomed tin.
6. Use the rolling pin to pick the pastry up and lay it over the tin. Gently press the pastry into the tin so that it fills all the contours. Be careful not to stretch the pastry or it will tear, or shrink back in the oven. Return it to the fridge for another 30 minutes, or more if the pastry still feels soft. Reserve the scraps.
7. Preheat the oven to 150°C (300°F). Line the pastry with tinfoil and fill with dried beans, raw rice or pastry weights.
8. Bake the pastry for 30 minutes. The pastry should be baked but not coloured.
9. Allow the pastry to cool before checking for any cracks or holes. Also make sure the pastry has not shrunk on the sides. Patch any low points, holes or cracks with your leftover pastry. Return to the oven to bake these patches.
10. Pour the freshly made warm lemon cream filling (see recipe below) into the baked pastry case.
11. Place the filled tart in the refrigerator and allow the filling to set (approximately 2 hours).
12. Cover with fruits of your choice.
13. Serve with fresh clotted cream.

Lemon Cream Filling

1. Place the sugar and lemon zest in a saucepan and rub together with the palms of your hands to infuse the sugar with lemon.
2. Add the lemon juice, eggs, egg yolks and butter. Whisk together to combine.
3. Heat until the mixture just reaches boiling point, stirring constantly with a wooden spoon. Do not boil rapidly or the eggs will scramble.
4. Pour into the baked pastry case immediately.

JOHN AND DONNA THOMSEN
COPENHAGEN BAKERY

*J*ohn Thomsen learnt the art of baking in an apprenticeship in Kloster, a tiny town on Denmark's west coast. He and his New Zealand wife Donna have a thriving bakery in the heart of central Christchurch, which is like a home away from home for Danish tourists who regularly gather to taste authentic Danish baking. There's even a guest book that Danes (having heard about the bakery in Australia, China or Bali) sign with sentimental comments, praising the hospitality.

The Thomsens' hard work has seen them purchase a traditional Kiwi bakery and build up such a following that they now have a highly successful retail outlet in the city and an offsite bakery in Bromley where the cakes, bread and pastries are baked. There has been a little compromise to cater for the Kiwi taste, but the rye bread, the pastries and the rund stykker, or fresh crusty bread rolls, are just as they are in Denmark.

'Baking is my life,' says this dedicated baker, who is ably assisted by Donna. Even their two sons, aged six and nine, are showing an interest in baking. Their idea of a treat is to spend a night 'helping' in the bakery, up to their elbows in flour and dough. Copenhagen Bakery's success is in the total family commitment and the philosophy that their shop is a stage where good service is paramount.

Danish Pastries

With their light pastry and sweet delicious fillings, true Danish pastries have grabbed the imagination of people all over the world. The range of Danish pastries in the Copenhagen Bakery makes a fabulous display and they are one of the fastest selling lines.

Dough

1. Sieve the flour onto your work surface. Make a well and add the gluten, salt, sugar, butter, egg, yeast and water.
2. Mix or knead the dough by hand using the technique shown in the All About Bread section. Every couple of minutes stop and check the gluten development and temperature of the dough. Only half develop your dough. This should take 5–7 minutes. At this stage the dough should be firm and cold.
3. Place the dough in a floured bowl. Cover with plastic and rest for 5 minutes in the refrigerator. While the dough is resting prepare the layering fat by placing the butter and flour into a mixing bowl fitted with a beater. Mix together on low speed until it forms a solid mass. Don't overmix or soften the butter too much. Place the layering fat between two layers of plastic and roll out to a flat square 17 cm x 17 cm (7 inches x 7 inches). Place in the refrigerator to firm up.
4. Remove the dough from the refrigerator (at this stage the yeast within the dough should not be gassing). Incorporate the layering fat into the dough using the French Method (see Mixing and Processing in the All About Pastries section). Ensure the dough is kept cool during the make up of Danish pastries.
5. You should now have an envelope of dough with the layering fat inside. Carefully roll out the dough on a lightly floured board lengthways to achieve a rectangle 15 mm (¹/₂ inch) in thickness. Give a half fold (see the laminating process in the All About Pastries section). Place on a floured tray, wrap in plastic and place in the freezer for 5 minutes.
6. Remove from the freezer and repeat the above process twice.
7. You should now give the Danish pastry three half folds, then rest the pastry for 15 minutes in the freezer.
8. Remove from the freezer and gradually roll the pastry out on a floured surface to 4 mm thick, ensuring that the pastry is freely moving during the rolling process. Keep the pastry as square and as even as possible. Trim the outside edges.
9. Cut the pastry into 10 cm x 10 cm (4 inches x 4 inches). Fill each square with 15 g (¹/₂ oz) of butter filling (see recipe on next page).
10. Fold each corner into the middle over the filling. Press firmly to hold down the ends (see photo opposite).
11. Place onto a greased tray or baking paper lined tray.
12. Cover the Danish lightly with a sheet of plastic.
13. Place in a warm place to proof for 45 minutes or until almost double in size.
14. After proofing, very gently brush the pastries with egg wash (two parts egg to one part milk or water). Push down the middle of each pastry with four fingers.

DOUGH
500 g (4 cups) strong flour (chilled in the refrigerator overnight)
15 g (1¹/₂ tablespoons) gluten flour
5 g (1 teaspoon) salt
30 g (2 tablespoons) sugar
60 g (¹/₄ cup + 1 tablespoon) butter
100 g (2) eggs (cold)
15 g (2 tablespoons) dried active yeast
200 ml (³/₄ cup + 4 tablespoons) chilled water (ice in the refrigerator overnight)
egg wash for finishing

Finished Dough Temperature:
15°C (60°F)

LAYERING FAT
500 g (2 cups + 6 tablespoons) butter (if using special butter sheets delete the flour)
100 g (²/₃ cup + 1¹/₂ tablespoons) strong flour

BUTTER FILLING

110 g (¹/₂ cup) softened butter

155 g (³/₄ cup + 2 teaspoons) sugar

10 g (1¹/₂ tablespoons) ground almonds

15 g (1 teaspoon) apricot jam

10 g (¹/₄ cup) white cake crumbs

CUSTARD

150 ml (²/₃ cup) milk

20 g (4 teaspoons) sugar

50 ml (5 tablespoons) milk

20 g (2¹/₂ tablespoons) custard powder

ICING

400 g (2¹/₃ cups) icing sugar

140 ml (¹/₂ cup) stock syrup (boil
100 ml (7 tablespoons) hot water
and 75 g (¹/₄ cup + 2 tablespoons)
sugar. Cool before use)

15. Fill the middle by piping one of the following into it: jam, thickened fruit filling, lemon curd, custard (see recipe below), fresh or well-drained tinned apricot halves.

16. Place directly into a preheated oven set at 210°C (410°F). Bake for 15–18 minutes until golden brown.

17. Cool and brush with apricot glaze (see recipe for Mediterranean Orange Cake).

18. Drizzle with white icing (see recipe below).

Butter Filling

Mix all the ingredients in a bowl with a wooden spoon until soft, creamy and smooth.

Custard

1. In a saucepan place the first amount of milk and sugar. Stir and bring to the boil.

2. Mix the second amount of milk with the custard powder in a bowl.

3. Add the boiled milk to the custard mix, then pour into the saucepan and return to a medium heat to thicken.

4. Cool before use.

White Water Icing

Sieve icing sugar and add stock syrup. You may have to warm it slightly to achieve the correct thickish, runny consistency.

Honey and Almond Tart

Prepared ahead, this tart would make a sweet ending to a dinner party. Serve it with coffee, as a dessert or as a special afternoon tea cake.

1. Lightly cream the butter and sugar in a mixing bowl fitted with a beater or beat in a bowl with a wooden spoon.
2. Add the egg and mix until combined.
3. Lastly add the flour and mix to a paste. Only mix until the paste comes clean off the bowl. Be careful not to overmix or the pastry will become too elastic and doughy.
4. Transfer to a bowl. Cover and refrigerate for 30 minutes or overnight.
5. On a lightly floured workbench roll the pastry out into a sheet about 5 mm (¼ inch) thick, and big enough to cover an 18 cm (7 inch) greased, loose bottomed fluted flan tin.
6. Use the rolling pin to pick the pastry up and lay it over the tin. Gently press the pastry into the tin so that it fills all the contours. Be careful not to stretch the pastry or it will tear, or shrink back in the oven. Return it to the fridge for another 30 minutes, or more if the pastry still feels soft. Reserve the scraps.

Almond Filling

1. Place the butter in a mixing bowl and soften in the microwave on a low heat.
2. Attach a beater, add the sugar, ground almonds and golden syrup and blend lightly together. Do not cream the mixture.
3. Slowly add the warmed eggs. Scrape down the sides of the bowl.
4. Add the flour and almond essence. Blend all ingredients together until well combined. Do not overmix.
5. Fill the tart base with the almond filling.
6. Place directly into a preheated oven set at 190°C (375°F). Bake for 18–20 minutes. Be careful not to overbake.
7. Once cool remove from the flan tin.
8. Spread the topping (see recipe below) on the cold almond tart.
9. Grill the top to a golden brown colour under a low heat. Be careful not to burn the top.

Honey and Almond Topping

1. Place all ingredients in a heavy bottomed saucepan.
2. Bring to the boil, stirring gently for 1 minute.
3. Use immediately.

PASTRY
170 g (¾ cup) salted butter
85 g (⅓ cup + 2 tablespoons) sugar
50 g (1) egg
260 g (1¾ cup + 5 tablespoons) plain flour

FILLING
75g (¼ cup + 1 tablespoon) butter
75 g (⅓ cup + 2 teaspoons) granulated sugar
50 g (½ cup) ground almonds
25 g (1¼ tablespoons) golden syrup
75 g (1½) eggs (warmed)
25 g (3½ tablespoons) plain flour
1–2 drops almond essence

TOPPING
50 g (2½ tablespoons) liquid honey
50 g (¼ cup) sugar
25 g (1¾ tablespoons) fresh cream
25 g (¼ cup) flaked almonds

DEAN BRETTSCHNEIDER

Dean (author of this book) is a committed professional baker and patissier, his expertise is well respected throughout the world and he is seen as an innovative and skilled craftsman with a perchant for troubleshooting in the bakery. His philosophy for successful baking is simple, 'commitment, dedication and passion combined with a little fun'. Here he shares some of his favourite recipes.

Panforte

This firm sweet cake is full of nuts, spices, white pepper and candied fruit. A specialty of Siena, it is traditionally served in winter, especially at Christmas. It will keep for several weeks in an airtight container.

1. To roast the hazelnuts, place on a baking tray and put into a preheated oven set at 180°C for 10–15 minutes. Rub the skins from the hazelnuts in a clean tea-towel. Roast the blanched almonds until they turn a very pale golden colour – 10–15 minutes. Once cool, coarsely chop the hazelnuts and almonds.

2. Mix the nuts, glazed fruits, mixed peel, spices, white pepper and flour thoroughly in a large bowl.

3. Place the sugar, honey and butter in a heavy-bottomed saucepan and cook over a medium heat until the mixture reaches 116°C (240°F) (soft ball) on a candy thermometer (or drop a little of the mixture into cold water and it should form a ball). Be careful as this will not take long. Remove from the heat.

4. Immediately pour the syrup into the nut and flour mixture and stir quickly using a wooden spoon until well combined.

5. Working quickly, place the mixture into a 20 cm (8 inch) springform cake tin, which has been lined, bottom and sides, with baking paper. The mixture will cool quickly and become very stiff, so work very fast. Smaller sizes can be made but remember to adjust the baking time.

6. Press the mixture evenly into the prepared tin by dipping the top of your hand in warm water and patting the mixture smooth and level. Again work quickly to avoid the mixture becoming stiff upon cooling.

7. Place the cake tin into a preheated oven set at 150–160°C (300–320°F) and bake for 30–40 minutes until the outside edges begin to firm up. The panforte won't colour or seem very firm even after baking, but will harden as it cools.

8. Cool in the tins until firm. Remove gently from the tin and remove the baking paper.

9. Before serving, dust with icing sugar and serve a thin slice with coffee. Or wrap in cellophane and tie with ribbon or raffia for that special gift.

115 g (³/₄ cup) hazelnuts

115 g (³/₄ cup) whole blanched almonds

35 g (¹/₄ cup) glazed/candied pineapple pieces

35 g (¹/₄ cup) glazed/candied apricots (cut into slices 5 mm in thickness)

35 g (¹/₄ cup) glazed/candied ginger (cut into slices 5 mm in thickness)

35 g (¹/₄ cup) dried figs (remove stems and cut into small pieces)

130 g (1 cup) finely chopped mixed peel

2 g (1 teaspoon) ground cinnamon

1 g (¹/₂ teaspoon) ground coriander

1 g (¹/₂ teaspoon) ground cloves

1 g (¹/₂ teaspoon) ground nutmeg

3 good pinches white pepper

90 g (²/₃ + 1 tablespoon) strong flour

150 g (³/₄ cup) granulated sugar

125 g (³/₄ cup + 1 tablespoon) honey

30 g (2 tablespoons) butter

Chocolate and Pecan Sourdough

This is an unusual but very moreish sourdough bread. The cocoa and chocolate chips make it rich, but it is not a very sweet bread. It is great served with freshly picked strawberries and cream cheese, or soft fresh white cheeses.

DOUGH

500 g (4 cups) strong flour

25 g (¼ cup) cocoa powder

250 g (1 cup) sourdough starter
  (see Pane Acido recipe)

330 ml (1⅓ cups + 3 tablespoons)
  water

10 g (2 teaspoons) salt

125 g (1 cup) pecans, chopped and
  lightly toasted

125 g (¾ cup) chocolate chips or small
  broken pieces of chocolate

STARCH GLAZE

165 ml (½ cup + 3½ tablespoons)
  cold water

5 g (1 teaspoon) cornflour or
  corn starch

Finished Dough Temperature:
  24–26°C (75–78°F)

1. Sieve the flour and cocoa powder onto your work surface. Make a well and add the sourdough starter and water, mixing well until it forms a mass.

2. Mix or knead the dough by hand using the technique shown in the All About Bread Section. Continue kneading until the ingredients are well combined, approximately 3–4 minutes (the dough is not fully developed at this stage).

3. Put the dough into a bowl and cover with plastic. Leave the dough for 20 minutes to rest.

4. Add the salt.

5. Continue to knead by hand. Every couple of minutes you should stop and check the gluten development and temperature of the dough. This final kneading should take about 10–15 minutes (check if you have fully developed the dough by using the stretch test).

6. Add the chopped pecans and chocolate pieces and knead into the dough until evenly mixed through – this should only take 1–2 minutes.

7. Lightly oil a bowl large enough to allow the dough to double in bulk. Put the dough in the bowl and cover with plastic. Leave in a warmish place (23–25°C/ 73–77°F) for 3 hours. By this time the dough should have started to gas and nearly doubled in size.

8. Gently knock back the dough in the bowl. This will deflate it slightly, but will develop more strength. Cover again and leave for another hour, by which time it should have well and truly doubled.

9. Tip the dough out onto a lightly floured bench and, using a dough scraper, cut the dough into 3 pieces at approximately 445 g (1 lb) each. Be gentle with the dough, do not aggressively punch it down or squeeze all the gas from within. Pick each piece up and gently tuck the edges underneath, pulling the surface tight around the mass. Lay the pieces back on the floured bench and cover with a proofing cloth (or tea-towel). Give an intermediate proof of 10 minutes. While you wait, lightly dust a proofing cloth or tea-towel with rye flour.

10. Uncover the dough and mould each dough piece into a vienna or baton shape. To achieve this, flatten the dough piece out then tightly roll the dough towards you as you would for a swiss roll. Apply pressure with your hands as you roll – the tighter the roll the better. Taper each end of the moulded loaf. Lay the first loaf on the proofing cloth. Before laying the second loaf down, pleat the cloth so that the loaves cannot touch as they rise. Repeat for the third loaf.

11. Final proof for approximately 2–2½ hours or until almost doubled in size. Cover with plastic to prevent skinning and chilling of the dough. Use the indentation test to tell when the dough is three-quarters proofed.

12. The oven should be preheated to 240–250°C (465–480°F), with a baking stone in place. Gently tip one loaf out onto a peel lightly dusted with semolina.

13. Using a razor blade or sharp knife, cut three 45° diagonal cuts in the top.

14. Just before you load the bread into the oven, spray water into the oven cavity with a spray gun. Close the door quickly so you don't lose any of the steam.

15. With the peel and loaf in one hand, open the oven with the other, and gently 'flick' the loaf off the peel and onto the baking stone. Close the oven door again immediately.

16. Repeat this for the second and third loaf, but be careful not to spray water directly onto the first loaf of bread. Close the door again and wait 2 minutes before opening the door slightly and spraying more water into the oven. Two minutes later, steam the oven again. Resist opening the door for another 20 minutes. While the bread is baking make the starch glaze.

17. After the first 20 minutes, turn the heat down to 200°C (390°F), and check the loaves for even baking. If necessary, turn to allow even browning.

18. After a total of 30–35 minutes the loaves will be ready. Check for correct baking by tapping the bottom of each loaf – it should sound hollow. As soon as you remove them from the oven, brush immediately with the prepared starch glaze. This will give an excellent shine to your baked loaves.

19. Cool on a wire rack.

Starch Glaze

1. Make a slurry with a little of the water and the cornflour.

2. Bring the rest of water to a boil in a saucepan, add the boiled water to the slurry mixture, whisk, then pour back into the saucepan.

3. Place back onto the heat and cook for 2 minutes on a medium heat.

4. Cool.

Ciabatta

Ciabatta is a favourite bread from Italy that has taken the world by storm and turns up in many innovative bakeries. It is a very complex bread to bake, requiring a lot of skill and knowledge. It has a golden brown crust and the moist interior has large airy holes. Dean has perfected the technique but warns that this bread should not be attempted by novice bakers.

STARTER

200 g (1½ cups) strong flour

¼ teaspoon dried active yeast

100 ml (⅓ cup + 2 tablespoons)
  water (25°C/77°F)

DOUGH

500 g (4 cups) strong flour

10 g (2 teaspoons) gluten flour

5 g (1¼ teaspoons) dried yeast

biga starter from above

450 ml (1¾ cups + 4 tablespoons)
  water (25°C/77°F)

10 g (2 teaspoons) salt

5 g (1 teaspoon) olive oil

semolina or flour for dusting

Day one: the biga starter

1. Place the flour and yeast onto your work surface. Make a well and add the water.
2. Knead the dough for 5 minutes until a very firm dough is formed.
3. Place in a lightly oiled container, cover and leave at room temperature overnight or for 12 hours.

Day two: the dough

1. Sieve the flour and gluten onto your work surface. Make a well.
2. Add the yeast, biga starter (cut into 8–10 pieces) and 320 ml (1½ cups) of the water to the well.
3. Knead the dough for 5 minutes.
4. Place the dough in a bowl, cover and rest for 15 minutes.
5. Add the salt and olive oil, and continue to knead until the dough is smooth, elastic and fully developed (15 minutes). Use the stretch test to tell when the dough is fully developed. Cover and rest for 5 minutes.
6. Very slowly, gently knead in the balance of the water, approximately 1 tablespoon at a time, kneading well before the next addition of water. Avoid adding too much water at once as this will cause the dough to slosh about and make it very difficult to knead. All the water must be added, so the dough will be very wet but when stretched it should still hold together and form a thin membrane. This process should take approximately 15 minutes.
7. Place the dough in a lightly oiled, flat container (to assist in transferring the dough from the bench to the container, dip your hands into water, as this will stop the dough sticking to your hands). Cover and rest for 15 minutes.
8. Gently knock back the dough by folding it inwards to expel the gases. Lightly oil the container again and return the dough, cover again and leave for 1 hour to double in size. Sprinkle your work surface heavily with semolina or flour.
9. Very gently tip or pour the dough out onto the floured bench. Sprinkle the top surface of the dough with semolina or flour.
10. Form a rectangle by gently pressing and stretching the dough until it is 4 cm (2 inches) thick. Avoid too much pressure with your hands as this will cause the dough to deflate and lose all the gases.
11. Leave the dough to rest for a further 5 minutes.
12. While the dough is resting, place a sheet of baking paper onto a clean baking tray. Sprinkle the baking paper heavily with semolina or flour.
13. Using your dough scraper, trim the outside edges and cut the dough into three equal rectangles.
14. Using your hands gently lift the dough pieces and place directly onto the baking

tray dusted with semolina or flour. Ensure there is a 2.5 cm (1 inch) gap between each piece.

15. Lightly sprinkle the top surface of the ciabatta again with semolina or flour. Cover with a proofing cloth or clean tea towel.

16. Place the ciabatta in a warm place for 35 minutes to proof. To test for readiness, lightly press your finger into the dough – it should feel soft and alive, no longer sticky and wet.

17. Preheat your oven to 250°C (480°F). With a baking stone or a hot oven tray in your oven, gently slide the ciabatta (which is still on the baking paper) directly onto the baking stone or a hot oven tray.

18. Spray the oven with water to create steam or have a pan filled with water within the oven. Repeat the spraying 2–3 times during the first 5 minutes of baking.

19. Reduce the oven temperature to 230°C (445°F) and bake for 25 minutes before opening the oven door.

20. Turn the ciabatta in the oven to ensure even baking. Bake for a further 15 minutes with the oven temperature set at 200°C (390°F). Ensure that the ciabatta are well baked and a hollow sound is heard when the bottom is tapped. The loaves should be light when picked up.

21. Place onto a wire cooling rack.

Dessert Pizza

Now that pizza appears on menus everywhere, from cafés through to upmarket restaurants, this dessert pizza is bound to be popular with young and old. It is a fun dessert with lots of delicious chocolate and caramel topped off with fresh fruit.

1. Sieve the flour onto your work surface. Make a well and add the salt, sugar and yeast.
2. Slowly add the water and ¾ of the egg. Knead the dough for 6–7 minutes or until the dough is almost fully developed (it is important to develop the gluten structure before all the egg is added).
3. Continue to add the balance of the egg slowly while the dough is still being kneaded. Add sufficient egg to achieve a very soft, elastic, smooth and shiny dough.
4. While kneading slowly add the softened butter in small amounts. Knead in all the butter to achieve a smooth, elastic, silky dough. Do not overmix the dough as this will cause overheating and the dough will become oily and greasy.
5. Transfer the dough into a lightly oiled container covered with plastic wrap, and give a bulk fermentation time of 1 hour in a warm, draught-free place. The dough should have doubled in size.
6. Gently knock back the dough to expel all the gases, reactivate the yeast and strengthen the gluten structure. Finally, push the dough out to a thickness of 5 cm (2 inches), place into a shallow container, and cover with plastic wrap.
7. Place in the refrigerator overnight (12 hours). This makes the dough easier to work and mould since the dough will be cold and firm.
8. The following day, cut the dough in half or into 250 g (8½ oz) pieces. Mould both pieces into a round ball, and rest for 5 minutes in the refrigerator. If you only require one base, wrap the other base in plastic wrap and return to the refrigerator. Use within 2 days.
9. On a lightly floured work surface, roll each dough ball out to a 30 cm (12 inch) circle, 3–4 mm (¼ inch) thick.
10. Place onto a baking tray lined with baking paper, ensuring that the circle is round and 3 mm (¼ inch) thick.
11. Using half the amount of moulding chocolate (see recipe overleaf) roll out into a 80 cm (32 inch) long rope. Place this rope around the outside edge of the dough, 2 cm (¾ inch) in from the edge.
12. Lightly brush or spray the dough with water. Fold the outside dough over the chocolate rope and seal firmly to ensure the chocolate rope is encased in dough (be careful not to break or puncture the dough). Egg wash the rim of the dough.
13. Spread half the amount of crème patisserie (see recipe overleaf) evenly over the base.
14. Place the warm caramel (see recipe overleaf) inside a paper piping bag and drizzle over the crème patisserie, ensuring an even amount is drizzled on.
15. Place the fruit (in order) over the crème patisserie and caramel (you may wish to add your own combination of fruits). Drizzle with melted chocolate after applying all the fruit.

BRIOCHE BASE
250 g (2 cups) strong flour
5 g (1 teaspoon) salt
25 g (2¼ tablespoons) granulated sugar
5 g (1¼ teaspoons) dried active yeast
25 ml (2 tablespoons) water
165 g (3½) eggs (variable)
125 g (½ cup + 1½ tablespoons) softened butter

Finished dough temperature:
27°C (80°F)

TOPPING
egg wash to seal
10–15 slices of banana
25 g (¼ cup) blueberries (fresh or frozen)
25 g (¼ cup) sliced peaches (fresh or frozen)
20 g (¼ cup) passionfruit pulp or sliced figs
15 g (1 tablespoon) broken milk chocolate pieces
30 g (2 tablespoons) broken white chocolate pieces
6–8 pecan halves
12 fresh raspberries
icing sugar and mint leaves for garnish

vanilla ice-cream to serve

16. Place the pizza base in a warm, draught-free place for 25–30 minutes to proof.
17. Place directly into a preheated oven set at 200°C (390°F) and bake for 12–15 minutes.
18. Remove from the oven and evenly place 12 fresh raspberries over the other toppings.
19. Lightly dust with icing sugar.
20. Garnish with fresh mint leaves.
21. Serve hot or cold with vanilla ice cream.

Crème Patisserie

CRÈME

125 ml (¹/₂ cup) milk

55 g (¹/₄ cup) granulated sugar

25 g (¹/₂) egg

35 g (4 tablespoons) plain flour

20 g (1¹/₄ tablespoons) butter

10 ml (2 tablespoons) rum, Kahlua or Baileys liqueur

1. Place the milk and half the sugar in a saucepan. Stir and bring to the boil.
2. Meanwhile in a bowl whisk the egg and the remaining sugar until the mixture becomes pale yellow and thick.
3. Slowly add the flour to the egg and sugar mixture while still whisking to avoid any lumps. Do not overmix.
4. Once the milk has come to the boil, add half of this to the sugar/egg and flour batter. Stir constantly with a whisk.
5. Return this mixture to the remaining milk in the saucepan and whisk together to avoid any lumps forming.
6. Place on a low heat and cook the mixture until it thickens, stirring all the time. Increase the heat to bring the mixture to the boil and cook for 3 minutes while still stirring.
7. Remove from the heat and whisk in the butter. Then whisk in the alcohol.
8. Transfer into a bowl and cover with plastic wrap. Cool completely before using. This is important.

Caramel

CARAMEL

100 g (¹/₃ cup) condensed milk

20 g (1¹/₄ tablespoons) butter

15 g (1 tablespoon) golden syrup

10 g (1 tablespoon) soft brown sugar

1. Place all the ingredients in a microwave-proof bowl and stir to combine all the ingredients.
2. Place into the microwave and cook on high for 1¹/₂ minutes, stirring every 20–30 seconds to avoid overcooking the caramel. This is possible due to the small amount of caramel in the bowl.

Moulding Chocolate

CHOCOLATE

55 g (2¹/₂ tablespoons) liquid glucose

110 g (¹/₃ cup) melted milk chocolate

1. Place the glucose in a small bowl and warm to approximately 30°C (85°F).
2. Add the melted chocolate and stir until the two ingredients are well combined (the mixture will appear to be very oily; do not panic at this stage).
3. Wrap the mixture in plastic wrap and leave overnight. The mixture will firm up.
4. Unwrap the moulding chocolate and soften by working it in your hands. Mould or roll as required. Any unused moulding chocolate should be stored in plastic wrap and kept in an airtight container to prevent skinning.

THE CHAIT FAMILY
DIXON STREET DELI

Three generations of the Chait family have been involved in the bustling Dixon St Deli in the heart of Wellington. From the 1930s through to the 1970s it was known as the Farm Poultry Supply Company and historic photos displayed around the walls today give a glimpse of the early retailing days.

Jayne, wife of second generation Martin Chait, learnt to bake traditional Jewish breads in a London deli in 1980. She returned to New Zealand and introduced Jewish rye bread, the first bagels in New Zealand, savoury pirogue, and a farmer's bread to the Wellington customers. The demand for these breads saw the business expand to a bakery in Brooklyn 10 years ago and it now supplies around 50 wholesale customers, some as far away as Auckland.

The bakery is now managed by third generation Ari Chait, who declares that 'baking is a very noble trade – in fact, the more I think about it, the more I like it!'

Authentic Bagels

The classic method of making bagels is revealed in this recipe. The interior should be soft and moist and the crust very chewy. As bagels are best eaten the day they're baked, use day-old bagels to make crisps which are excellent with spreads and dips.

1. Sieve the flour onto your work surface. Make a well and add the gluten, salt, sugar, olive oil, yeast and water.
2. Mix or knead the dough by hand using the technique shown in the All About Bread section. Every couple of minutes stop and check the gluten development and temperature of the dough. This final kneading should take about 10–15 minutes (check if you have fully developed the dough by using the stretch test). At this stage the dough should be firm and cool.
3. Using your dough scraper divide the dough into 100 g (3½ oz) pieces. You should have 12 dough pieces.
4. Round each dough piece into a tight ball, cover with plastic or a clean tea towel. Give an intermediate proof of 10 minutes.
5. Roll each ball into a 20 cm (8 inch) long sausage shape, ensuring that it is an even thickness from end to end.
6. Wrap the elongated dough piece around your four fingers with the two ends meeting together underneath your fingers. Applying pressure on the bench, roll the ends together to create a seal and ultimately forming the distinctive ring shape (see photograph opposite).
7. Once the bagels are formed place onto a baking tray (or suitable trays that will fit into your refrigerator) dusted with fine corn grits or semolina and place in the refrigerator overnight (maximum of 16 hours). Allow approximately 2 cm (¾ inch) space around each bagel.
8. Remove from the refrigerator and stand at room temperature for 45–60 minutes. While the bagels are recovering, put a large saucepan of hot water onto a high heat (with the lid on) and bring to the boil.
9. While the water is boiling, remove the lid and place three bagels at a time into the boiling water. Blanch for 30 seconds on each side, a total of 1 minute.
10. Using a slotted spoon gently remove the bagels, ensuring that all the water has drained off. Place bottom side down onto a greased or baking paper-lined baking tray (allow approximately 2 cm (1 inch) space around each bagel).
11. Toppings can be applied at this stage, for example, sesame seeds, poppy seeds, grated cheese or finely sliced onion, etc.
12. Place a full tray of bagels into a preheated oven set at 200°C (390°F). Bake for 20–25 minutes until shiny and golden brown.
13. Place on a cooling rack.

750 g (5¾ cups) strong flour
30 g (3 tablespoons) gluten flour
20 g (4 teaspoons) salt
25 g (2 tablespoons) soft brown sugar
15 g (3 teaspoons) olive oil
10 g (2½ teaspoons) dried active yeast
430 ml (1¾ cups + 2 tablespoons) chilled water (placed in the refrigerator overnight)

Finished Dough Temperature:
25°C (77°F)

Variations

Onion Bagel
- If using dried onions add an extra 60 ml (4 tablespoons) of water.
- Add 65 g (1 cup) of dried onion flakes (or finely chopped fresh onion) directly to the dough at step 1.
- Process as for standard bagel.

Cinnamon and Raisin Bagel
- Increase the dried yeast to 16 g (3 teaspoons).
- Increase the water by 60 ml (4 tablespoons).
- Add 15 g (3 teaspoons) of ground cinnamon directly to the dough after three-quarters of the dough development (near the end of step 2). Knead in well until the cinnamon is evenly dispersed.
- Add 115 g ($^3/_4$ cup) of raisins to the dough once full dough development has been achieved (at the end of step 2). Knead in gently to avoid crushing the raisins.
- Process as for standard bagel.

Chocolate Chip Bagel
- Add 45 g ($^1/_2$ cup) of cocoa powder to the dough at step 1.
- Increase the water by 60 ml (4 tablespoons).
- Add 115 g ($^3/_4$ cup) of chilled chocolate chips to the dough once full dough development has been achieved (at the end of step 2). Knead in gently.
- Process as for standard bagel.

Bagel Crisps
- Once the bagels are 2–3 days old, using a sharp bread knife, carefully slice the bagel horizontally as thinly as possible to form 3–4 mm ($^1/_4$ inch) thick bagel discs. In a commercial bakery you can use a bacon slicer.
- Place the thinly sliced bagel discs onto a baking tray and toast under the grill set at 150°C until light golden brown; turn over and repeat. These are great served with guacamole or your favourite dip. You can also place them into a cellophane bag tied with a ribbon for that special gift.

Caraway Rye Bread

Jane Chait learnt this classic Jewish bread recipe while working in London and introduced it to Dixon St Deli customers in the early 80s. It is enormously popular and full of flavour. The process of making this bread involves making the 'sour' over three days before actually mixing the dough.

Day one: the sour

1. Mix all the ingredients together in a clean bowl.
2. Using a wooden spoon stir until combined, then scrape down the sides of the bowl.
3. Cover with muslin cloth and place in a warm place to ferment until the next day (maximum of 18 hours).

Day two

Mix ingredients as for Day 1.

Day three

Mix ingredients as for Day 1.

Day four: the dough

1. Sieve the two flours onto your work surface. Make a well and add the rye sour, salt, caraway seeds, yeast and water.
2. Mix or knead the dough by hand using the technique shown in the All About Bread section. Continue to knead the dough by hand. Every couple of minutes stop and check the gluten development and temperature of the dough. This final kneading should take about 10–15 minutes (check if you have fully developed the dough by using the stretch test).
3. Lightly oil a bowl large enough to allow the dough to double in bulk. Put the dough in the bowl and cover with plastic. Leave in a warmish place (23–25°C/ 73–77°F) and give a bulk fermentation time of 30 minutes.
4. Gently knock back the dough, cover with plastic again and leave for a further 15 minutes.
5. Tip the dough out onto the bench which has been lightly dusted with flour.
6. Using a dough scraper, divide the dough in half.
7. Gently shape each dough piece into a ball or cob shape.
8. Place on a lightly floured bench and give an intermediate proof of 10 minutes, covered with plastic. While you wait, lightly dust a proofing cloth or tea towel with rye flour.
9. Uncover the dough and remould into a smooth tight vienna shape. The surface of the dough should be stretched tightly over the mass, and there should be a neat seam along one side. Lay the first loaf on the proofing cloth, but before laying the second loaf down pleat the cloth so that the loaves cannot touch as they rise.
10. Final proof for approximately 45–55 minutes in a warm, draught-free place. Cover with plastic to prevent skinning and chilling of the dough. Use the

DAY ONE
40 g (5 tablespoons) rye flour (not ryemeal)
40 ml (3 tablespoons) water at 28°C (90°F)
¹/₄ teaspoon dried active yeast

DAY TWO
sour from above
80 g (²/₃ cup) rye flour
80 ml (6 tablespoons) water at 32°C (90°F)

DAY THREE
sour from above
240 g (1³/₄ + 2¹/₂ tablespoons) rye flour
120 ml (8 tablespoons) water at 32°C (90°F)

DAY FOUR
100 g (³/₄ cup) rye flour
700 g (5¹/₂ cups) strong flour
sour from above
20 g (4 teaspoons) salt
25 g (¹/₄ cup) caraway seeds
10 g (2¹/₂ teaspoons) dried yeast
460 ml (1³/₄ cups + 5 tablespoons) water

Final Dough Temperature:
28°C (80°F)

indentation test to tell when the dough is three-quarter proofed. These loaves are dense in texture so you will not achieve the same volume as a white loaf.

11. The oven should be preheated to 220°C (430°F), with a baking stone in place. Gently tip one loaf out onto a peel lightly dusted with semolina.

12. Dust the loaves lightly with rye flour (optional).

13. Using a razor blade or sharp knife, make four diagonal cuts in the top of the loaves.

14. Just before you load the bread into the oven, spray water into the oven cavity. Close the door quickly so you don't lose any of the steam.

15. With the peel and loaf in one hand, open the oven door with the other, and gently 'flick' the loaf off the peel and onto the baking stone. Close the oven door immediately.

16. Repeat this for the second loaf, but be careful not to spray water directly onto the first loaf. Close the door again and wait 2 minutes before opening the door slightly and spraying more water into the oven. Two minutes later, 'steam' the oven again. Resist opening the door for another 20 minutes.

17. Turn the heat down to 200°C (390°F), and check the loaves for even baking. If necessary, turn them around. For the remaining time leave the door of the oven slightly ajar to thicken and dry the crust.

18. After a total of 30–40 minutes the loaves will be ready. Cool on a wire rack.

DOVEDALE FOODS

Deep in the valley beyond Moutere, about 50 kilometres from Nelson, the Dovedale bakery hides in an old tobacco kiln set amongst leafy trees and surrounded by paddocks, views of the distant hills and absolute peace. Roland Dallas, his wife Christine and their two daughters sought a quieter, calmer lifestyle after running a busy Sydney bakery, Dallas Bread, and now bake on three days a week for numerous retail outlets and private customers throughout New Zealand.

Roland is totally committed to baking bread with wholesome organic ingredients, and produces a mere five product lines including a popular rice bread which is the mainstay of the business. This is free of yeasts, gluten and wheat flour so it finds favour throughout the country with those on special diets. Uncompromising in standards, with the best organic flours and grains sourced from Australia, Roland has perfected the art of natural yeasts for fermentation. (See following notes for his philosophy on this.)

A creative baker, ably assisted by Paula Williamson (below), he does occasionally produce pastries and Italian-style rustic breads for special local events. His fruity buns and a smooth Scottish bannock, available year round, are supplemented at Christmas and Easter with a fruity stollen. His business is more than passion for baking: it is about a lifestyle and a niche market that work remarkably well.

A Note on Ingredients and Leavens

We at Dovedale Foods use only organic stoneground flours and grains in our breads. We recommend their use in leaven breads. The power of a leaven ferment can be affected by many factors, including chemicals in over-refined flours, pesticide residues in conventional flour and chlorine in water.

In addition, stoneground flours are ground at lower temperatures, ensuring that nutritional properties are left intact, thus providing more food for the leaven to feed on.

It is important to understand the difference between the wild yeasts of leaven fermentation and the commercial baker's yeast used in most breads. There are over 400 different species of yeast microfungi. Baker's yeast is one single species (Saccharomyces cerevisiae), a purified virulent strain bred for fast, uniform development.

Leavens or sourdoughs, however, are usually leavened by multiple wild yeast species of lower virulence, and less uniform characteristics. True leaven or sourdough breads are the product of not only wild yeasts but also beneficial bacteria called lactobacilli, which produce lactic acid and contribute to the piquant flavour.

The longevity of the people of the Caucasus Mountains has been attributed to their high intake of lactobacilli and acidophillus, through the consumption of yoghurt and traditionally fermented bread.

Lactobacilli require at least eight hours to develop in a leaven. Since the introduction of commercial baker's yeast last century, shorter proving times have meant that lactobacilli have been missing from the modern loaf.

Lactobacilli and wild yeasts are in the air all around us. They are diverse in their composition, reflecting differences in flavour from area to area.

Here in Dovedale we enjoy a rural environment with close proximity to beech and pine forests and hedgerows of hawthorn and barberry. Just as the juniper bushes of the Yukon and the sourdoughs of San Francisco give a distinct flavour to those regions' traditional breads, so too does our Dovedale environment dictate the flavour of our ferments.

Dovedale Rye and Linseed

With the nutty crunch of the linseed and the full flavour of rye, this is a bread that you will want to cook often. It is quite moist and will keep well for a few days. Try it toasted when the flavour really comes out well.

1. Mix all ingredients in a bowl, then knead on the bench for 10–15 minutes. The dough will be sticky in texture, similar to that of a stiff biscuit dough. You will not achieve a smooth elastic developed dough as rye flour does not contain any elastic and extensible gluten-forming proteins.

2. Using your dough scraper divide the dough into three pieces at 800 g (1 lb 10½ oz) each.

3. On a lightly floured bench, shape the dough into a oblong roll.

4. Place into greased bread tins, ensuring the smooth side is at the top and the seam is at the bottom.

5. Cover the tins with plastic and proof in a warm place for 3–4 hours. Correct proof has been achieved when the dough has small bubbles and holes on the dough's surface and when the dough has risen approximately 3.5 cm (1½ inches) from its original height. This indicates that maximum gassing has been achieved.

6. Place the proved loaves directly into a preheated oven set at 215°C (420°F). Bake the tins on the oven stone to achieve a solid bake.

7. Bake for 1 hour, or until the hollow sound is heard when the bottom is tapped.

8. Place on a cooling rack.

80 g (½ cup) linseed (soaked for 12 hours in 120 ml (8 tablespoons) of boiling water)
1 kg (8 cups) organic rye flour
15 g (3 teaspoons) sea salt
600 g (2¾ cups) rye leaven (see making a leaven, using only rye flour)
600 ml (2½ cups) water (25°C/77°F)

Making a Dovedale Leaven

A leaven is a mixture of flour and water of porridge-like consistency. Two parts flour to three parts water should make a wet mix with the pouring qualities of a batter.

STAGE ONE

200 g (1¹/₂ cups + 1 tablespoon) organic white flour

(or this can be replaced with any organic flour)

200 g (³/₄ cup + 2 tablespoons) filtered water (25°C/77°F)

STAGE TWO

600 g (4¹/₂ cups) organic flour

900 g (4 cups + 1¹/₂ tablespoons) filtered water (25°C/77°F)

Stage one

Mix the initial starter in an earthenware or stainless steel bowl; cover with a tea towel and leave for a minimum of 48 hours at room temperature.

At this point, the flour and water should have separated. It will have a slightly sour odour with a few bubbles on the surface and the flour will be discoloured.

Stage two

Add more flour and water to the starter, this time with three times the amount of flour and water used in the initial starter.

Cover again and leave at least 8 hours.

Stage three

The leaven will now be at optimum gassing power with a thick, foaming consistency bubbling with life and a distinct beer-like sour aroma. This is the time to harness the wild yeast activity and make your final dough.

Dovedale Gluten-Free Rice-Millet Bread

The perfect answer for people who have allergies to mainstream breads, this is Dovedale's most popular selling line. It contains no wheat, gluten or yeast and the resulting loaf is moist and dense.

300 g (2 cups) millet

1 lt (4¹/₂ cups) water (25°C/77°F)

1 kg (8 cups) organic brown rice flour

20 g (4 teaspoons) sea salt

60 g (¹/₂ cup) maize starch

1 litre (4 cups + 2 tablespoons) rice flour leaven (see making a leaven, using only rice flour)

1. Bring the millet and 660 ml (2³/₄ cups) of the water to the boil and simmer for 20 minutes. Cool before use.
2. Mix all ingredients in a mixing bowl, including the balance of the water, then knead on the bench for 10–15 minutes. The dough will be sticky in texture, similar to that of a stiff biscuit dough. You will not achieve a smooth elastic developed dough as rice flour does not contain any elastic and extensible gluten-forming proteins.
3. Using your dough scraper, divide the dough into five pieces at 800g each.
4. On a lightly floured bench, shape the dough into an oblong roll.
5. Place into greased bread tins, ensuring the smooth side is at the top and the seam is at the bottom.
6. Cover the tins with plastic and proof in a warm place for 3–4 hours. Correct proof has been achieved when the dough has small bubbles and holes on the dough's surface, and when the dough has risen approximately 3.5 cm (1¹/₂ inches) from its original height. This indicates that maximum gassing has been achieved.
7. Place the proved loaves directly into a preheated oven set at 200°C (390°F). Bake the tins on the oven stone to achieve a solid bake.
8. Bake for 1¹/₂–2 hours, or until a hollow sound is heard when the bottom is tapped.
9. Place on a cooling rack.

FLEISCHER CONTINENTAL CAKES

*F*or over 60 years this quiet unassuming business in the Melbourne suburb of Malvern has supplied wedding and special occasion cakes to the élite of the city. Present owner Lori Leidler has continued the tradition of baking the fine cakes and pastries that was begun by a Jewish family, the Fleischers, in 1938. The original shop was in South Yarra, close to the area's large immigrant population who enjoyed their favourite European style strudels, kugelhopfs, cheese pastries and rich chocolate cakes.

Lori Leidler trained as a pastrycook in his native Vienna and came to Australia in 1961, first working at Paterson's Cakes. He bought Fleischers in 1967 and, even though it was a small operation, had 'queues out the door from 8.30 am until the early afternoon'. He is a committed baker, and chooses to work with the 'best of ingredients at all times'. He has shifted the business three times, from the original site to the present premises on Glenferrie Road and his loyal customer base has always followed, enjoying coffee and cakes, and ordering the specialty cakes (including stunning white chocolate wedding cakes) for which he has built a reputation.

Lori's son Michael followed his dad into the business, training there and keeping up with new innovations and trends. They both enjoy their craft, and the next generation is assured that the established traditions and reputation will continue.

Chocolate, Vanilla and Hazelnut Buttercake

Use a kugelhopf mould for this cake. When sliced, it looks quite dramatic as the chocolate and vanilla mixtures create a swirling pattern. It is moist and rich – perfect as an afternoon teacake.

One hour before making the cake batter

1. Sieve the icing sugar, instant coffee, cinnamon and cocoa powder into a bowl, then add the sugar and hazelnuts and combine using a wooden spoon.
2. Add the rum and vanilla essence and stir until all the ingredients are well combined. Scrape down the sides of the bowl, cover with plastic wrap then leave for 1 hour to infuse.

Cake Batter

1. In a mixing bowl fitted with a beater, cream the butter and sugar until light and fluffy.
2. Add the eggs and egg yolks slowly over 2–3 additions, beating well between each to avoid curdling. While the batter is mixing, lightly grease the kugelhopf mould with the melted butter. Set aside until required.
3. Sieve the flour and baking powder together, then use a wooden spoon to gently fold into the creamed mixture. Add the milk once the flour is three-quarters mixed in. Do not overmix.
4. Divide the mixture into thirds, placing each third into a separate bowls.
5. Into one add the cocoa paste mixture, mixing with a wooden spoon until well combined. Do not beat too much as this will toughen the batter.
6. Pour one-third of the plain batter into the prepared kugelhopf mould, followed by the chocolate batter and finally pour on the remaining plain batter (ensuring that the batters are evenly layered into the mould).
7. Using the handle end of a wooden spoon, lightly mix the batters together to give a marbling effect – this can be done by moving the wooden spoon handle through the batter in a circular waving motion.
8. Place the cake directly into a preheated oven set at 180°C (355°F) and bake for approximately 25–30 minutes or until a cake skewer comes out clean.
9. Allow the cake to cool for 10 minutes before gently removing and placing onto a serving plate.
10. Cool and lightly dust with icing sugar.

COCOA PASTE
20 g (1 tablespoon) icing sugar
5 g (1 teaspoon) instant coffee powder
1 teaspoon ground cinnamon
10 g (2 teaspoons) cocoa powder
10 g (2 teaspoons) granulated sugar
50 g (1½ cups) ground hazelnuts or almonds
3 tablespoons rum
1 teaspoon vanilla essence

CAKE BATTER
250 g (1 cup + 3 tablespoons) softened butter
225 g (1½ cups + 2 tablespoons) caster sugar
150 g (3) eggs
4 egg yolks
250 g (2 cups) plain flour
8 g (2 teaspoons) baking powder
50 ml (2½ tablespoons) milk

melted butter for greasing the kugelhopf mould
icing sugar for dusting

Linzer Torte

A traditional middle European cake, this is a delectable treat, as the pastry is fragrant with spices and the jam provides a light fruity richness. Ensure that you make it with a very high quality jam that is full of fruit.

PASTRY

200 g (1¹/₂ cups) plain flour

¹/₈ teaspoon ground cloves

¹/₄ teaspoon cinnamon

170 g (1¹/₂ cups + 2 tablespoons) ground almonds

110 g (¹/₂ cup + 1 tablespoon) caster sugar

1 teaspoon lemon zest

2 hardboiled egg yolks, mashed and cooled

225 g (1 cup) unsalted butter, softened

2 raw egg yolks, lightly beaten

¹/₂ teaspoon vanilla essence

FILLING

300 g (1 cup + 1 tablespoon) good quality blackcurrant, redcurrant or raspberry jam

GLAZE

1 egg and 50 ml (3 tablespoons) fresh cream, lightly beaten together

GARNISH

icing sugar for dusting

fresh redcurrants

1. Sieve the flour, cloves and cinnamon together into a mixing bowl. Add the almonds, sugar, lemon zest and mashed egg yolks.
2. Using a wooden spoon, beat in the butter, raw egg yolks and vanilla essence. Continue to beat until the mixture is well combined and forms a mass.
3. Form into a ball and wrap in plastic wrap. Place in the refrigerator for approximately 1¹/₂ hours or until the dough is firm enough to roll out into a circle.
4. Remove the pastry from the refrigerator and using approximately three-quarters (return the rest to the refrigerator) roll it out on a lightly floured surface to approximately 5–6 mm (¹/₄ inch) in thickness and large enough to cover a 200 mm x 25 mm (8 inch x 1 inch) high round open-bottomed flan ring (or a 200 mm x 25 mm (8 inch x 1 inch) fluted flan ring with a loose bottom). The dough is very soft so take care.
5. Gently roll it up on the rolling pin and unroll it into the greased flan ring, taking care not to rip or tear the pastry. Patch any holes up with the reserved pastry. Trim the edges to ensure an even surface is achieved.
6. Spoon the jam into the pastry case and spread it evenly over the bottom.
7. On a floured surface roll the remaining pastry out to a 150 mm x 200 mm x 5 mm (6 inch x 8 inch x ¹/₄ inch) thick rectangle. With a sharp knife cut the dough into strips approximately 10–12mm (¹/₂ inch) in width.
8. Carefully pick up each strip and arrange in a lattice pattern over the edges of the flan ring and filling.
9. Gently brush the lattice top with the egg glaze and return the completed unbaked Linzer Torte to the refrigerator for approximately 1 hour.
10. Place the torte directly into a preheated oven set at 175–180°C (350–355°F) and bake for 30–35 minutes or until the pastry is lightly brown.
11. Cool completely and remove the flan ring, lightly dust with icing sugar and garnish the outside edges with redcurrants. Place onto a serving dish.

IAIN BANFIELD AND LYNDALL FRANCIS

FRUITION

From their tiny bakery in the hills, Iain Banfield and Lyndall Francis have a sweeping view over the picturesque Yarra Valley. Theirs is a very boutique operation, as they combine their choice of a rural lifestyle with Iain's enthusiasm for baking traditional artisan sourdough breads.

They originally fled the fast city pace to grow organic vegetables, supplying families throughout the valley. It was not long before Iain began baking bread to supplement the boxes of veges they delivered, and Lyndall's brother was called in to help construct a wood-burning brick-hearthed Alan Scott-designed oven in a farm shed. It's now a full-time occupation for the pair, who bake several times a week for various outlets, restaurants and the farmers' market in the valley.

Totally dedicated to their craft, Iain and Lyndall ensure that they plant at least a hundred trees each year to replace the sawmill offcuts that they use to fire their oven. They are committed to sourcing organic or bio-dynamic flours and ingredients for all their products, and display real passion for ensuring that their breads are easily digestible and great tasting.

Olive and Rosemary Focaccia

Redolent of fresh rosemary and garnished with meaty olives, this focaccia is a perfect bread to serve with a salad for a summer lunch, or to complement a hearty winter soup. It is soft and chewy and will disappear in a flash if served while still warm from the oven.

Preparation of the Topping

1. Cut the onions in half and slice into vertical strips.
2. Heat the olive oil in a frying pan and sauté the onion, garlic and chopped rosemary for approximately 10 minutes over a low heat or until the mixture slightly caramelises.
3. Place into a bowl and cool.

Dough

1. Sieve the flour and salt onto your work surface. Make a well and add the wholemeal flour, sourdough starter and water, mixing well until it forms a mass.
2. Mix or knead the dough by hand using the technique shown in the All About Bread Section. Continue kneading until the ingredients are well combined and the dough is three-quarters mixed (the dough is not fully developed at this stage).
3. Add half of the caramelised onions and continue to knead by hand. This final kneading should take a further 5–8 minutes (check if you have fully developed the dough by using the stretch test). This will be a little sticky at the start but it will come right.
4. Lightly oil a bowl large enough to allow the dough to almost double in bulk. Put the dough in the bowl and cover with plastic. Leave in a warmish place (23–25°C/73–77°F) for 3 hours. By this time the dough should have started to gas and nearly doubled in size.
5. Tip the dough out onto a lightly floured bench and gently mould the dough piece into a round ball. Do not aggressively punch it down, or squeeze all the gas from within. Pick each piece up and gently tuck the edges underneath, pulling the surface tight around the mass.
6. Place the moulded dough piece onto a well-oiled 250 mm (10 inch) pizza tray or a baking tray, cover with a sheet of plastic and allow to rest for 15 minutes.
7. Uncover the dough and, using the palm of your hand, flatten the dough piece to a disc of 200 mm (8 inches) in diameter.
8. Mix the remaining rosemary leaves with the caramelised onion and spread evenly over the surface of the dough.
9. Final proof for approximately 3 hours or until almost reached the sides of the pizza tray. Cover with plastic to prevent skinning and chilling of the dough. Use the indentation test to tell when the dough is fully proofed.
10. Stud the dough evenly with the olives sliced-side down, then push small sprigs of rosemary evenly into the dough.
11. Place directly into a preheated oven set at 250°C (480°F) and bake for approximately 15–18 minutes.
12. Cool on a wire rack.
13. Serve warm.

TOPPING

¾ *medium-sized organic brown onion*

35 ml (3½ tablespoons) olive oil

1–2 garlic cloves, finely chopped

1 sprig fresh rosemary, remove leaves and finely chop half the amount, keeping the rest of the leaves whole for later

DOUGH

275 g (2 cups + 2 tablespoons) organic white flour

5 g (1 teaspoon) salt

25 g (3 tablespoons) organic wholemeal flour

100 g (½ cup) sourdough starter (see Pane Acido)

165 ml (¾ cup) water

GARNISH

10 Kalamata olives, pitted and sliced in half lengthwise

half the caramelised onion mixture from above

1 sprig fresh rosemary (broken into smaller sprigs)

Finished Dough Temperature:
24 –26°C (75–78°F)

Photo of recipe on front cover.

Sprouted Wheat and Rye Bread

Don't just soak the wheat and rye berries, but take the time to sprout them. The sprouted wheat makes the bread sweet and moist, the texture dense and the nuttiness very satisfying. Many followers of good nutrition are turning to such sprouted wheat breads and finding them beneficial to their diet.

GRAINS

30 g (3 tablespoons) whole wheat berries

30 g (3 tablespoons) whole rye berries

warm water, enough to cover the berries

DOUGH

300 g (2¼ cups) organic white flour

5 g (1 teaspoon) salt

50 g (⅓ cup) organic rye meal flour

110 g (½ cup + 1 tablespoon) sourdough starter (see Pane Acido recipe)

200 ml (½ cup + 6 tablespoons) water

sprouted wheat and rye berries from above

Finished Dough Temperature:
24–26°C (75–78°F)

Four days in advance

1. Place the berries into a large bowl and soak in the water overnight. The next day drain and rinse the berries, then place into either a colander sitting in a bowl or container with holes in the bottom sitting on a plate. Place a damp towel over the top to prevent the berries from drying out during the sprouting process.

2. The sprouting of the berries should take 3 days in summer and 4 days in winter if kept in a warm place. They are ready to use when the white shoot is approximately two-thirds the length of the berry. During the sprouting process, the starch is converted to simple sugars (maltose), which in turn give the finished loaves a sweet, malty and nutty flavour.

Dough

1. Sieve the flour and salt onto your work surface. Make a well and add the rye meal flour, sourdough starter and water, mixing well until it forms a mass.

2. Mix or knead the dough by hand using the technique shown in the All About Bread Section. Continue kneading until the ingredients are well combined and the dough is three-quarters mixed (the dough is not fully developed at this stage).

3. Add the sprouted berries and continue to knead by hand. This final kneading should take a further 5–8 minutes (check if you have fully developed the dough by using the stretch test).

4. Lightly oil a bowl large enough to allow the dough to almost double in bulk. Put the dough in the bowl and cover with plastic. Leave in a warmish place (23–25°C/73–77°F) for 3 hours. By this time the dough should have started to gas and nearly doubled in size.

5. Tip the dough out onto a lightly floured bench and gently mould the dough piece into a round ball. Do not aggressively punch it down or squeeze all the gas from within. Pick each piece up and gently tuck the edges underneath, pulling the surface tight around the mass.

6. Lay the dough back on the floured bench and cover with a proofing cloth (or tea-towel). Give an intermediate proof of 20 minutes. While you wait, lightly dust a large cane proofing basket with flour, or alternatively line a large round bowl with a clean tea-towel and dust with flour.

7. Uncover the dough and mould it into a boule shape by cupping your hands around and moving in a circular motion, pulling the skin tight over the dough. Don't overdo it though, or the skin will rip and this will spoil the appearance of the finished product. The final shape will look like a smooth ball, but with a rough, scrunched-up bottom.

8. Place the moulded boule smooth-side down into the proofing basket or prepared bowl.

9. Final proof for approximately 2½–3 hours in a warm, draft-free place. Cover with plastic to prevent skinning and chilling of the dough. Use the indentation test to tell when the dough is three-quarters proofed.

10. The oven should be preheated to 240°C (465°F), with a baking stone in place. Gently tip the dough piece out onto a peel lightly dusted with semolina (so that the top of the dough piece has now become the bottom). Using a razor blade or sharp knife, slash 90° cuts in the top of the boule in a decorative pattern.

11. Just before you load the bread into the oven, spray water into the oven cavity with a spray bottle. Close the door quickly so you don't lose any of the steam.

12. With the peel and loaf in one hand, open the oven with the other, and gently 'flick' the boule off the peel and onto the baking stone. Spray the oven again with water, quickly closing the oven door. Wait for a further 2 minutes and spray the oven again, quickly closing the door. Resist opening the door.

13. Bake for 20 minutes, then check the loaves for even baking and turn down the oven to 220°C (430°F). If necessary, turn for even browning. For the remaining time leave the door of the oven slightly ajar to thicken and dry the crust.

14. After a total of 35–40 minutes the loaves will be ready to come out of the oven. Tap the bottom and listen for a hollow sound.

15. Cool on a wire rack.

JENNIFER JOHNSON AND LOUIS VAUSSENAT

IL FORNAIO

Not far from Melbourne's St Kilda Beach, tucked into a small side street, Il Fornaio is one of those bakery cafés where people of all ages and backgrounds can sit, pass the time of day and feel very comfortable. Louis Vaussenat's bakery products shine and glisten in a glass-fronted case, a wonderful aroma of coffee, wine and freshly baked bread mingles in the air and Jennifer Johnson has that warm personality to reassure regulars and new customers.

Louis has been very influential in the Melbourne baking scene since he arrived in Australia from Chamonix in 1980. Many of the top bakers have spent time learning from this talented and passionate baker who produces superb cakes, bread and pastries in traditional French style. He frequently returns to France to refresh and update his skills.

Jennifer, originally from North Queensland, is a chef. While running her own tiny restaurant where she served great cakes for afternoon tea, she decided she would love to work with Louis. When the opportunity to purchase Il Fornaio came up, the partnership was formed and they have been busy from the day they opened, serving a wide variety of breads, savoury dishes and patisserie items. The pair also operate a local retail store and supply many top restaurants with their daily bread.

Fougasse Provençale

A classic bread from south eastern France, where Louis hails from, the fougasse is a ladder-like flat bread that was traditionally topped with tiny pieces of pork fat. Louis adds bacon and onions to this version and makes a tasty savoury delicacy that is at its best when warm from the oven.

Day one: fermented dough

1. In a bowl, mix all the ingredients together to form a dough, place onto the bench and knead until fully developed. This should take 8–10 minutes.
2. Place into a lightly oiled container, cover with plastic wrap and leave overnight to ferment – at least 12 hours.

Sautéed Onions and Bacon

1. Heat a frying pan with a small amount of olive oil and lightly sauté the onion and bacon. Season with salt and pepper.
2. Remove from the heat and place onto a paper towel to absorb any oil. Place in a container to cool, cover and place in the fridge.

Day two: the dough

1. Sieve the flour onto your work surface. Make a well and add the salt, fermented dough, yeast and butter.
2. While mixing by hand, slowly add the water to the well.
3. Mix or knead the dough by hand using the technique shown in the All About Bread Section. Continue to knead the dough by hand. Every couple of minutes you should stop and check the gluten development and temperature of the dough (and take a quick breather!). This final kneading should take about 15 minutes (check if you have fully developed the dough by using the stretch test). It is important to ensure that the dough is fully developed.
4. Add the pre-cooked onions and bacon and continue to knead – this will take a while to become incorporated.
5. Lightly oil a bowl large enough to allow the dough to double in bulk. Put the dough in the bowl and cover with plastic. Leave in a warmish place (23–25°C/73–77°F) for 1½ hours. By this time the dough should be nearly double in size.
6. Gently knock back the dough in the bowl. This will deflate it slightly, but will develop more strength. Cover again and leave for 30 minutes.
7. Tip the dough out onto a lightly floured bench and, using a dough scraper, cut the dough into 4 pieces at approximately 315 g (11 oz) each. Mould each dough piece into a cob shape by cupping your hands around and moving in a circular motion, pulling the skin tightly over the dough. Don't overdo it though, or the skin will rip and this will spoil the appearance of the finished product. The final shape will look like a smooth ball, but with a rough, scrunched-up bottom. Lay the pieces back on the floured bench and cover with a proofing cloth or plastic. Give an intermediate proof of 15 minutes.
8. Uncover the dough and then, on a floured bench, use a rolling pin to roll each dough piece into an oval shape, approximately 200 mm (8 inches) long by 100 mm (4 inches) wide and 10 mm (½ inch) thick.

FERMENTED DOUGH
100 g (³/₄ cup) strong flour
good pinch of salt
¼ teaspoon dried yeast
60 ml (5 tablespoons) water

SAUTÉED ONIONS AND BACON
olive oil
150 g (1 cup) sliced onions
150 g (1 cup) bacon (trimmed and cut into thin slices)
salt and black pepper

DOUGH
500 g (4 cups) strong flour
10 g (2 teaspoons) salt
fermented dough from the day before (about 160 g)
5 g (1¼ teaspoons) dried yeast
20 g (1 tablespoon) butter
315 ml (1½ cups) water
pre-cooked onions, from the day before
pre-cooked bacon, from the day before
dried herbs for topping (optional)

Finished Dough Temperature:
26°C (78°F)

9. Using a sharp knife or razor blade, cut 3–4 diagonals down each side, 50 mm (2 inches) in length and all the way through, then pull each cut apart to create a wide open effect (see photo on page 35 in the All About Bread Section). Repeat for the remaining dough pieces.

10. Place each dough piece onto a baking tray lined with baking paper, 2 per baking tray. Allow about 50 mm (2 inches) between each piece of dough, keeping the cut wide open. The more wide apart the better.

11. Cover each baking tray with plastic and put in a warm place. Allow to final proof for 30–40 minutes or until fully proofed. If desired, lightly spray the dough with warm water and sprinkle with dried herbs.

12. Place the baking trays into a preheated oven set at 230–240°C (445–465°F) and bake for 15–18 minutes. Fougasse should be well baked so that they are crisp and not pale.

13. Remove from the oven and, if desired, immediately brush lightly with olive oil. Cool on a wire rack.

Madeleines

This 'seashell cake, so strictly pleated on the outside and so sensual inside' (Marcel Proust) is one of the pinnacles of French patisserie. It must be made in Madeleine moulds and is a melt-in-the-mouth experience that is perfect with fragrant tea or steamy coffee. It is often flavoured with either orange flower essence or lemon, as in Louis' recipe.

1. Place the eggs and sugar into a mixing bowl fitted with a whisk, and whisk until thick and creamy and the mixture has reached the ribbon stage (see section on All About Cakes, Sponges and Biscuits).
2. While the above is whisking, sieve the flour, baking powder and salt, then add the lemon zest. Set aside. Lightly grease your Madeleine mould with melted butter.
3. Slowly add the milk and vanilla essence to the egg and sugar mixture while still mixing on slow speed.
4. Gently fold the dry ingredients into the egg and sugar mixture, taking care not to overmix and knock all the air out. When the dry ingredients are three-quarters mixed in, gently fold through the melted butter until you achieve a creamy supple paste.
5. Using a tablespoon, three-quarter fill each pre-greased Madeleine shape with approximately 20–25 g (1 oz) of mixture and place directly into a preheated oven set at 210°C (410°F). Bake for approximately 9–10 minutes or until each Madeleine springs back when lightly touched with your fingertip. The amount of filling and baking times will vary depending on the size of your Madeleine mould.
6. Remove the Madeleines from their moulds immediately and cool on a wire rack. Wipe the Madeleine mould clean with a paper towel, cool quickly in the freezer for a few minutes and then re-grease before using immediately.
7. Using the balance of the mixture, repeat step 5 until all the mixture has been used up. This recipe should make approximately 30 Madeleines at approximately 20–25 g (1 oz) each.

Note: The mixture will become fluffy as time goes on. This is due to the baking powder reacting with the warmth and moisture within the batter. This may result in a denser crumb structure.

150 g (3) eggs
200 g (1 cup + 1 tablespoon) caster sugar
250 g (1³/₄ cups + 2 tablespoons) plain flour
5 g (1 teaspoon) baking powder
pinch of salt
zest of 1 lemon, finely chopped
80 ml (5¹/₂ tablespoons) warm milk
125 g (¹/₂ cup + 2 tablespoons) melted butter
2–3 drops of vanilla essence

Mushroom Brioche

Rather like a gourmet pizza, Louis' mushroom brioche is a flavourful experience that makes a super snack to eat on the run or, better still, to enjoy with a fresh green salad or simple tomato salad. The cream is cooked with the mushrooms to make them rich and smooth.

BRIOCHE BASE

250 g (2 cups) strong flour

5 g (1 teaspoon) salt

25 g (2¼ tablespoons) granulated sugar

5 g (1¼ teaspoons) dried active yeast

25 ml (2 tablespoons) water, cold

160 g (3½) eggs, cold

125 g (½ cup + 1½ tablespoons) softened butter

Finished Dough Temperature:
  27°C (80°F)

MUSHROOM FILLING

75 g (⅓ cup) butter

500 g (1 lb) button mushrooms, cleaned and thinly sliced

200 ml (¾ cup) fresh cream

50 g (½ heaped cup) grated tasty cheese

salt and pepper for seasoning

eggwash for the brioche discs

100 g (1 heaped cup) grated tasty cheese for sprinkling on the top

Day one: the brioche base

1. Sieve the flour onto your work surface. Make a well and add the salt, sugar and yeast.

2. Slowly add the water and three-quarters of the egg, then knead the dough for 6–7 minutes or until the dough is almost fully developed (it is important to develop the gluten structure before all the egg is added).

3. Continue to add the balance of the egg slowly while the dough is still being kneaded. Add sufficient egg to achieve a very soft, elastic, very smooth and shiny dough.

4. While kneading, slowly add the softened butter in small amounts. Knead in all the butter to achieve a smooth, elastic, silky dough. Do not overmix as this will cause overheating and the dough will become oily and greasy.

5. Transfer the dough into a lightly oiled container covered with plastic wrap, give a bulk fermentation time of 1 hour in a warm draft-free place. The dough should have doubled in size.

6. Gently knock back the dough to expel all the gases, reactivate the yeast and strengthen the gluten structure. Finally push the dough out to a thickness of 5 cm (2 inches) and place into a shallow container. Cover with plastic wrap.

7. Place into the refrigerator overnight (12 hours). This makes the dough easier to workoff and mould.

Mushroom Filling

1. Heat the butter in a saucepan over a medium heat, add the mushrooms and fry until soft and the moisture has come out – this should take approximately 10–15 minutes. Drain well.

2. Return the mushrooms to the saucepan and add the cream. Cook over a medium heat until the cream has nearly reduced by half, stirring all the time – this should take approximately 10 minutes. Remove from the heat.

3. Add the grated cheese and salt and pepper to taste. Stir until the cheese is incorporated.

4. Cool then place into a container, cover and refrigerate overnight.

Day two: assembly

1. Remove the dough from the refrigerator and scale off into 10 dough pieces at 60 g (2 oz) each. Mould each piece into a round ball, place onto a floured tray and return to the refrigerator for 5 minutes.

2. On a floured surface, use a rolling pin to roll out each ball into a circle 150 mm (6 inches) in diameter.

3. Roll back the edges of each circle 10 mm (½ inch) to create an edging. Ensure

this is firmly rolled back otherwise it will unroll during baking. This will prevent the mushroom filling from running out during baking. Place the brioche discs onto 2 baking trays lined with baking paper, 5 per tray.

4. Cover with plastic to prevent the dough from skinning and then put in a warm place for 30 minutes to allow the dough pieces to proof.

5. Gently brush the outside edges of each disc with eggwash and then evenly spoon the mushroom filling into each disc, starting from the middle and working outwards, taking care not to overflow the edges.

6. Lightly sprinkle grated cheese over the mushroom filling.

7. Place each tray directly into a preheated oven set at 180°C (355°F) and bake for 15–20 minutes.

8. Cool or serve warm with your favourite salad.

JOCELYN HANCOCK

JOCELYN'S PROVISIONS

Walk into Jocelyn Hancock's store in New Farm, Brisbane, and you know immediately that she's a baker who loves her chosen profession. The atmosphere exudes character and personality, and the slightly French provincial feel is a perfect backdrop for Jocelyn's excellent breads, cakes, biscuits, tarts and provisions. The five years since she established her business have seen three changes of premises, as she has expanded what was originally a wholesale-only bakery for cakes, biscuits and tarts to the large warehouse space with a busy retail outlet that she works in today.

After pursuing training as a chef in Brisbane in the late eighties, Jocelyn headed overseas to Britain and there found two sets of mentors who laid the foundation for her appreciation and enthusiasm for superb produce and fantastic flavours. Her first job was in a Norfolk country house working for a busy London couple who had a true love of good food, and they encouraged Jocelyn to develop her skills further. She then moved on to work at Sally Clarke's where New Zealander Maureen Challender helped her develop excellent technical baking skills. The pair worked very hard, spending six days a week in the kitchen on a minimum of 12-hour shifts.

It's Brisbane's good fortune that, after returning to Australia and working at Phillippa's in Melbourne, Jocelyn decided to open her own business and returned to her home town. Today she cooks her superior products for appreciative customers, and supplies restaurants, caterers and airlines.

Eggplant, Sweet Potato, Fennel & Goats Cheese Brioche Tart

The brioche crust for this excellent tart must be begun a day ahead. There are several components to the filling and, although it is rather complex to make, the finished tart will be much admired and quickly devoured.

Day one: the brioche base

1. Sieve the flour onto your work surface. Make a well and add the salt, sugar and yeast.
2. Slowly add the water and three-quarters of the egg, knead the dough for 6–7 minutes or until it is almost fully developed (it is important to develop the gluten structure before all the egg is added).
3. Continue to add the balance of the egg slowly while the dough is still being kneaded. Add sufficient egg to achieve a very soft, elastic, very smooth and shiny dough.
4. While kneading, slowly add the softened butter in small amounts. Knead in all the butter to achieve a smooth, elastic, silky dough. Do not overmix as this will cause overheating and the dough will become oily and greasy.
5. Transfer the dough into a lightly oiled container covered with plastic wrap, give a bulk fermentation time of 1 hour in a warm draft-free place. The dough should have doubled in size.
6. Gently knock back the dough to expel all the gases, reactivate the yeast and strengthen the gluten structure. Finally push the dough out to a thickness of 5 cm (2 inches) and place into a shallow container. Cover with plastic wrap.
7. Place into the refrigerator overnight (12 hours). This makes the dough easier to workoff and mould.

Day two: filling and assembly

1. Remove the dough from the refrigerator and divide into 2 equal pieces, approximately 295 g (10 oz) each. Mould both pieces into ball shapes. Place one ball into a bowl and cover with plastic wrap, return to the refrigerator and use the following day or process as for brioche or dessert pizza (see recipe for brioche or dessert pizza). Place the other ball back into the refrigerator for 10–15 minutes to rest and firm up.
2. Remove one ball from the refrigerator and on a lightly floured surface, using a rolling pin, roll the pastry out to a sheet about 3–4mm (¼ inch) thick and big enough to cover a 250 mm (10 inches) round x 30 mm (1½ inches) high greased fluted or non-fluted loose-bottomed flan tin.
3. Use the rolling pin to pick the pastry up and lay it over the tin. Gently press the pastry into the tin so that it fills all the contours. Be careful not to stretch the pastry or it will tear or shrink back in the oven. Return it to the fridge for another 30 minutes, or more if the pastry feels soft. Reserve the scraps.
4. Spread the caramelised onion filling (see recipe) over the base and then fill with the oven roasted vegetables (see below), ensuring that they are placed in a rustic fashion.

BRIOCHE BASE
250 g (2 cups) strong flour
5 g (1 teaspoon) salt
25 g (2¼ tablespoons) granulated sugar
5 g (1¼ teaspoons) dried active yeast
25 ml (2 tablespoons) water
160 g (3½) eggs, cold
125 g (½ cup + 1½ tablespoons) softened butter

Finished Dough Temperature: 27°C (80°F)

CARAMELISED ONION
3 tablespoons olive oil
300 g (2 cups) brown onions, cut in half and chopped
15 ml (1 tablespoon) balsamic vinegar
15 g (1 tablespoon) brown sugar
1 tablespoon mustard seeds
salt and freshly ground pepper to taste
good pinch grated nutmeg

OVEN ROASTED VEGETABLES
2 tablespoons olive oil
100 g (1 cup) sweet potato, peeled and roughly diced
150 g (1 cup) fennel, roughly sliced
150 g (1 cup) eggplant, roughly sliced
100 g (1 cup) red capsicums, lightly grilled then cut into strips
150 g (1 cup) zucchini, sliced
salt and pepper for seasoning
2 fresh thyme sprigs, leaves removed

SAVOURY ROYALE FILLING
300 g (6) eggs
200 ml (³/₄ cup) fresh cream
¹/₄ teaspoon ground nutmeg
good pinch of salt
freshly ground pepper

TOPPING
120 g (³/₄ cup) goats cheese, cut into
* small slices*
4–5 spears of asparagus

5. Pour the savoury royale mixture (see recipe) evenly into the filled case. Dot the surface with small slices of goats cheese and place on the spears of asparagus.
6. Place the tart into a preheated oven set at 175–180°C (350°F) and bake for 35–40 minutes or until the mixture is just set and firm to the touch. Do not overbake.
7. Remove from the oven and cool before removing from the flan tin.

Caramelised Onion

1. In a frying pan, heat the olive oil, add the onions and cook over a medium heat for a few minutes until the onions begin to soften. Add the balsamic vinegar, brown sugar and mustard seeds.
2. Angle a lid on the frying pan to allow the steam to escape, reduce the heat to low and slowly cook the onions for approximately 30–40 minutes, stirring from time to time to prevent the onions from burning or catching on the bottom.
3. Towards the end of cooking remove the lid and add the seasoning and nutmeg, stirring well to combine. The onions should be soft, caramelised and not too brown.
4. Cool before use.

Oven Roasted Vegetables

1. Place the olive oil into a heated roasting dish, add the sweet potato and roast for 15 minutes, then add the remaining prepared vegetables, thyme and seasoning, and roast for a further 10–15 minutes.
2. Remove from the roasting pan and cool on a plate until required.

Filling

1. Place the eggs into a mixing bowl and whisk by hand until smooth and broken up.
2. Pour in the cream and add the nutmeg, salt and pepper, then whisk to combine. Do not overwhisk or the mixture will become too fluffy. Set aside until required.

Fruit Brioche

A fabulous dessert with a great brioche base. The fresh fruit is given a delicious spiciness with the cinnamon sugar, and it should be served warm with cream or ice cream for a real treat.

Day one: the brioche base

1. Sieve the flour onto your work surface. Make a well and add the salt, sugar and yeast.
2. Slowly add the water and three-quarters of the egg, knead the dough for 6–7 minutes or until the dough is almost fully developed (it is important to develop the gluten structure before all the egg is added).
3. Continue to add the balance of the egg slowly while the dough is still being kneaded. Add sufficient egg to achieve a very soft, elastic, very smooth and shiny dough.
4. While kneading, slowly add the softened butter in small amounts. Knead in all the butter to achieve a smooth, elastic, silky dough. Do not overmix as this will cause overheating and the dough will become oily and greasy.
5. Transfer the dough into a lightly oiled container covered with plastic wrap and give a bulk fermentation time of 1 hour in a warm draft-free place. The dough should have doubled in size.
6. Gently knock back the dough to expel all the gases, reactivate the yeast and strengthen the gluten structure. Finally push the dough out to a thickness of 5 cm (2 inches) and place into a shallow container, cover with plastic wrap.
7. Place into the refrigerator overnight (12 hours). This makes the dough easier to workoff and mould.

Day two: poached fruit of your choice

If you prefer you can use fresh fruit without poaching, e.g. raspberries, mango, nectarines, apricots, apples, etc.

1. Place water and sugar into a saucepan and gently bring to the boil. Reduce the heat to a simmer.
2. Place your selected fruit into the simmering sugar syrup and poach until tender. Do not overcook the quince otherwise it will become too soft. Different fruit will require different poaching time.
3. Remove the fruit from the syrup and cool. Slice larger fruits into slices 3–4mm (¹/₄ inch) thick. Cover and set aside.
4. Place the sugar, cinnamon and oil into a bowl.
5. Using your hands, rub the oil into the cinnamon and sugar to ensure an even distribution and prevent separation. Set aside until required.

Assembly

1. Remove the dough from the refrigerator and scale off into 10 dough pieces at 60 g each. Mould each piece into a round ball, place onto a floured tray and return to the refrigerator for 5 minutes.
2. On a lightly floured surface, use a rolling pin to roll out each ball into a circle or disc 10 cm (4 inches) in diameter.

BRIOCHE BASE

250 g (2 cups) strong flour

5 g (1 teaspoon) salt

25 g (2¹/₄ tablespoons) granulated sugar

5 g (1¹/₄ teaspoons) dried active yeast

25 ml (2 teaspoons) water

160 g (3¹/₂) eggs, cold

125 g (¹/₂ cup + 1¹/₂ tablespoons) softened butter

POACHED FRUITS

500 ml (2 cups) water

250 g (1¹/₄ cups) sugar

6 halves of fruit of your choice, e.g. quince, pear, apricots, prunes, etc.

1 cinnamon stick

CINNAMON SUGAR

100 g (¹/₂ cup) granulated sugar

1¹/₂ teaspoons cinnamon

2–3 small drops of olive oil

Finished Dough Temperature: 27°C (80°F)

3. Place the brioche discs onto 2 baking trays lined with baking paper, 5 per tray. Lightly sprinkle each disc with cinnamon sugar.

4. Cover with plastic to prevent the dough from skinning and then put in a warm place for 30–45 minutes to allow the dough pieces to proof. Then place a selection of poached fruits on top, pressing down slightly to prevent the fruit from coming off during baking.

5. Place each tray directly into a preheated oven set at 180°C (355°F) and bake for 15–20 minutes or until golden brown.

6. Allow to cool or serve warm with cream or ice cream.

ROBERT HILT
LA BRETAGNE

Sydney's Rose Bay is a far cry from the tiny village of Ittenheim, near Strasbourg, where Robert Hilt grew up in his father's patisserie. But there's a real village atmosphere in the Plumer Road specialty food shops, and it's here that Robert owns a tiny genuine French patisserie not unlike the family business in France.

Robert spent the first part of his working life following in the paternal footsteps, learning the art of patisserie and following seasonal work in the south of France during the summer months before heading to the winter snow resort scene of Austria and Switzerland. He then worked as a patissier with Club Med and saw the world.

He has been in Australia for the past 10 years, and purchased La Bretagne in 1999. All the delights of the French patissier's kitchen are baked daily in his tiny workshop, with Robert as the sole operator. There's a jewel-like array of glazed fruit pastries, quiches and tiny savouries, and tempting éclairs, tarts and meringues. A constant stream of customers crowd into the store to purchase his specialty cakes and tarts to take to parties and celebrations.

Chocolate Kugelhopf

This kugelhopf is classic, dark and daringly rich. It is an advanced patissier's recipe and requires careful management and a lengthy preparation that will prove very rewarding when the final cake emerges from the oven. Serve as a dessert or as an accompaniment to strong hot coffee.

Day one: the chocolate filling preparation

1. Place the cream into a saucepan and gently bring to the boil.
2. Remove from the heat and add the chocolate.
3. Stir using a wooden spoon until the chocolate has melted. You may need to put the saucepan back onto the warm element to melt the chocolate, stirring to prevent sticking.
4. Place into a bowl, cover and leave out at room temperature overnight. Do not put in the fridge.

Day two: the ferment

1. Place the flour, yeast and sugar into a mixing bowl. Stir together to combine.
2. Pour in the milk and, using a wooden spoon, stir until a smooth batter has been achieved.
3. Cover the bowl and leave the mixture in a warm place to ferment for 20 minutes until it becomes a frothy spongy batter.

Day two: the creamed mixture

1. In a separate bowl and using a wooden spoon, cream the butter and sugar until light and fluffy.
2. Slowly beat in the eggs and egg yolks, beating between each addition until light and fluffy. Set aside.

Day two: the final dough

1. Place onto your work surface the flour and salt. Make a well and add the ferment and creamed egg/sugar mixture.
2. Mix or knead the dough by hand using the technique shown in the All About Bread Section. The dough will seem sticky, but don't worry as it will firm up as you are kneading. Don't be tempted to add more flour at this stage. Continue kneading until the ingredients are well combined. This final kneading should take about 10–15 minutes (check if you have fully developed the dough by using the stretch test). The dough will be smooth, elastic and a little sticky.
3. Place the dough into a large lightly oiled container and cover. Give a bulk fermentation time of 1 hour in a warm place (24–25°C/75–77°F).
4. Gently knock back the dough in the bowl. This will deflate it slightly, but it will develop more strength. Cover again and leave for 30 minutes. Mould the dough into a ball and place back into the lightly oiled container.
5. Tip the dough out onto a lightly floured work surface and divide the dough into 2 equal pieces (375 g/13 oz each) or leave as one large piece (750 g/ 1 lb 10½ oz). Weights will vary depending on the size of the kugelhopf mould. The rest of the instructions that follow are for a 750g (1 lb 10½ oz) kugelhopf.

CHOCOLATE FILLING

50 ml (2½ tablespoons) fresh cream

100 g (¾ cup) dark chocolate, finely chopped

DOUGH

75 g (½ cup + 1 tablespoon) strong flour

8 g (1 tablespoon) dried active yeast

good pinch of sugar

150 ml (½ cup + 2 tablespoons) milk (30°C/85°F)

110 g (½ cup) softened butter

70 g (¾ cup) sugar

50 g (1) egg

40 g (2) egg yolks

300 g (2¼ cups) strong flour

5 g (1 teaspoon) salt

6. Flatten the dough piece on a lightly floured bench into a rectangular shape. Using a rolling pin, roll the dough piece to an even rectangle shape of 450 mm x 250 mm (17½ inches x 10 inches) and 5 mm (¼ inch) in thickness. This will take some time so be patient and allow the dough to relax for a few minutes when the rolling becomes difficult.

7. Using a palette knife, spread the chocolate filling evenly over the sheet of dough. If the chocolate filling is too firm, place in the microwave for only a few seconds at a time to soften. Do not melt the filling otherwise it will cause problems later on during baking.

8. Starting at the top, roll the long edge downwards to form a swiss roll shape (as for Chelsea buns). The length of the rolled kugelhopf will depend on what size mould is used. Join the ends together to form a ring shape.

9. Place the dough piece smooth-side down and with the seam facing upwards into a prepared kugelhopf mould or moulds. To prepare the kugelhopf mould, lightly grease with melted butter and place whole blanched almonds in the bottom ribs of the mould.

10. Proof the kugelhopf for approximately 1½ hours in a warm place, covered with a sheet of plastic to prevent the surface from drying out. The dough will have doubled in size. Use the indentation test to tell when the dough is fully proofed.

11. Place the moulds directly into a preheated oven set at 190–200°C (375°F) and bake for approximately 30 minutes. If the surface becomes too dark, place a sheet of greaseproof paper on top during the final stages of baking.

12. Tip onto a wire rack to cool.

13. Dust with icing sugar if desired.

Concorde Gateau

This is another advanced recipe from La Bretagne. There are several steps to cover in the preparation before this magnificent cake is assembled with its moist and luscious chocolate filling, and the crisp meringue covering. Customers demand Robert's Concorde for special occasions and gifts.

Day one: the chocolate meringue preparation

1. Before starting, thoroughly wash a stainless steel mixing bowl and whisk in hot soapy water, then rinse in hot water and dry well with a clean tea-towel.
2. Place the egg whites into the mixing bowl and whisk for 2–3 minutes on medium speed to allow the egg whites to double in volume.
3. Slowly add the sugar over 5 additions, continuing to whisk on high speed until the meringue has reached stiff peaks.
4. Sieve the second amount of sugar and cocoa powder together then, using a large metal spoon, fold through the stiff meringue until well combined.
5. Place the meringue mixture into a piping bag, fitted with a 1 cm (½ inch) plain piping nozzle.
6. Pipe straight and even lines of meringue directly onto a baking tray lined with baking paper. Ensure the meringue lines are approximately 2 cm (1 inch) apart. You should have enough mixture for 2 full baking trays.
7. Place the baking trays directly into a preheated oven set at 100°C (215°F), turn off the heat and allow the meringues to dry out overnight in the oven. Ensure the oven door is slightly ajar to allow any moisture to escape. If the meringues are soft in the middle, turn the oven on again to 100°C (215°F) and bake until dry.
8. Once the meringues are dry and cool, cut each strip into approximately 2.5 cm (1 inch) long pieces and store for later use.

Day two: the sponge cake base

1. Place the egg yolks and sugar into a mixing bowl. Whisk until thick and creamy and the mixture has reached the ribbon stage (see section on All About Cakes, Sponges and Biscuits).
2. In a separate clean grease-free bowl whisk the egg whites until fluffy and holding a stiff peak.
3. In 3 additions gently fold the egg whites into the egg yolk and sugar mixture.
4. Sieve the flour and cocoa and fold in until half mixed through.
5. Add the melted butter and melted chocolate, gently folding until evenly distributed. Do not overmix at this stage, as this will cause the air bubbles to escape and result in a low volume sponge base.
6. Gently pour the mixture into a greased 23 cm (9 inch) round cake tin.
7. Place directly into a preheated oven set at 180°C (355°F) and bake for 35–40 minutes or until the cake springs back when lightly pressed in the centre.
8. Cool for 15 minutes before removing from the tin.
9. Cool completely.

CHOCOLATE MERINGUE
150 g (4) egg whites
225 g (1 cup + 1 tablespoon) caster sugar
75 g (¼ cup + 2 tablespoons) caster sugar
25 g (¼ cup) cocoa powder

SPONGE CAKE BASE
6 only eggs (separated)
175 g (¾ cup + 1½ tablespoons) caster sugar
125 g (1 cup) self raising flour
25 g (¼ cup) cocoa powder
90 g (⅓ cup + 2 tablespoons) melted butter
150 g (¼ cup) melted chocolate

GANACHE FILLING AND COATING
500 g (3¼ cups) chocolate, finely chopped
250 ml (1 cup) fresh cream
Kahlua liqueur for soaking the layers of sponge

DECORATION
cocoa powder for sieving
icing sugar for sieving

Ganache Filling and Coating

1. Place the cream into a saucepan and gently bring to the boil.
2. Remove from the heat and add the chocolate.
3. Using a wooden spoon, stir until the chocolate has melted.
4. Place into a mixing bowl fitted with a beater, and on medium speed beat until the ganache filling has begun to cool, thicken and change colour – this should take approximately 10–12 minutes. Do not beat too much as you do not want to incorporate air into the filling. The consistency should be that of three-quarters whipped cream (soft peak) and be able to be spread easily with a palette knife.

Note: Do this just prior to kneading, or the ganache will go firm.

Gateau Assembly

1. Slice the cake horizontally into 3 even layers. Place the top layer upside down on the bench so that it becomes the base of the gateau.
2. Using a pastry brush, lightly brush the base with the Kahlua liqueur.
3. Using a palette knife, spread a thin layer (approximately 5 mm/¼ inch thick) of the soft filling onto the base.
4. Place the middle layer of the sponge cake on top of the filling and brush with the Kahlua, pressing down lightly.
5. Repeat steps 3 and 4.
6. Ensure that the last layer of sponge cake has the smooth side on top.
7. Holding the palette knife vertically coat the outside sides of the gateau with the filling, ensuring that there is an even coating all around.
8. Again using the palette knife spread an even layer of the filling on the top surface of the gateau. To achieve a smooth and clean finish, dip the palette knife into hot water and give the surface one last even spread.
9. Tidy up any rough edges.
10. Use a palette knife to lift the gateau up and then slide your hand underneath. Gently place the gateau onto a large flat serving plate.
11. Place the meringue sticks around the outside edge of the gateau in a random manner.
12. Once you have completed the sides, roughly place the meringue sticks on the top surface, starting from the outside and working inwards to finish off with the effect of the meringue sticks coming out from the middle (see photo).
13. Lightly dust the meringue sticks (top of gateau only) with cocoa powder and then lightly dust with icing sugar.
14. Place in the refrigerator for 1 hour before serving.

Note: When cutting a slice of gateau always ensure that you dip your knife in hot water first.

LA TARTINE

Most La Tartine customers purchase this unique bread in one of the crop of farmers' markets that have sprung up around Sydney. Nick and Laurence are extremely happy to see their breads sold in this manner because it makes them feel connected to the people who eat their bread.

They are dedicated to offering breads baked from certified organic ingredients, and made with filtered water so that any La Tartine loaf is wholesome and made without harm to the environment. The pair met in the USA, both keen skiers working in a small resort, and they worked together in the Haute Savoie, where Laurence had grown up. This part of France is renowned for traditional crusty hearth loaves, so it was these breads that they turned out of their bakery that they established when they arrived in Australia, Nick's homeland.

Finding Sydney very expensive, they established their bakery in an industrial area at Somersby, north of the city but close to the major roads, and installed a huge purpose-built wood-fired oven. Nick's brother Mark has joined them and this very hands-on, very intensive operation is now turning out a range of authentic organic sourdoughs unequalled in the city.

Fruited Sourdough

So popular is this bread in the farmers' markets that 300 to 400 loaves sell out by 10 am each day that the La Tartine team appear. It is dense and full of organic fruits, and keeps well. Nick and Laurence feel it's important that their customers know that their bread is better eaten 24 hours after baking as the increased acidity ensures a more complete digestion.

1. Sieve the flour and salt onto your work surface. Make a well and add the leaven and water, mixing well until it forms a mass.

2. Mix or knead the dough by hand using the technique shown in the All About Bread Section. Continue kneading until the ingredients are well combined and the dough is fully developed. This should take approximately 15 minutes (check if you have fully developed the dough by using the stretch test).

3. Gently knead in the figs, apricots and sultanas until evenly mixed through the dough. Avoid excessive kneading at this stage as this could result in crushing the fruit.

4. Place the dough piece into a bowl, cover and allow to rest for 10–15 minutes. While you wait, lightly grease a bread tin (size of the bread tins should be approximately 230 mm (9 inches) in length, 80 mm (3 inches) in width and 75 mm (3 inches) in height).

5. Tip the dough out onto the bench and divide in half. Mould each piece into a boule shape. For the boule, shape each piece into a ball by cupping your hands around and moving in a circular motion, pulling the skin tight over the dough. Don't overdo it though, or the skin will rip and this will spoil the appearance of the finished product. The final shape will look like a smooth ball, but with a rough, scrunched-up bottom.

6. Firmly press the bottom and halfway up the sides of each boule into the chopped almonds.

7. Place the moulded boules almond-side down into the greased bread tin.

8. Final proof for approximately 5–6 hours in a warm, draft-free place (ideal temperature 28°C). Cover with plastic to prevent skinning and chilling of the dough. Use the indentation test to tell when the dough is three-quarters proofed.

9. Using a razor blade or sharp knife, make a cut lengthways down the middle of the proofed dough pieces.

10. Just before you load the bread into the preheated oven set at 230–240°C (445–465°F), spray water into the oven cavity with a spray bottle. Close the door quickly so you don't lose any of the steam.

11. Place the bread directly into the oven, spray again with water and bake for 20 minutes, then reduce the heat to 200°C (390°F) and bake for a further 15–20 minutes or until a hollow sound is heard when the bottom is tapped.

12. Cool on a wire rack.

300 g (2¼ cups) strong flour

10 g (2 teaspoons) sea salt

200 g (1 cup) leaven (using the same leaven recipe as for the Pumpkin Sourdough)

200 ml (½ cup + 6 tablespoons) chlorine-free water (25°C/77°F)

100 g (½ cup) dried figs, organic if available (remove the stems and cut into small pieces)

100 g (½ cup) dried apricots, organic if available (cut into quarters)

100 g (½ cup) sultanas, organic if available

50 g (¼ heaped cup) natural whole almonds, roughly chopped into thirds, for decoration

Finished Dough Temperature:
26°C (78°F)

Pumpkin Sourdough

The sweet nutty flavour of this sourdough bread is quite unique. The pumpkin must be cooked and mashed and incorporated into the dough, and the finished loaf has a crusty exterior and an even, dense interior.

STARTER

120 g (1 cup) wholemeal flour

80 ml ($^1/_3$ cup) chlorine-free water (25°C/77°F)

DOUGH

360 g (12 oz) raw pumpkin

270 g (2 cups + 1$^1/_2$ tablespoons) strong flour

5 g (1 teaspoon) sea salt

120 g (1$^1/_4$ cups) leaven (from above)

90 ml ($^1/_3$ cup + 1 tablespoon) water (25°C/77°F)

Finished Dough Temperature: 26°C (79°F)

Forty-eight hours in advance: La Tartine starter

1. Place the flour onto your work surface. Make a well and add the water, mixing well until it forms a mass.

2. Mix or knead the dough by hand using the technique shown in the All About Bread Section. Continue kneading until the ingredients are well combined and the dough is fully developed. This should take approximately 15 minutes (check if you have fully developed the dough by using the stretch test).

3. Place the dough into a clean glass jar or bowl and cover with the lid slightly ajar or a clean tea-towel (this is important as it will allow the starter to breathe). Leave in a warmish place (23–25°C/73–77°F) for 36–48 hours. By this time the dough should have started to bubble and ferment. If it hasn't, leave it longer or you may have to start the process again.

4. Take 30 g (2 tablespoons) of the starter (throw away the rest) and remix it with 100 g ($^3/_4$ cup) of wholemeal flour and 70 ml ($^1/_3$ cup) warm water (25°C/77°F). Knead this for approximately 15 minutes or until the dough is fully developed. This is the leaven for your dough.

5. Place the dough back into the bowl and cover, leave in a warm place for a further 8 hours to fully develop and ripen the leaven. The leaven should be very active by this stage.

Dough

1. Remove the skin and seeds from the pumpkin, cut into pieces then place on a baking tray and bake in the preheated oven set at 220°C (430°F) until soft. This should take approximately 45 minutes. Place in a food processor and purée. Cool before use.

2. Sieve the flour and salt onto your work surface. Make a well and add the leaven, pumpkin purée and water, mixing well until it forms a mass. Depending on how much water is in the pumpkin an adjustment of water or flour may be necessary to achieve soft dough (not too firm or too wet).

3. Mix or knead the dough by hand using the technique shown in the All About Bread Section. Continue kneading until the ingredients are well combined and the dough is fully developed – this should take approximately 15 minutes (check if you have fully developed the dough by using the stretch test).

4. Place the dough piece into a bowl, cover and allow to rest for 10–15 minutes. While you wait, lightly dust a large cane proofing basket with flour or alternatively line a medium to large round bowl with a clean tea-towel and dust with flour.

5. Tip the dough out onto the bench and mould each piece of dough into a boule shape by cupping your hands around and moving in a circular motion, pulling the skin tight over the dough. Don't overdo it though, or the skin will rip and

this will spoil the appearance of the finished product. The final shape will look like a smooth ball, but with a rough, scrunched-up bottom.

6. Place the moulded boule smooth-side down into the proofing basket or prepared bowl.

7. Final proof for approximately 5–6 hours in a warm, draft-free place (ideal temperature 28°C/82°F). Cover with plastic to prevent skinning and chilling of the dough. Use the indentation test to tell when the dough is three-quarters proofed.

8. The oven should be preheated to 240°C (465°F), with a baking stone in place. Gently tip the dough piece out onto a peel lightly dusted with semolina (so that the top of the dough piece has now become the bottom). Using a razor blade or sharp knife, slash 90° cuts in the top in a decorative pattern.

9. Just before you load the bread into the oven, spray water into the oven cavity with a spray bottle. Close the door quickly so you don't lose any of the steam.

10. With the peel and loaf in one hand, open the oven with the other, and gently 'flick' the boule off the peel and onto the baking stone. Spray the oven again with water, quickly closing the oven door. Wait for a further 2 minutes and spray the oven again, quickly closing the door. Resist opening the door.

11. Bake for 20 minutes, then check the loaves for even baking and turn down the oven to 220°C (430°F). If necessary, turn for even browning. For the remaining time leave the door of the oven slightly ajar to thicken and dry the crust.

12. After a total of 30–35 minutes the loaves will be ready to come out of the oven. Tap the bottom and listen for a hollow sound.

13. Cool on a wire rack.

HELEN RICHARDS
MUFFIN TIME

Helen Richards came from a business background to start her muffin bakery in Dunedin. In 1990 she set up the retail outlet for her tasty muffins, which quickly won the approval of customers throughout the city and the South Island. In order to expand her business Helen worked extensively with the Otago University Food Science Department to develop a frozen muffin batter, which is marketed nationwide. The business has grown, producing an extremely high quality product, which has won two Carter Holt Harvey Food Awards.

Muffin Time's muffins are made with the best available ingredients, and a large selection of freshly baked muffins are enjoyed every day by customers.

Chocolate Ecstasy Muffins

Chocolate lovers will revel in these rich chocolate muffins that are layered with chocolate chips and chocolate buttons.

1. Place the butter in a large bowl, and microwave to melt.
2. Add eggs and milk, and mix well together.
3. Sieve the flour, baking powder, sugar and cocoa. Add the chocolate chips. Add to the liquid mixture.
4. Using a wooden spoon stir until all ingredients are just combined. Don't overmix.
5. Pour one third of the batter into greased muffin pans or 12 muffin paper cases.
6. Place a white chocolate button in each muffin mould.
7. Pour more batter on top of the chocolate button. Total batter weight in each mould is approximately 120 g (4 oz).
8. Sprinkle with chocolate chips or place a milk chocolate button on top of each muffin.
9. Bake in a preheated oven set at 180°C (355°F) for 20–25 minutes.
10. Remove from the tray while still warm.
11. Cool and dust with icing sugar.

115 g (¹/₂ cup + 1 teaspoon) butter
75 g (1¹/₂) eggs
425 ml (2 cups) milk
450 g (3¹/₃ cups) plain flour
25 g (5 teaspoons) baking powder
210 g (1 cup + 1 tablespoon) granulated sugar
60 g (¹/₂ cup + 1 tablespoon) cocoa
115 g (³/₄ cup) chocolate chips

FILLING
white and milk chocolate buttons or chocolate chips
icing sugar to dust

Orange Cheesecake Muffins

Sweet and fruity, these orange flavoured muffins are quite refreshing. The cream cheese centre adds a smooth dimension to the crumbly texture.

1. Wash the oranges and remove half the zest. Quarter the oranges, removing any pips.
2. Place the orange quarters into a blender and blend for 15 seconds.
3. Add the chopped butter and blend for 30–60 seconds.
4. Add the egg and water, and blend for a further 2–3 minutes.
5. Pour the blended mixture into a large bowl.
6. Sieve the flour, sugar and baking powder, and add to the above.
7. Using a wooden spoon stir until all ingredients are just combined. Don't overmix.
8. Pour one third of the batter into greased muffin pans or 12 muffin paper cases.
9. Pipe or spoon approximately 15 g (1 tablespoon) of softened cream cheese into each muffin mould.
10. Pour more batter on top of the cream cheese. Total batter weight in each mould is approximately 105 g (3³/₄ oz).
11. Place a thinly sliced piece of orange on top of each muffin and sprinkle with a little granulated sugar.
12. Bake in a preheated oven set at 180°C (355°F) for 20–25 minutes.
13. Remove from the tray while still warm.
14. Cool and brush with apricot glaze (see recipe for Mediterranean Orange Cake).

1¹/₂ medium fresh oranges
135 g (¹/₂ cup + 2 tablespoons) softened butter
75 g (1¹/₂) eggs
240 g (1 cup) water
445 g (3¹/₃ cups) plain four
215 g (1 cup + 2 tablespoons) granulated sugar
20 g (4 teaspoons) baking powder

FILLING
180 g (³/₄ cup) cream cheese (approximately 15 g (1 tablespoon) per muffin)

Spinach and Parmesan Muffins

A top seller at Muffin Time, this delicious savoury muffin is almost a meal. The cream cheese filling eliminates the need for butter, and provides a surprise in the centre.

240 ml (1 cup) milk
65 ml (¼ cup + 1 tablespoon) oil
95 g (1 heaped cup) grated cheese
80 g (¾ cup) parmesan cheese
135 g (5 oz) spinach (chopped well)
10 g (1 tablespoon) chilli sauce
150 g (3) eggs
480 g (3¾ cups) plain flour
20 g (4 teaspoons) baking powder
pinch of salt

FILLING
180 g (¾ cup) cream cheese
   (approximately 15 g (1 tablespoon)
   per muffin)
sesame and pumpkin seeds to sprinkle
   on top

1. Place the milk, oil, grated and parmesan cheeses, spinach, chilli sauce and eggs into a large bowl and stir well.
2. Sieve the flour, baking powder and salt, and add to the above mixture.
3. Using a wooden spoon stir until all ingredients are just combined. Don't overmix.
4. Pour one third of the batter into greased muffin pans or 12 muffin paper cases.
5. Pipe or spoon approximately 15 g (1 tablespoon) of softened cream cheese on top of each muffin.
6. Pour more batter on top of the cream cheese. Total batter weight in each mould is approximately 105 g (3¾ oz).
7. Sprinkle the muffin batter with sesame and pumpkin seeds.
8. Bake in a preheated oven set at 180°C (355°F) for 20–25 minutes.
9. Remove from the tray while still warm.

Maple Muffins (without egg)

The distinctive flavour of maple syrup shines through in these unusual muffins. Look for authentic maple syrup as there are some cheaper imitation maple syrups around that are more sugary and less nutty.

130 g (½ cup + 1½ tablespoons)
   softened butter
200 g (½ cup) granulated sugar
360 g (2½ cups + 3 tablespoons) plain
   flour
20 g (4 teaspoons) baking powder
pinch of salt
140 g (1½ cups) rolled oats
240 g (½ cup + 2 tablespoons) maple
   syrup
210 ml (½ cup + 8 tablespoons) water
chopped walnuts (optional)

ICING
25 g (1½ tablespoons) softened butter
70 g (3½ tablespoons) maple syrup
150 g (1 cup + 3 tablespoons) icing
   sugar
walnuts to garnish

1. Soften the butter in a microwave on low. Do not melt.
2. Add the sugar and beat until lightly creamed.
3. Sieve the flour, baking powder and salt, and add the rolled oats. Then add this to the creamed butter mixture.
4. Mix until the mixture resembles the consistency of coarse breadcrumbs.
5. Combine the maple syrup and water.
6. Add to the dry ingredients and mix until just combined. Don't overmix.
7. Pour batter into greased muffin pans or 12 muffin paper cases. Batter weight for each muffin should be approximately 105 g (3¾ oz). Sprinkle chopped walnuts onto the batter if desired.
8. Bake in a preheated oven set at 180°C (355°F) for 20–25 minutes.
9. Remove from the tray while still warm.
10. Cool before icing.

Maple Icing
1. Mix all ingredients well in a bowl.
2. Add a little milk if the icing is too firm.
3. Spread or pipe icing onto the cooled muffins.
4. Place half a walnut in the middle of the icing before it sets.

PETER GRAY
NADA BAKERY

Peter Gray (below) exemplifies the traditional, hard-working New Zealand baker. Following a humble Johnsonville childhood, he worked long hours to build his very successful bakery, Nada Cakes, and has worked equally hard for the New Zealand Baking Society. Currently president of the society, Peter has taken special interest in all aspects of the industry. He has overseen the formation of a buying group, which has led to wider training opportunities for apprentices, and the ongoing education and development of existing bakers.

He passionately believes that the status of the baker should be raised, and that the industry be proactive in education and research. He leads tours to the large baking shows of Europe and has been extremely innovative in organising training videos and fostering business plans for bakers.

His own bakery in his hometown of Johnsonville has a neverending stream of customers through the door, seeking special breads, pies and the mainstay of his business, specialty cakes. Peter has observed changes in Kiwi tastes in the past 20 years, and continues to develop baked products with less sugar, lower salt and gluten-free content.

Boiled Festive Fruit Cake

Easy to make, this sultana cake is a classic recipe from Nada. The boiling of the fruit ensures that the cake is moist and spicy. The recipe includes decoration of the top for festive occasions, especially Christmas.

1. Place the sultanas and ground ginger in a saucepan and just cover with water. Bring to the boil and simmer on a medium heat for 5 minutes. Drain in a large sieve and leave to cool. Reserve the juices.
2. Place the eggs, sugar, brandy, essence and reserved juice in a mixing bowl fitted with a beater. Beat together for 2 minutes on medium speed.
3. Sieve the flour and baking powder into a bowl. Place the butter in a bowl and melt in the microwave.
4. Add the cooled sultanas, melted butter and dry ingredients to the egg/sugar mixture.
5. Mix on medium speed for 1 minute until a smooth batter is formed, scrape down the sides of the bowl and mix for 20 seconds. Do not overmix.
6. Prepare a 20 cm (8 inch) round cake tin by lining the edges and bottom with greaseproof paper, two-ply thick.
7. Pour the batter into the tin and pat the mixture flat leaving a dip in the middle.
8. Place into a preheated oven (with a pan of water in it) at 140°C (285°F), and bake for 1³/₄ hours or until baked. Place a piece of greaseproof paper over the cake halfway through baking.
9. Leave in the tin to cool.
10. Remove from the tin and remove the greaseproof paper.
11. Brush the top surface of the cake with an apricot glaze. Decorate in a pattern with a variety of nuts, glacé cherries, crystallised fruit, etc.
12. Brush the nuts and glacé fruits with the apricot glaze. This seals the festive topping and gives a nice sheen.

CAKE
315 g (2 cups) sultanas
5 g (1 teaspoon) ground ginger
water to just cover sultanas and ginger
125 g (2¹/₂) eggs
175 g (1 cup + 1 tablespoon) soft brown sugar
5 ml (1 tablespoon) brandy
280 g (2 cups + 4 tablespoons) strong four
5 g (1 teaspoon) baking powder
175 g (³/₄ cup + 1 tablespoon) melted butter (still warm)
2 drops almond essence

DECORATION
apricot glaze (see Mediterranean Orange Cake)
assorted nuts, e.g., pecans, brazil, blanched whole almonds, walnuts, etc.
red and green glacé cherries
crystallised fruits, e.g., pineapple, ginger, etc.

KINGSLEY SULLIVAN

NEW NORCIA BAKERY

Kingsley Sullivan opted for a career change from marketing and advertising and together with his wife Chrissie established a small gourmet food shop in the suburbs of Perth. A chance meeting with the Benedictine monks of New Norcia led to the re-establishment of breadmaking in Australia's only monastic town, about an hour and a half from Perth. A large wood-fired oven, built there 120 years before, was revived as Kingsley, believing that good bread is the basis of all good food, was keen to fire it up again. He supervised the production there of hand-crafted bread using quality ingredients.

The New Norcia Bakery baked for the many visitors to this unique town, and supplied Kingsley's shop in Perth and many other customers with authentic crusty wood-fired sourdough breads that won acclaim from food lovers locally and across Australia. Three years later, having developed a long-life export product, the world famous New Norcia Nut Cake, Kingsley located another wood-fired oven at Mt Hawthorn in Perth and opened a second bakery to produce breads and cakes for city customers.

Kingsley has won many awards for his bread and bakery products and continues to be totally uncompromising on quality and authenticity. Between his bread bakes, New Norcia uses the retained heat of the oven to produce biscuits and slices, pastries and delicious wood-fired oven roasted vegetables.

Hot Cross Buns

Traditionally, produced by all bakeries over Easter, these buns are fragrant and spicy, and the sticky lemon-flavoured glaze makes them a very special holiday treat. Ensure that you soak the fruit ahead of time so that it is moist and plump. Try to serve these buns warm, even if it means gently reheating.

Day one: the fruit preparation

1. Place the sultanas and currants in a bowl, cover with 40°C (105°F) warm water and leave to soak for at least 10 minutes. Drain the fruit into a sieve and add the mixed peel. Sit overnight in the sieve to absorb the moisture.

Day two: the dough

1. Place onto your work surface the flour, salt, sugar, and butter. Make a well and add the yeast, egg and milk.
2. Mix or knead the dough by hand using the technique shown in the All About Bread Section. Continue kneading until the ingredients are well combined – approximately 8 minutes until the dough is three-quarters developed. Place the dough into a bowl and rest for 10 minutes (this allows the yeast to begin to work before the spices are added).
3. Add the spices and continue to knead the dough until it is fully developed, approximately 6–7 minutes (check if you have fully developed the dough by using the stretch test).
4. Add the prepared fruit and gently incorporate into the dough, taking care not to damage the fruit too much – this should take a further 1–1½ minutes.
5. Place the dough into a lightly oiled bowl large enough to allow it to double in bulk. Cover with plastic and leave in a warmish place (23–25°C/73–77°F) until the dough has doubled in size – approximately 1 hour.
6. Gently knock back the dough in the bowl then tip the dough out onto a lightly floured bench and, using a dough scraper, cut the dough into 12 pieces at approximately 95 g (3 oz) each.
7. Mould each piece of dough into a round ball. This is done by cupping your hand over the dough piece on a flourless bench, applying downwards pressure and moving your hand around in a circular motion.
8. Place the buns on a baking tray, lightly greased or lined with baking paper, 12 per tray, 4 across and 3 down. Ensure the buns are not placed too close together – they should be almost individual buns once baked.
9. Final proof in a warm place for approximately 35–40 minutes or until almost doubled in size. Cover with plastic wrap to prevent skinning and chilling of the dough. Use the indentation test to tell when the buns are fully proofed.
10. Using a piping bag fitted with a 3 mm (¼ inch) piping nozzle and filled with the crossing mixture (see recipe), pipe crosses on top of the buns.
11. Place the baking tray into a preheated oven set at 200°C (390°C) and bake for 15–20 minutes. For even browning, turn the oven tray around halfway through baking. The buns should be lightly coloured on the sides and slightly darker on the tops.
12. Remove from the oven and immediately brush each bun all over with the prepared bun glaze (see recipe).
13. Cool on a wire rack.

FRUIT

120 g (³/₄ cup) sultanas

80 g (¹/₂ cup + 2 tablespoons) currants

50 g (¹/₄ cup + 1 tablespoon) candied mixed peel (finely chopped)

DOUGH

500 g (4 cups) strong bakers flour

10 g (2 teaspoons) salt

25 g (2 tablespoons) raw sugar

65 g (¹/₃ packed cup) unsalted butter, softened

10 g (1 tablespoon) dried yeast

50 g (1) egg

250 ml warm milk (30°C/86°F)

¹/₂ teaspoon ground nutmeg

¹/₂ teaspoon ground ginger

¹/₂ teaspoon ground coriander

1 teaspoon ground cloves

1 teaspoon ground cinnamon

Finished Dough Temperature: 26°C (79°F)

CROSSING MIXTURE

150 g (1 cup + 3 tablespoons) soft flour

50 g (¹/₄ cup) vegetable oil (soya or canola oil)

150 ml (¹/₂ cup + 2 tablespoons) water

BUN GLAZE

40 ml (3 tablespoons) water

80 g (¹/₄ cup + 2¹/₂ tablespoons) caster sugar

2 teaspoons lemon zest

The Cross

1. Place the flour and oil in the mixing bowl fitted with a whisk.
2. Add the water and whisk until the mixture is smooth and lump free.
3. Transfer the crossing mixture into a container and cover with a lid to avoid a skin forming. Use when required.

The Glaze

1. Place all the ingredients into a saucepan and bring to the boil.
2. Remove from the heat and cool to ensure the lemon is fully infused into the glaze.
3. Pass through a sieve before use.

Bread Cases with Olive Tapenade
and Roasted Tomato

Bread Cases with Olive Tapenade & Roasted Tomato

A fantastic use of stale bread, these bread cases can be made in whatever size you like. If you make them in muffin pans, as in the recipe, they can be a lunchtime snack or to serve when you have to 'take a plate'. Make them in the tiny cocktail-sized muffin pans and you will have a savoury treat to serve with drinks. The tapenade filling has a real Mediterranean flavour with the combination of anchovies, olives and tuna. Use the best quality ingredients for this mixture.

1. Place all the ingredients except the olive oil into a food processor and blend to a smooth and fine paste.
2. Slowly pour the olive oil through the opening while the food processor is turning. Stop once you have a smooth, well combined mixture.
3. Season with pepper to taste.
4. Store in an airtight container in the refrigerator for up to 2 weeks. This recipe is enough for 2 batches.
5. Using a large sourdough loaf, cut 12 thin slices, then remove the crusts.
6. Using a rolling pin, roll each slice out to approximately 150 mm x 150 mm (6 inches x 6 inches) square.
7. Cut a 110 mm (4½ inch) diameter circle out of each slice. This can be done with a cutter or by using a cardboard template to cut around.
8. Lightly butter one side of the circles and then gently push into a standard muffin pan, buttered-side down.
9. Place into a preheated oven set at 200°C (395°F) and bake for 10–15 minutes or until crisp and golden brown.
10. Cool on a wire rack. (The bread cases can be stored for up to one week in an airtight container.)
11. Wash the tomatoes and cut in half horizontally.
12. Remove the stem.
13. Place each tomato half cut-side up onto a grilling rack or fine wire rack with a baking tray underneath.
14. Brush each tomato half generously with olive oil then sprinkle with 6–7 grains of sea salt and some freshly ground black pepper. Finally add a pinch of sugar to neutralise the acidity.
15. Place into a preheated oven set at 180°C (355°F) and bake for approximately 1 hour until the edges of each tomato start to turn brown.
16. Use while still warm or cool if desired.

Assembly

1. Place 12 prepared bread cases onto a large serving dish or individual plates.
2. Place approximately 20 g of tapenade into each bread case. Top with a roasted tomato and then garnish with a basil leaf, tucking one end of the basil leaf underneath each tomato, ensuring that it sticks out slightly.
3. Top with a dollop of sour cream.
4. If desired, serve as an entrée with a rocket salad dressed with extra virgin olive oil and roasted walnuts.

TAPENADE

200 g (1 cup) Kalamata black olives, pitted and drained
125 g (4½ oz) tuna in oil, drained
20 g (½ cup) fresh basil, washed and dried
4 anchovy fillets, drained
1 garlic clove, crushed
zest of 1 lemon
35 ml (2 tablespoons) lemon juice
ground black pepper, good pinch
35 ml (2½ tablespoons) extra virgin olive oil

BREAD CASES

12 thin slices of sourdough bread
softened butter

ROASTED TOMATOES

6 medium tomatoes
extra virgin olive oil
Maldon sea salt and freshly ground pepper
sugar, approximately 1 teaspoon

GARNISH

12 fresh basil leaves, washed and dried
sour cream

Goats Cheese & Caramelised Onion Tart

BRISÉE PASTRY

120 g (1 cup) plain flour

90 g ($^1/_3$ cup + 1 tablespoon) cold butter

good pinch of salt

25 ml (2 tablespoons) cold water

CARAMELISED ONION

3 tablespoons olive oil

300 g (2$^1/_2$ cups firmly packed) brown onions, cut in half and then chopped

salt and freshly ground pepper to taste

good pinch of grated nutmeg

FILLING

150 g (3) eggs

100 g ($^1/_2$ cup) crème fraîche or fresh cream

$^1/_2$ teaspoon salt

freshly ground black pepper

150 g (1 heaped cup) fresh goats cheese, cut into strips and then slices

3-4 sprigs of thyme

1 slice of tomato

1. Place the flour, butter and salt into a mixing bowl fitted with a dough hook or beater and mix until all the ingredients are rubbed in or resemble breadcrumbs. Do not overmix.
2. Add the water and mix until a dough is formed.
3. Transfer to a bowl. Cover and refrigerate for 30 minutes or overnight.
4. On a lightly floured workbench, roll the pastry out to a sheet about 5 mm ($^1/_4$ inch) thick and big enough to cover a 200 mm (8 inch) round x 25 mm (1 inch) high greased fluted loose-bottomed flan tin.
5. Use the rolling pin to pick the pastry up and lay it over the tin. Gently press the pastry into the tin so that it fills all the contours. Be careful not to stretch the pastry or it will tear or shrink back in the oven. Return it to the fridge for another 30 minutes, or more if the pastry feels soft. Reserve the scraps.
6. Preheat the oven to 200°C (395°F). Line the pastry with tinfoil and fill with dried beans, raw rice or pastry weights.
7. Bake the pastry base for 20–30 minutes until it is almost completely baked. Remove the tinfoil and pastry weights and set aside.
8. In a frying pan, heat the olive oil, then add the onions and cook over a medium heat for a few minutes until the onions begin to soften.
9. Angle a lid on the frying pan to allow the steam to escape, reduce the heat to low and slowly cook the onions for approximately 30–40 minutes, stirring from time to time to prevent the onions from burning or catching on the bottom.
10. Towards the end of cooking remove the lid and add the seasoning and nutmeg, stirring well to combine. The onions should be soft, caramelised and not too brown.
11. Cool before use.

Goats Cheese Filling and Assembly

1. Place the eggs, crème fraîche, salt and pepper into a mixing bowl and whisk by hand until smooth. Set aside until required.
2. Place the caramelised onion into the bottom of the pre-baked pastry flan, ensuring an even coating.
3. Place the sliced goats cheese evenly over the caramelised onion and the tomato slice in the middle.
4. Finally, pour the cream mixture around the slices of cheese and sprinkle with the thyme leaves.
5. Place the tart into a preheated oven set at 200°C (395°F) and bake for 25–30 minutes or until the mixture is just set and firm to the touch and the pastry is golden brown. Do not overbake. Ensure the tart is on the lowest rack in the oven to bake the tart case completely.
6. Cool in the tin.
7. Serve warm or at room temperature.

KAYE AND RICHARD TOLLENAAR
PANDORO PANETTERIA

Authentic Italian artisan breads and cakes are the passion of this talented couple who operate a busy Parnell store and two large wholesale bakeries in Auckland and Wellington. Kaye was inspired to bake handcrafted breads while cooking alongside visiting chef Tony Papas at a Parnell restaurant in the early 90s. As newlyweds, Kaye and Richard Tollenaar opened Pandoro Panetteria and within six weeks the bakery was at maximum capacity, forcing them to open a wholesale plant to cater for the unprecedented demand.

They travel the world in search of new breads, ideas and techniques and have almost traded places in the management of the company. While it is Kaye's expertise that got them up and running, Richard has developed a passion for baking that now sees him at the helm of the production, while Kaye manages the business details. Richard travelled to the Culinary Institute of America to spend a week with some of the USA's top artisan bakers and has a newfound fascination with tasty sourdoughs and artisan-style organic loaves that are popular lines with their customers.

Pandoro breads are sought by foodlovers, top restaurants and even airlines because the best possible ingredients are used, and there is no compromise in production. The shelves are crammed with a large variety of rustic-looking breads and rolls, toothsome European cakes and biscotti which are baked each day. No artificial flavourings, extenders or preservatives are used, which means that their bread is best eaten the day it is bought.

Kaye and Richard are as passionate about their craft as it is possible to be. They manage to juggle their businesses with their family of two young daughters, while continually seeking out potential new products and developing an even greater range of delicious breads and cakes.

Mediterranean Orange Cake

A moist cake that is perfect as a light dessert or with coffee. The orange slush should be made ahead, preferably a day before, and refrigerated. Totally flour and gluten free!

Orange Slush

1. Wash the oranges, then cut off the tops and bottoms and place in a large pot.
2. Fill with enough water to cover half the oranges, and simmer uncovered for 2 hours.
3. Drain off the excess water, place the oranges in a food processor and purée.
4. Place in a bowl and cover; refrigerate overnight.

Cake

1. Prepare a 23 cm (11 inch) round cake tin by greasing and lining the bottom and sides with baking paper. Preheat the oven to 170°C (340°F).
2. Mix the baking powder and ground almonds together to ensure even dispersal of the baking powder within the cake.
3. Mix the eggs and sugar together until just combined. Be careful not beat the eggs as this will aerate the mixture.
4. Add the orange slush and baking powder mixture, then mix gently until well combined.
5. Pour the mixture into the tin and bake for approximately 80 minutes.
6. Cool overnight in the tin, covered loosely with plastic wrap.
7. The next day remove the baking paper and place on a wire cooling rack.
8. Using a pastry brush, brush the entire cake (excluding the bottom) with apricot glaze (see recipe below), ensuring an even, glossy finish.
9. Toast natural flaked almonds on a baking tray, in a oven set at 200°C (395°F), until light amber. Keep a close eye on the almonds as they colour quickly. Cool before use.
10. Gently sprinkle the toasted almonds around the top edge of the cake, creating a ring of toasted almonds approximately 2.5 cm (1 inch) wide.

Apricot Glaze

1. Mix apricot jam and water together in a saucepan.
2. Bring to the boil, but do not boil too long as this will evaporate the water.
3. Once boiled, pass through a sieve to remove any lumps or coarse apricot pulp.
4. Use hot, reheating if necessary in the microwave.

Note: the consistency can be adjusted with water.

SLUSH
4 oranges (medium size)
water

CAKE
15 g (3 teaspoons) baking powder
310 g (3 cups) ground blanched almonds
400 g (8) eggs
310 g (1½ cups + 1 tablespoon) caster sugar
orange slush from above
natural flaked almonds for decoration

GLAZE
300 g (1 cup + 1 tablespoon) apricot jam
150 g (½ cup) water

Citron Tart

A real favourite at Pandoro, this tart is filled with melt-in-the-mouth tangy lemon cream that will appeal to everyone.

PASTRY

170 g (¹/₂ cup + 1¹/₂ tablespoons) salted butter

85 g (¹/₃ cup + 1 tablespoon) sugar

50 g (1) egg

260 g (2 cups + 1 tablespoon) plain flour

FILLING

3 fresh lemons

350 g (7) eggs

300 g (1¹/₂ cups) caster sugar

240 ml (1¹/₄ cups) fresh cream

Sweet Pastry

1. Lightly cream the butter and sugar in a mixing bowl fitted with a beater or beat in a bowl with a wooden spoon.
2. Add the egg and mix until combined.
3. Lastly add the flour and mix to a paste. Only mix until the paste comes clean off the bowl. Be careful not to overmix or the pastry will become too elastic.
4. Transfer to a bowl, cover and refrigerate for 30 minutes or overnight.
5. On a lightly floured workbench roll the pastry out into a sheet about 5 mm (¹/₄ inch) thick, and big enough to cover a 28 cm (11 inch) greased flan or tart tin.
6. Use the rolling pin to pick the pastry up and lay it over the tin. Gently press the pastry into the tin so that it fills all the contours. Be careful not to stretch the pastry or it will tear, or shrink back in the oven, causing the filling to leak or spill. Return it to the fridge for another 30 minutes, or more if the pastry still feels soft. Reserve the scraps for later.
7. Preheat the oven to 150°C (300°F). Line the pastry with tinfoil and fill with dried beans, raw rice or pastry weights.
8. Bake the pastry for 30 minutes. It should be baked but not coloured.
9. Allow the pastry to cool before checking for any cracks or holes. Also make sure the pastry has not shrunk on the sides. Patch any low points, holes or cracks with your leftover pastry.

The Citron Mix

This can be prepared while you wait for the pastry to rest or bake, but you will get better results if the mix is made a day in advance and refrigerated overnight.

1. Wash the lemons in warm water. Zest and squeeze out their juice.
2. Combine the eggs and sugar and mix gently until the sugar is dissolved.
3. Lightly beat the cream with a whisk, then add the egg mixture and stir to combine.
4. Add the juice and zest. Stir only until slightly thickened (1–2 minutes).
5. Transfer the citron mix to a container and rest in the fridge, preferably overnight.
6. Preheat the oven to 170°C (340°F). Pour the citron mix into the patched pastry case.
7. Bake for 40–50 minutes until a nice golden brown and set. Cool before removing from the tin.

Pane Acido (Organic Sourdough Starter)

Pane acido is the Italian sourdough starter (the French refer to this as a leaven), however, they both serve the same purpose and are largely used in the production of sourdough-based breads. The difference between a biga and pane acido is the biga contains a percentage of commercial baker's yeast, whereas the pane acido relies on capturing the wild yeasts in the air. Stoneground organic flour can be replaced with standard flour.

*S*ourdough is both the oldest and newest way of making bread. Thousands of years ago people noticed that their porridge-like mixtures of flour and water started to bubble when left for a few days. Over time they learnt how to control this activity and use it to make bread – a universal staple. Until commercial yeast was discovered in the late 18th century, sourdough was the only way of baking. In the last 20 to 30 years these old methods have been revived and refined, resulting in more consistent products produced on a commercial scale – albeit only by dedicated bakers!

Day one: capturing the wild yeast
Equipment:
1 large bowl
1 piece of muslin cloth

400 g (3 cups + 3 tablespoons) stoneground organic flour
500 ml (2 cups) filtered water (about 25°C/77°F)

Mix the flour and water together to a smooth batter in the bowl. The temperature of the water is important. If it is too cold, the yeasts will lie dormant. If it is too hot, they will die. Cover the bowl with the muslin and place somewhere outside where it will get plenty of fresh air, but no direct sunlight.

Day two
Twenty-four hours later, some bubbles may appear on the surface. This is a good sign. Use a wooden spoon to beat air into the mixture, cover with the muslin and leave for another 24 hours.

Days three and four: breeding the yeasts
If there are no bubbles by day three you should start again. Assuming there is some activity, it's now time to bring the culture inside and increase the concentration of yeasts. To do this, feed the culture with:

200 ml (³/₄ cup + 1¹/₂ tablespoons) filtered water (about 25°C/77°F)
200 g (1¹/₂ cups + 1¹/₂ tablespoons) stoneground organic flour

Pour the water in first and break up the culture in the water. This helps disperse the yeast spores throughout the liquid. Then add the flour and mix well. Don't worry about it being a bit lumpy as that will all go as the yeasts ferment. Cover the bowl with the muslin again and let it stand in a warm place. (In summertime almost anywhere is fine. In winter try on top of the fridge, or somewhere else that gets to about 23–25°C/73–77°F.) Leave the starter about 24 hours before feeding it again with the same quantities of flour and water.

There is a risk from this point on that mould may appear. All this means is that the balance of yeasts and lacto-bacteria needs to be corrected. Scrape off any hairy bits from the starter, transfer to a clean bowl, and give it another feed. This will encourage more yeasts to multiply.

Days five and six

As the yeast spores multiply they start getting through their food a bit quicker, so you need to feed them more regularly. About 12 hours after the last feeding on day four, you should pour off half the culture, and feed the remainder with the same quantities of flour and water as above. Twelve hours later feed the culture again. The next day, pour off half the culture and feed twice, as you did on day five.

Day seven onward: feeding yeasts

Having captured the yeasts, you now need to keep them alive. This is where having a sourdough starter becomes a bit like owning a pet. Yeast needs to eat three times a day if it is to perform well.

Equipment:
starter container with lid (with a small air-hole in the lid)
rubber spatula (or a keen pair of hands)

FIRST FEED

100 g (¹/₂ cup) starter (discard the rest)
50 g (¹/₃ cup) stoneground organic flour
50 ml (4 tablespoons) water (25°C/77°F)

Allow to ferment for about eight hours.

SECOND FEED

200 g (1 cup) starter
100 g (³/₄ cup) stoneground organic flour
100 ml (¹/₃ cup + 3 tablespoons water (25°C/77°F)

Allow to ferment for about eight hours.

THIRD FEED

400 g (2 cups) starter
200 g (1¹/₂ cups + 1¹/₂ tablespoons) stoneground organic flour
200 ml (³/₄ cup + 1¹/₂ tablespoons) water (25°C/77°F)

Allow the starter to ferment for eight hours before starting again with the first feed. After a couple of weeks, if all has gone well, you should have a happy and healthy sourdough starter. From about day 10 it will be strong enough to make bread, and this strength will increase as your starter matures. As your starter ages it will develop consistency, balance and, to a certain extent, immunity from foreign invaders.

The difference between sourdough and regular bread is basically in the yeast. Commercial, or baker's yeast, is a particular strain that is hybridised to ferment quickly and consistently. Sourdoughs utilise wild yeast spores present in grain flours, fruits, vegetables, or in the air. Before making bread the yeasts need to be captured, bred and fed in order to get as many of them as you can into enough of a feeding frenzy to leaven the bread. These yeasts work a lot slower than their high-speed commercial cousins, but the resulting bread has a much better flavour, texture, aroma and keeping qualities. Many books recommend that only advanced or experienced bakers attempt to make sourdough. All you really need, though, is enthusiasm and dedication. Remember, our ancestors used this method in their homes centuries ago, and thought nothing of it.

The Feeding Schedule

The timing of your feeding schedule can be organised to suit your day, and your baking plans. I prefer to make my dough first thing in the morning, so my feeding schedule looks something like this:

8 am	*first feed*	*}*
4 pm	*second feed*	*} the days before baking*
10 pm	*third feed*	*}*
6 am	*make dough*	

However, if you wanted to bake your bread late at night, you might try something like this:

2 pm	*first feed*	*}*
10 pm	*second feed*	*} the days before baking*
7 am	*third feed*	*}*
3 pm	*make dough*	

If you are just maintaining your starter, but not planning to make bread, throwing out nearly a kilogram of starter every day may seem quite wasteful. And it is. Once your starter is bubbling along in a healthy way (at least two weeks after day one), you can store it in the fridge while you are not using it. This should be done just after the first feed, so the yeast has some food for its hibernation. In the fridge most of the yeasts will go dormant, just snoozing until you wake them up. As time goes on, though, these dormant spores will start to die off. So while the starter is in cold storage it will still need the occasional feed. This can be done once a week, with the feeding amounts below (discarding the excess as required), but with slightly warmer water (about 35°C/95°F). This will allow the yeasts to feed for a while before going dormant in the cold again.

A word of warning, though: you will need to get the starter back on three feeds a day at room temperature at least two days before you bake with it again. If you try to make bread with starter straight from the fridge you will fail.

Feeding Amounts

The amount of water and flour fed to the sourdough starter once it is healthy varies from bakery to bakery and person to person. The feeding amounts below are a good guide. The amount of healthy sourdough can vary, but the formula should stay the same.

Total weight of sourdough starter should be fed with $1/2$ its amount of water and $1/2$ its amount of flour.

Example: 500 g (4 cups) healthy (active) sourdough starter
250 g (2 cups) flour
250 ml (1 cup) water
————————————————————
1000 g ($6^{1}/_2$–7 cups) sourdough starter (approximately)

Organic Sourdough Bread

Although a lot of effort, this bread is a very rewarding experience. The loaf is full of flavour, with a great chewy crust. Take time to read the notes on the organic sourdough starter (pane acido).

1. Sieve the flour onto your work surface. Make a well and add the pane acido and water, mixing well as you would for the feeding of the pane acido.
2. Mix or knead the dough by hand using the technique shown in the All About Breads section. Continue kneading until the ingredients are well combined (the dough is not fully developed at this stage).
3. Put the dough into a bowl, and cover with plastic. Leave for 20 minutes to rest. (This rest is called autolysis and it is an extremely useful baking trick. Allowing the dough to rest without salt is achieving a number of desirable ends. First, the flour, without salt, absorbs water faster, resulting in a moister, springier loaf. Second, as the dough rests the fermentation begins. A side-effect of fermentation is gluten development, which is what we are trying to achieve by mixing the dough in the first place. The good thing about the autolysis is that the gluten is developed very gently. Finally, as the dough ferments it relaxes and softens, making it easier to knead.)
4. Add the sea salt.
5. Continue to knead the dough by hand. Every couple of minutes stop and check the gluten development and temperature of the dough. This final kneading should take about 10–15 minutes (check if you have fully developed the dough by using the stretch test).
6. Lightly oil a bowl large enough to allow the dough to double in bulk. Put the dough in the bowl and cover with plastic. Leave in a warmish place (23–25°C/73–77°F) for 3 hours. By this time the dough should be nearly double in size.
7. Gently knock back the dough in the bowl. This will deflate it slightly. Cover again and leave for another 60 minutes, by which time it should have well and truly doubled. After baking a few times you will know the feel of a dough that has fermented fully.
8. Tip the dough out onto a lightly floured bench and using a dough scraper cut the dough in half. Be gentle with the dough; do not aggressively punch it down, or squeeze all the gas from within. Pick each piece up and gently tuck the edges underneath, pulling the surface tight around the mass. Lay the pieces back on the floured bench and cover with a proofing cloth (or tea towel). Give an intermediate proof of 20 minutes. While you wait, lightly dust two round proofing baskets with rye flour.
9. Uncover the dough and shape each piece into a ball by cupping your hands around and moving in a circular motion, pulling the skin tight over the dough. Don't overdo it though, or the skin will rip and this will spoil the appearance of the finished product. The final shape will look like a smooth ball, but with a rough, scrunched-up bottom. This is called the seam. When the shaping is complete, place the breads in the proofing baskets, seam up. Cover the baskets with plastic or a proofing cloth, and leave in a warm, draught-free place, to rise.

1 kg (8 cups) organic white flour
300 g (¹/₂ cup) organic sourdough starter (see pane acido)
600 ml (2¹/₂ cups) filtered water
20 g (4 teaspoons) sea salt

Finished Dough Temperature:
  24°C (75°F)

10. Final proof for approximately 2¹/₂–3 hours. Cover with plastic to prevent skinning and chilling of the dough. Use the indentation test to tell when the dough is three-quarters proofed.

11. The oven should be preheated to 240°C (465°F), with a baking stone in place. Gently tip one loaf out onto a peel lightly dusted with semolina. The seam that was on the top is now on the bottom.

12. Using a razor blade or sharp knife, score the top of the loaf.

13. Just before you load the bread into the oven, spray water into the oven cavity. Close the door quickly so you don't lose any of the steam.

14. With the peel and loaf in one hand, open the oven with the other, and gently 'flick' the loaf off the peel and onto the baking stone. Close the oven door immediately.

15. Repeat this for the second loaf, but be careful not to spray water directly onto the first loaf. Close the door again and wait 2 minutes before opening the door slightly and spraying more water into the oven. Two minutes later, 'steam' the oven again. Resist opening the door for another 20 minutes.

16. Turn the heat down to 220°C (430°F), and check the loaves for even baking. If necessary, turn them around. For the remaining baking time leave the door of the oven slightly ajar to thicken and dry the crust (remember to tap the bottom of the loaf; if it sounds hollow it is baked).

17. After 30–35 minutes the loaves will be ready. Cool on a wire rack.

Pane Italiano

A crusty white loaf that is made by the biga or sponge method. Not to be confused with sourdough, pane Italiano is made with commercial yeast, but unlike most commercial yeasted breads, this method results in a very flavourful bread with great texture that keeps quite well.

Day one (at about 9 pm): the biga

1. In a large bowl dissolve the dried yeast and honey in the warm water, then add the flour and knead roughly together by hand (do not over knead at this stage).
2. Cover with plastic and leave to ferment overnight.

Day two (at about 9 am): the dough

1. Sieve the flour and semolina onto your work surface. Make a well and add the biga or sponge.
2. In a bowl, dissolve the yeast in the water. Add the water and yeast to the well.
3. Mix or knead the dough by hand using the technique shown in the All About Bread section. Continue kneading until the ingredients are well combined (the dough is not fully developed at this stage).
4. Put the dough into a bowl, and cover with plastic. Leave the dough for 20 minutes to rest.
5. Add the sea salt.
6. Continue to knead the dough by hand. Every couple of minutes stop and check the gluten development and temperature of the dough. This final kneading should take about 10–15 minutes (check if you have fully developed the dough by using the stretch test).
7. Lightly oil a bowl large enough to allow the dough to double in bulk. Put the dough in the bowl and cover with plastic. Leave in a warmish place (23–25°C/73–77°F) for 30 minutes. By this time the dough should be nearly double in size.
8. Gently knock back the dough in the bowl. This will deflate it slightly. Cover again and leave for another 30 minutes, then knock it back again. After resting in the bowl for another 30–40 minutes the dough should be fully fermented.
9. Tip the dough out onto a lightly floured bench and using a dough scraper cut the dough in half. Be gentle with the dough; do not aggressively punch it down, or squeeze all the gas from within. Pick each piece up and gently tuck the edges underneath, pulling the surface tight around the mass. Lay the pieces back on the floured bench and cover with a proofing cloth (or tea towel). Give an intermediate proof of 10 minutes. While you wait, lightly dust a proofing cloth or tea towel with rye flour.
10. Uncover the dough and mould each piece into a vienna or baton shape. The surface of the dough should be stretched tightly over the mass, and there should be a neat seam along one side. Lay the first loaf on the proofing cloth, seam up, and then shape the second loaf in the same way. Before laying the second loaf down pleat the cloth so that the loaves cannot touch as they rise.
11. Final proof for approximately 45–60 minutes in a warm, draught-free place. Cover with plastic to prevent skinning and chilling of the dough. Use the indentation test to tell when the dough is three-quarters proofed.

BIGA
1/4 teaspoon dried active yeast
10 g (1 tablespoon) honey
250 ml (1 cup) water
250 g (2 cups) strong four

DOUGH
500 g (4 cups) strong flour
50 g (1/3 cup) semolina
biga or sponge from day before
8 g (1 tablespoon) dried active yeast
250 ml (1 cup) water
10 g (2 teaspoons) sea salt

Finished Dough Temperature:
* 27°C (80°F)*

12. The oven should be preheated to 220°C (430°F), with a baking stone in place. Gently tip one loaf out onto a peel lightly dusted with semolina. The seam that was on the top is now on the bottom.

13. Using a razor blade or sharp knife, slash a single, long, deep 45° cut in the top of the loaf (see diagram).

14. Just before you load the bread into the oven, spray water into the oven cavity. Close the door quickly so you don't lose any of the steam.

15. With the peel and loaf in one hand, open the oven with the other, and gently 'flick' the loaf off the peel and onto the baking stone. Close the oven door immediately.

16. Repeat this for the second loaf, but be careful not to spray water directly onto the first loaf. Close the door again and wait 2 minutes before opening the door slightly and spraying more water into the oven. Two minutes later, 'steam' the oven again. Resist opening the door for another 20 minutes.

17. Turn the heat down to 200°C (395°F), and check the loaves for even baking. If necessary, turn them around. For the remaining time leave the door of the oven slightly ajar to thicken and dry the crust.

18. After 30–35 minutes the loaves will be ready. Cool on a wire rack.

Olive Bread

Almost a meal by itself, this decorative bread has a fragrant, sweet onion jam filling. Choose full-flavoured olives for the best taste, and serve this bread warm.

DOUGH

15 g (2 tablespoons) dried active yeast
275 ml (1 cup + 2 tablespoons) water
500 g (4 cups) strong four
10 g (2 teaspoons) salt
10 g (1 tablespoon) olive oil
70 g (¹/₂ cup) pitted sliced olives

FILLING

150 g (³/₄ cup) onion jam
  (see recipe following)
1 sprig fresh rosemary
rock salt
olive oil

Finished dough temperature:
  28°C (80°F)

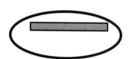

1. In a small bowl dissolve the yeast in the warm water. Let stand for 10 minutes.
2. Sieve the flour onto your work surface and make a well. Add the salt and olive oil.
3. Mix or knead the dough by hand using the technique shown in the All About Bread section. Continue to knead the dough by hand. Every couple of minutes stop and check the gluten development and temperature of the dough. This final kneading should take about 10–15 minutes (check if you have fully developed the dough by using the stretch test).
4. Add the well-drained olives and continue mixing until the olives are evenly distributed.
5. Lightly oil a bowl large enough to allow the dough to double in bulk. Put the dough in the bowl and cover with plastic. Leave in a warmish place (23–25°C/ 73–77°F) to ferment for 30–40 minutes.
6. Gently knock back the dough after 25 minutes, cover with plastic again. By this time the dough should be nearly double in size.
7. Tip the dough out onto the bench, which has been lightly dusted with flour.
8. Using a dough scraper, divide the dough in half.
9. Shape each piece into a ball or cob shape.
10. Place on a lightly floured bench and give an intermediate proof of 10 minutes, covered with plastic.
11. Using a rolling pin, roll each ball out into a long, flat, oval shape.
12. Place 75 g (¹/₄ cup) of onion jam and a few rosemary leaves slightly off centre on the dough (see diagram).
13. Fold the dough over and pinch the edges together.
14. Lightly brush the top with olive oil and smear 35 g (2 tablespoons) of onion jam all over the top surface. Sprinkle with a few more rosemary leaves and some rock salt to finish.
15. Bend slightly to form a crescent shape and pinch along the edge to scallop shape the bread.
16. Place the two dough pieces on a lightly greased baking tray, allowing enough room for the dough to almost double in size.
17. Final proof for 30–40 minutes in a warm, draught-free place. Do not overproof.
18. The oven should be preheated to 220°C (430°F). Place the baking tray into the oven and steam the oven.
19. Bake for 20–25 minutes until golden brown. Avoid excessive oven heat and baking time as this will burn the onion jam.
20. Remove from the oven and brush immediately with olive oil.
21. Cool on a wire rack.

Onion Jam (filling for the olive bread)

Onion jam is great on an antipasto platter or served with a steak. Otherwise it can be used as a filling in olive bread, making this loaf virtually a meal in itself.

1. Heat the oil and add the onion, bayleaves and rosemary.
2. Brown well over a low-medium heat, stirring regularly to prevent sticking.
3. Add the vinegar and stir well to deglaze the pan.
4. Finally, add the sugar and mustard seeds and cook over a low heat, covered, for about 30 minutes.
5. The finished product should be quite thick and a shiny, rich brown. Cool completely before using to fill the olive bread.

Note: the onion jam can be made in advance and kept in an airtight container for 2–3 days in the refrigerator.

2 tablespoons olive oil

3 medium onions, chopped

2 bayleaves

1 sprig fresh rosemary

2 tablespoons red wine vinegar (balsamic is even better)

50 g (¼ cup) brown sugar

1 tablespoon yellow mustard seeds

1 tablespoon black mustard seeds

PATERSON'S CAKES

*P*eter Schneider and his sister Pamela are the third generation involved in this popular cake and coffee shop in Melbourne's Chapel Street. Their Swiss grandfather left an immigrant ship and was hired as a pastry cook when Mrs Paterson opened the business in 1917. Grandfather Schneider bought the business from the original owners in 1952 and his son and grandson rose to the expectations that they too would become patissiers or pastry cooks. Peter oversees the bakery today, having served his apprenticeship there and had several years' experience baking in Zurich and Cologne. Pamela joined him in the business recently to supervise the administration.

Historic photos line the walls of the café where regular customers stop off to order coffee, snacks and enjoy the cakes that have won wide recognition. A variety of baked goods are produced and Paterson's specialty cakes are sought for weddings, birthdays and many other occasions. Fresh cream cakes, iced 'fancies', petits-fours, and small individual cakes are offered.

There's a large loyal customer base and many rely on home deliveries that are done within a 20 kilometre radius. More than 50 staff are employed at Paterson's and it is a tribute to the business that many of them have served there for 20 to 30 years. In 1999 a large fire destroyed much of the bakery and the Schneiders were really touched by the concern that the Melbourne community demonstrated as they rebuilt and modernised this successful business.

Quince & Ricotta Tart

The quince is an old fashioned fruit that has recently enjoyed renewed popularity. The flavour of the quince, combined with the ricotta cheese and cream filling is excellent in this tart. If fresh quinces are not available, substitute a juicy pear for an equally good result.

Sweet Pastry Base

1. Lightly cream the butter and sugar in a mixing bowl fitted with a beater or use a bowl and beat with a wooden spoon.
2. Add the egg and mix until combined.
3. Lastly, add the flour and mix to a paste. Only mix until the paste comes clean off the bowl. Be careful not to overmix or the pastry will become too elastic and doughy.
4. Transfer to a bowl. Cover and refrigerate for 30 minutes or overnight.
5. On a lightly floured workbench roll the pastry out into a sheet about 5 mm (¼ inch) thick, and big enough to comfortably cover an 18 cm (7 inch) greased fluted loose-bottomed tin.
6. Use the rolling pin to pick up the pastry and lay it over the tin. Gently press the pastry into the tin so that it fills all the contours. Be careful not to stretch the pastry or it will tear or shrink back in the oven. Return it to the fridge for another 30 minutes, or more if the pastry still feels soft. Reserve the scraps for later use.
7. Preheat the oven to 150°C (300°F). Line the pastry with tinfoil and fill with dried beans, raw rice or pastry weights.
8. Bake the pastry for 30 minutes. The pastry should be cooked but not coloured.
9. Allow the pastry to cool before checking for any cracks or holes that have opened up. Also make sure the pastry has not shrunk on the sides. Patch any low points, holes or cracks with your leftover pastry.

Poached Quince

1. Place water and sugar in a saucepan and gently bring to the boil. Reduce the heat to a simmer.
2. Place the quince halves in the simmering syrup and poach until tender – do not overcook the quince or it will become too soft. This should take 40–45 minutes.
3. Remove the quince from the syrup and cool, then slice each half into slices 5 mm (¼ inch) thick, cover and keep for later on.

Filling and Assembly

1. Place the ricotta cheese and sugar in a mixing bowl fitted with a beater and mix until smooth.
2. Add the egg, cream and lemon zest, and blend together until smooth. Do not overbeat the mixture at this stage.
3. Pour one-third of the filling into the baked sweet pastry flan case and then evenly place the slices of quince over the filling.
4. Pour the remainder of the filling over the quinces and sprinkle generously with cinnamon sugar (see recipe for Fruit Brioche).

PASTRY

170 g (¾ cup + 1 tablespoon) butter

85 g (¼ cup + 3 tablespoons) caster sugar

50 g (1) egg

260 g (2 cups + 1½ tablespoons) plain flour

POACHED QUINCE

1 quince (cut in half, peel and remove the core)

500 ml (2 cups) water

250 g (1½ cups + 4 tablespoons) sugar

FILLING

125 g (1 cup) ricotta cheese

55 g (¼ cup + ½ tablespoon) caster sugar

50 g (1) egg

60 g (3½ tablespoons) fresh cream

zest of 1 lemon

5. Place directly in a preheated 190°C (375°F) oven and bake for 25–30 minutes or until the filling has set.
6. Cool before removing the flan case.
7. Before serving, dust generously with icing sugar.

Old-fashioned Lemon Tea Cake

Old-fashioned Lemon Tea Cake

This light syrupy cake is moist, delicious, and makes a perfect cake for picnics and summer occasions. It will keep fresh for several days with the high syrup content maintaining the moisture.

Lemon Syrup

1. Place lemon strips, cinnamon stick, water and sugar in a saucepan and gently bring to the boil. Reduce the heat to a simmer.
2. Simmer for 5–10 minutes.
3. Allow the lemon strips to sit in the sugar syrup to infuse with the cinnamon.
4. Cover and reheat when required.

Cake

1. In a mixing bowl fitted with a beater, on medium speed beat the butter, flour and lemon zest until well blended. The colour and consistency of the batter should be light but not too light and fluffy (this should take approximately 3 minutes on medium speed). Be careful not to overbeat the mixture as this will result in a dry cake.
2. Using a wooden spoon mix the eggs, sugar and yoghurt together in a separate bowl and then add to the butter and flour mixture. Beat well but do not beat too much – approximately 1½ minutes on medium speed.
3. Divide the mixture into two empty fruit cans (100 mm/4 inches diameter) lined with baking paper on the bottom and sides. Alternatively, use greased spring-form tins.
4. Place both cakes in a preheated 190°C (375°F) oven and bake for 35–40 minutes or until a cake skewer comes out clean.
5. As soon as the cakes are removed from the oven, pour approximately 75–100ml (⅓ cup) of the hot syrup onto each cake. This must be done immediately otherwise the cakes will become soggy.
6. Once the cakes have cooled, carefully remove from the tins.
7. Glaze the top of each cake, if desired, with a thin layer of apricot glaze (see recipe for Mediterranean Orange Cake, use half the amounts) and immediately place strips of lemon rind on top (from the infused lemon syrup) or dust with icing sugar and place a lemon twist on the top.
8. Tie a wide lemon-coloured ribbon around the cake for extra eye appeal, if desired.

SYRUP
lemon rind strips (made by peeling 1 lemon with a potato peeler)
1 cinnamon stick
250 ml (1 cup) water
150 g (¾ cup) sugar

CAKE BATTER
85 g (⅓ cup + 1 tablespoon) butter (softened)
85 g (½ cup + 2 tablespoons) plain flour
10 g (2 teaspoons) lemon zest
110 g (2) egg
170 g (¾ cup + 2 tablespoons) caster sugar
65 g (⅓ cup) natural yoghurt

PHILLIPPA'S

'*Flavour and texture*' *are of paramount importance to Phillippa Grogan and Andrew O'Hara in their bread baking, so it is no wonder that the revered food commentator Stephanie Alexander regards the breads from Phillippa's as the best in Melbourne. The pair operate a commercial bakery in Richmond which supplies a large base of retail and restaurant customers with great bread and pastries that are made without stabilisers, gluten or additives.*

Phillippa quotes her philosophy from Elizabeth David, 'The true essence of good bread lies in the slow fermentation and unhurried ripening of the dough.'

New Zealand born Phillippa and Andrew met while working at Sally Clarke's well regarded patisserie and bakery in London, and married after Phillippa employed Andrew as a baker in the bakery/café she established in 1994 in Melbourne's Armadale. This bakery, in a charming original shop building, is one of the food hubs on High Street, as an endless stream of customers arrive to purchase bread, pastries and provisions and take time out to sip coffee and relax. A special feature is the selection of cheese, and there's always advice on which of the superb range of Phillippa's breads will complement the cheese.

Corn Bread

Refreshingly different, this corn bread adds cooked polenta to the dough mix to provide a very interesting texture in the final product. Shape the loaf into a boule and try it toasted after a day or two to bring out the flavour. Phillippa suggests it can be brushed with olive oil and sage and served under veal, lamb or chicken.

1. Place the polenta and water into a saucepan and bring to the boil, reduce the heat to low and cook for 2 minutes, stirring all the time. Cover and cool, preferably overnight.

2. Sieve the flour onto your work surface. Make a well and add the polenta, sugar and yeast.

3. Slowly add the milk to the well.

4. Mix or knead the dough by hand using the technique shown in the All About Bread Section. Continue kneading until the ingredients are well combined, 3–4 minutes (the dough is not fully developed at this stage).

5. Put the dough into a bowl, and cover with plastic. Leave the dough for 10 minutes to rest. (This rest is called autolysis and it is an extremely useful baking trick. Allowing the dough to rest without salt is achieving a number of desirable ends. Firstly, the flour, without salt, absorbs water faster, resulting in a moister, springier loaf. Secondly, as the dough rests the fermentation begins. A side-effect of fermentation is gluten development, which is what we are trying to achieve by mixing the dough in the first place. The good thing about the autolysis is that the gluten is developed very gently. Finally, as the dough ferments it relaxes and softens, making it easier to knead).

6. Add the salt.

7. Continue to knead the dough by hand. Every couple of minutes stop and check the gluten development and temperature of the dough (and take a quick breather!). This final kneading should take about 15 minutes (check if you have fully developed the dough by using the stretch test). It is important to ensure that the dough is fully developed.

8. Lightly oil a bowl large enough to allow the dough to double in bulk. Put the dough in the bowl and cover with plastic. Leave in a warmish place (23–25°C/ 73–77°F) for 1½ hours. By this time the dough should be nearly double in size.

9. Gently knock back the dough in the bowl. This will deflate it slightly, but it will develop more strength. Cover again and leave for another 45 minutes by which time the dough should be fully fermented.

10. Tip the dough out onto a lightly floured bench and, using a dough scraper, cut the dough into 2 pieces (approximately 450 g/1 lb each). Be gentle with the dough, do not aggressively punch it down, or squeeze all the gas from within. Pick each piece up and gently tuck the edges underneath, pulling the surface tight around the mass. Lay the pieces back on the floured bench and cover with a proofing cloth (or tea-towel). Give an intermediate proof of 10 minutes. While you wait, lightly dust a proofing cloth or tea-towel with rye flour.

POLENTA

25 g (2½ tablespoons) coarse polenta or cornmeal
175 ml (¾ cup) water (cold)

DOUGH

500 g (4 cups) strong flour
cooked polenta from above
40 g (3 tablespoons) raw sugar
½ teaspoon dried active yeast
210 ml (1 cup, less 1 tablespoon) milk (25°C/77°F)
10 g (2 teaspoons) salt

Finished Dough Temperature:
24-26°C (75–79°F)

11. Uncover the dough and mould each piece of dough into a boule shape. For the boule, shape each piece into a ball by cupping your hands around and moving in a circular motion, pulling the skin tight over the dough. Don't overdo it though, or the skin will rip and this will spoil the appearance of the finished product. The final shape will look like a smooth ball, but with a rough, scrunched-up bottom.

12. Place the boules onto the lightly floured proofing cloth.

13. Final proof for approximately 70–80 minutes in a warm, draft-free place. Cover with plastic to prevent skinning and chilling of the dough. Use the indentation test to tell when the dough is three-quarter-proofed, do not overproof.

14. The oven should be preheated to 230–240°C (445–465°F), with a baking stone in place. Gently place one loaf out onto a peel lightly dusted with semolina. Lightly dust each loaf with flour then, using a razor blade or sharp knife, slash 90° cuts in the top of each boule, four cuts vertically and four cuts horizontally to achieve a trellis pattern.

15. Just before you load the bread into the oven, spray water into the oven cavity with a spray gun. Close the door quickly so you don't lose any of the steam.

16. With the peel and loaf in one hand, open the oven with the other, and gently 'flick' the boule off the peel and onto the baking stone. Repeat with the second boule, being careful not to spray the first loaf with water. Close the oven door again immediately.

17. Bake for 20 minutes, then check the loaves for even baking and turn down the oven to 220°C (430°F). If necessary, turn for even browning. For the remaining time leave the door of the oven slightly ajar to thicken and dry the crust.

18. After approximately 30–35 minutes the loaves will be ready to come out of the oven. Tap the bottom and listen for a hollow sound.

19. Cool on a wire rack.

Smoked Salmon Savoury Tart

This rustic savoury tart is perfect as a luncheon dish, accompanied by a crisp salad. The salmon combines well with the eggs and sour cream for a rich and creamy filling which is counterbalanced by the leeks and spinach. It will be a favourite with everyone.

1. Place the flour, butter and salt into a mixing bowl fitted with a dough hook or beater and mix until all the ingredients are rubbed in or resemble breadcrumbs, do not overmix.
2. Add the water and mix until a dough is formed.
3. Transfer to a bowl. Cover and refrigerate for 30 minutes or overnight.
4. On a lightly floured workbench roll the pastry out to a sheet about 5 mm (1/4 inch) thick and big enough to cover a 250 mm (10 inch) round x 30 mm (1 inch) high greased fluted loose-bottomed flan tin.
5. Use the rolling pin to pick the pastry up and lay it over the tin. Gently press the pastry into the tin so that it fills all the contours. Be careful not to stretch the pastry or it will tear, or shrink back in the oven. Return it to the fridge for another 30 minutes, or more if the pastry feels soft. Reserve the scraps.
6. Preheat the oven to 200°C (390°F). Line the pastry with tinfoil and fill with dried beans, raw rice or pastry weights.
7. Bake the pastry base for 30–40 minutes. Remove the tinfoil and pastry weights.

Savoury custard

1. Place the sour cream into a mixing bowl and whisk by hand until smooth.
2. Add the eggs and whisk in.
3. Finally, pour in the cream and add the salt and pepper, then whisk to combine all the ingredients. Do not over whisk at this stage or the mixture will become too fluffy.

Filling and assembly

1. Toss the smoked salmon, leeks and spinach together in a bowl, then place into the pre-baked pastry case in a rustic fashion.
2. Pour the custard mixture evenly into the filled pre-baked case.
3. Place the tart into a preheated oven set at 175–180°C (355°F) and bake for 20–25 minutes or until the mixture is just set and firm to the touch. Do not overbake.
4. Allow to cool before removing from the flan tin.
5. Serve warm or cold with a refreshing summer salad and chilled glass of wine.

BRISÉE PASTRY
240 g (2 cups) plain flour
180 g (3/4 cup + 2 tablespoons) butter
good pinch of salt
60 ml (3 tablespoons) cold water

SAVOURY CUSTARD MIXTURE
70 g (1/2 cup) sour cream
225 g (41/2) eggs
210 ml (1 cup) cream
good pinch of salt
pepper

FILLING
240 g (1/2 lb) smoked salmon, diced
200 g (2 cups) leeks, cut into rings and lightly cooked in butter then seasoned with salt and good pinch of freshly ground pepper
150 g (1 cup) spinach leaves, quickly blanched in salted water

Vinefruit and Rosemary Bloomer

The fresh rosemary adds a tantalising perfume to this bread. It is crusty with added grain making it very textural and chewy. It's excellent for serving with sharp cheddar or cured meats.

GRAIN MIXTURE

10 g (1 tablespoon) kibbled wheat

10 g (1 tablespoon) kibbled rye

10 g (2 tablespoons) rolled oats

10 g (1 tablespoon) sunflower seeds

10 g (1 tablespoon) linseed

10 g (1 tablespoon) coarse polenta or cornmeal

60 ml ($^1/_4$ cup) hot water

DOUGH

450 g (3$^1/_3$ cups) strong flour

50 g ($^1/_3$ cup) rye flour

Soaked Grain Mixture from above

10 g (2 teaspoons) salt

$^1/_2$ teaspoon dried active yeast

310 ml (1$^1/_3$ cups + 2 tablespoons) water (25°C/77°F)

225 g (1$^1/_4$ cups) sultanas

10 g (2 tablespoons) fresh rosemary leaves (roughly chopped)

Finished Dough Temperature: 26°C (79°F)

STARCH GLAZE

5 g (1 teaspoon) cornflour or corn starch

165 ml ($^1/_2$ cup + 3$^1/_2$ tablespoons) cold water

Day one: soaking the grain

1. Place all the grains in a bowl and mix.
2. Add the hot water. Using a wooden spoon mix together.
3. Cover and soak for 10–12 hours or overnight.

Day two: the dough

1. Place on your work surface the white flour, rye flour, soaked grain and salt. Make a well and add the yeast and water.
2. Mix or knead the dough by hand using the technique shown in the All About Bread Section. Continue kneading until the ingredients are well combined. This final kneading should take about 10–15 minutes (check if you have fully developed the dough by using the stretch test).
3. Add the sultanas and rosemary and gently incorporate into the dough, taking care not to crush the fruit too much.
4. Place the dough into a lightly oiled bowl large enough to allow the dough to double in bulk. Cover with plastic wrap and leave in a warmish place (23–25°C/73–77°F) until the dough has doubled in size – approximately 1$^1/_2$ hours.
5. Gently knock back the dough in the bowl. This will deflate it slightly, but it will develop more strength. Cover again and leave for 30 minutes.
6. Tip the dough out onto a lightly floured bench and, using a dough scraper, cut the dough into 2 pieces. Be gentle with the dough, do not aggressively punch it down, or squeeze all the gas from within. Pick each piece up and gently tuck the edges underneath, pulling the surface tight around the mass. Lay the pieces back on the floured bench and cover with a proofing cloth (or tea-towel). Give an intermediate proof of 10 minutes. While you wait, lightly dust a proofing cloth or tea-towel with rye flour.
7. Uncover and mould the dough pieces into a vienna or baton shape. To achieve this, flatten the dough piece out then tightly roll the dough towards you as you would for a swiss roll. Apply pressure with your hands as you roll – the tighter the roll the better. Lay the first loaf on the proofing cloth, but before laying the second loaf down pleat the cloth so that the loaves cannot touch as they rise.
8. Final proof for approximately 50–60 minutes or until almost doubled in size. Cover with plastic to prevent skinning and chilling of the dough. Use the indentation test to tell when the dough is three-quarter-proofed.
9. The oven should be preheated to 220–230°C (430–445°F), with a baking stone in place. Gently tip one loaf out onto a peel lightly dusted with semolina.
10. Using a razor blade or sharp knife, cut two 45° diagonal cuts in the top of the loaves.
11. Just before you load the bread into the oven, spray water into the oven cavity with a spray bottle. Close the door quickly so you don't lose any of the steam.

12. With the peel and loaf in one hand, open the oven with the other, and gently 'flick' the loaf off the peel and onto the baking stone. Close the oven door again immediately.
13. Repeat this for the second loaf, but be careful not to spray water directly onto the first loaf of bread. Close the door again and wait two minutes before opening the door slightly and spraying more water into the oven. Two minutes later, steam the oven again. Resist opening the door for another 20 minutes. While the bread is baking, make the starch glaze.
14. After the first 20 minutes, turn the heat down to 200°C (390°F), and check the loaves for even baking. If necessary, turn for even browning.
15. After a total of 30–35 minutes the loaves will be ready. As soon as you remove them from the oven immediately brush each loaf with the prepared starch glaze. This will give an excellent shine to your baked loaves.
16. Cool on a wire rack.

Starch Glaze
1. Make a slurry with a little of the water and the cornstarch.
2. Bring the rest of the water to a boil in a saucepan and add the boiled water to the slurry mixture, whisk, then pour back into the saucepan.
3. Place back onto the heat and cook through for 2 minutes on a medium heat.
4. Cool and use later.

QUINTON'S BAKERY

Warwick Quinton claims to have been a food adventurer all his life. He fell into being a baker while working in the organics industry as buyer for a whole foods company. Warwick discovered organic wheat farmers who needed a market for their products, and also a baker who was seeking to source organic flours. While matching these people up, Warwick became fascinated with the art of bread baking and from very humble beginnings of merely experimental baking at home, he grew his hobby into a viable business.

At first he carried a tray of his breads around the markets. But, armed with a New Enterprise government grant, he established a bakery at Clovelly in Sydney, and dealt with a few high profile food industry customers like Simon Johnson. After this start, Warwick moved his family to Leura in the Blue Mountains, and opened a small café/bakery that was a huge hit from the first day. Warwick had someone who would drive the bread down to Sydney customers each morning, and it was not long before he grew out of 'the smallest bakery in the Southern hemisphere'. He opened Quinton's, a commercial bakery in North Katoomba, and maintains a tiny attractive retail café and store in the main street of Leura.

An avid fan of farmers' markets, Warwick still loves to get amongst the customers who truly appreciate the fabulous sourdoughs and organic loaves he bakes. He has developed his skills in patisserie too and makes light-as-air croissants and Danish pastries, which are equally sought after and full of the same good quality ingredients.

Warwick's Seven Day Leaven

This leaven can be used as a basis for many of the sourdough starters called for in this book.

Day one

Mix the flour and water in a large jar with a whisk. Leave out of the fridge until a froth forms on the top 2 cm (1 inch) of the batter. In the early stages, bubbles don't usually form. In winter, you may need to leave the jar in a warm place; in the summer a cooler place. The following recipe makes 1½ kg (15 cups) of starter.

100 g (²⁄₃ cup) organic flour (wholemeal, white or a combination of 80 percent white and 20 percent wholemeal)
500 ml (2 cups) lukewarm water

Days two to six

Feed according to the recipe below at the same time each morning.

	Day two	Day three	Day four	Day five	Day six	Day seven
Flour	100 g (²⁄₃ cup)	–	100 g (²⁄₃ cup)	100 g (²⁄₃ cup)	100 g (²⁄₃ cup)	
Water	100 ml (¹⁄₃ cup + 2 table-spoons	–	100 ml (¹⁄₃ cup + 2 table-spoons	100 ml (¹⁄₃ cup + 2 table-spoons	200 ml (²⁄₃ cup + 2 table-spoons	

Day eight onwards

After the end of the first week, use or pour off up to two-thirds of the leaven (use or pour off more if very active, less if not active. Measure activity visually by the concentration of bubbles in the leaven in the morning before feeding. The more bubbles, the more active it is. The smell of the leaven changes according to its maturity. A young leaven, or one that has been recently fed, will smell like bananas. As it matures, a slight vinegar smell develops. If the vinegar smell is too strong, or if the banana smell is completely masked by the vinegar smell, feed to double the volume of the leaven).

Once this initial cycle has been completed, continue to feed the leaven at a ratio of one part flour to two parts water. The leaven will keep in the fridge without feeding for a week. It will then need whisking, pouring off and feeding, whether you use it or not.

If you have forgotten about your leaven and wish to revive it after an extended period, weigh it and divide the total weight by three. This is the amount of flour to use, and the water follows in the same ratio as above. The leaven will revive in a day. If it smells too vinegary after this time, pour off half again and repeat the procedure. It will then be ready for use. If you are not sure as to whether your leaven will work, use up to 25 percent leaven against flour weight in a normal bread recipe, with 0.5–1 percent yeast maximum. This will simply add a good flavour to your yeasted dough, in the same way a skilled baker would make a sponge or a biga the day before making their dough.

Once the leaven is healthy and strong, feed once every 24 hours and ensure 24 hours has elapsed since its last feed before using it in the recipe, as this will allow for a full-bodied sour flavour.

Sourdough Stick

This dense loaf with a crunchy crust and plenty of texture and flavour is ideal for picnics, for everyday use and for all occasions where bread is called for to accompany a meal. It is very popular with Warwick Quinton's customers.

300 g (2½ cups) organic flour

150 g (¾ cup) Warwick's seven day leaven

6 g (2 teaspoons) olive oil

6 g (1 teaspoon) malt flour

150 g (½ cup) filtered or spring water (cold)

7 g (1 teaspoon) sea salt

Finished Dough Temperature:
  22–24°C (72–75°F)

1. Place the flour, leaven, oil and malt flour onto your work surface. Make a well and add three-quarters of the water.

2. Mix or knead the dough by hand using the technique shown in the All About Bread Section. Continue kneading until the ingredients are well combined (the dough will be firm at this stage). Continue to add the remaining water slowly, kneading well between each addition. Finally add the salt and knead the dough to full development – this should have taken about 10–15 minutes. Check if you have fully developed the dough by using the stretch test – the finished dough should be shiny, well developed and a little on the firm side, as this is not a particularly wet or soft dough.

3. Place the dough in a lightly oiled bowl large enough to allow it to double in bulk. Cover with plastic and leave in a warmish place (23–25°C/73–77°F) for approximately 1½ hours.

4. Place the covered dough in the refrigerator for 10–12 hours.

5. Remove the dough from the refrigerator and tip it out onto a lightly floured bench and, using a dough scraper, cut the dough into 2 pieces (300 g/10 oz each). Be gentle with the dough, do not aggressively punch it down, or squeeze all the gas from within. Gently mould the dough into semi-round shapes, lay the pieces back on the floured bench and cover with a proofing cloth (or tea-towel).

6. Allow the dough to ferment again at room temperature – this should take approximately 3 hours. While you wait, grease a special fluted baguette tray that is approximately 400 mm (15½ inches) in length or a standard flat baking tray can be used.

7. Uncover and mould each dough piece into a French baguette shape. To achieve this flatten the dough piece out then tightly roll the dough towards you as you would for a swiss roll. Apply pressure with your hands as you roll – the tighter the roll the better. Do not expect to roll and stretch the dough to its correct length of 350 mm (13½ inches) straight away. Do this in stages, work on one piece and then allow it to relax while working on the second piece. Take your time!

8. Once you have achieved the correct length, place each dough piece seam-side down on the greased baguette tray.

9. Cover the dough with a sheet of plastic and allow the dough to ferment for 45 minutes in a warm place then place in the refrigerator (while still covered) for 18–24 hours.

10. Remove from the refrigerator and final proof – this can take anywhere from 1–3 hours, depending on the temperature of the room. Use the indentation test to tell when the dough is three-quarters to fully proofed.

11. The oven should be preheated to 230–240°C (445–465°F). Using a razor blade or sharp knife, cut four 45° diagonal cuts in the top of each stick.

12. Just before you load the sticks into the oven, spray water into the oven cavity with a spray bottle. Place the baking tray in the oven. Close the door quickly so

you don't lose any of the steam. Two minutes later, steam the oven again. After 15 minutes, open the door to allow the steam to escape. If necessary, turn for even browning.

13. Bake for 20–25 minutes or until a deep golden brown colour. If the maturation is correctly achieved, light coloured blisters will appear on the crust.

14. Cool on a wire rack.

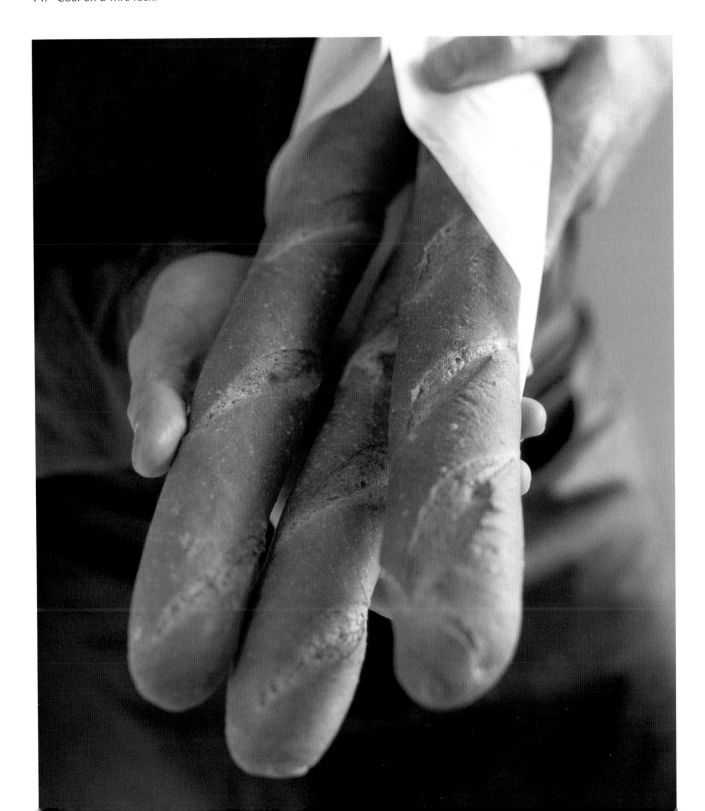

Fig and Nut Round Cob

This bread bursts with figs and nuts. Eat it fresh with a generous spread of nut butter or to accompany cheese. And try it for breakfast as the flavours really come through when it is toasted.

DOUGH

150 g (1¼ cups) organic wholemeal flour

150 g (1¼ cups) organic white flour

3 g (1 teaspoon) dried active yeast

12 g (1 tablespoon) olive oil

5 g (1 teaspoon) malt flour

6 g (1 teaspoon) sea salt

6 g (2 teaspoons) apricot jam

180 ml (¾ cup) filtered or spring water (cold)

50 g (¼ heaped cup) whole natural almonds or cashew nuts (roughly chopped)

50 g (½ cup) dried figs, remove stems and cut into small pieces

Finished Dough Temperature:
  26°C (78°F)

DECORATION

150–200 g (2 cups) sliced/flaked almonds

1 whole fig

GLAZE

70 g (¼ cup) good quality apricot jam

35 ml (2½ tablespoons) water

1. Place the flours, yeast, oil, malt flour, salt and apricot jam onto your work surface. Make a well and add the water.

2. Mix or knead the dough by hand using the technique shown in the All About Bread Section. Continue kneading until the ingredients are well combined (the dough will be firm at this stage). Knead the dough to full development – this should take about 10–15 minutes. Check if you have fully developed the dough by using the stretch test – the finished dough should be shiny, well developed and a little on the firm side, as this is not a particularly wet or soft dough.

3. Lastly add the almonds and figs. Knead into the dough until evenly mixed through – this should only take 1–2 minutes.

4. Place in a lightly oiled bowl large enough to allow the dough to double in bulk. Cover with plastic and leave in a warmish place (23–25°C/73–77°F) for approximately 1½ hours.

5. Tip the dough out onto a lightly floured bench. Be gentle with the dough, do not aggressively punch it down, or squeeze all the gas from within. Gently mould the dough into a semi-round shape, lay back on the floured bench and cover with a proofing cloth (or tea-towel).

6. Allow the dough to fully ferment again – this should take approximately 30–45 minutes. While you wait, line a baking tray with baking paper.

7. Uncover the dough and mould into a cob shape. For the cob, shape the dough piece into a ball by cupping your hands around and moving in a circular motion, pulling the skin tight over the dough. Don't overdo it though, or the skin will rip and this will spoil the appearance of the finished product. The final shape will look like a smooth ball, but with a rough, scrunched-up bottom.

8. Lightly dampen the surface of the moulded cob with water, roll the complete cob in almond flakes. Then firmly push one whole fig into the middle of the cob so that it is submerged 30 mm (1¼ inches) deep into the loaf.

9. Place on the prepared baking tray.

10. Cover with a sheet of plastic and allow the dough to final proof for approximately 1–1½ hours in a warm place. Use the indentation test to tell when the dough is fully proofed.

11. The oven should be preheated to 190°C (375°F). Just before you load the loaf into the oven, spray water into the oven cavity with a spray bottle. Place the baking tray in the oven. Close the door quickly so you don't lose any of the steam. Two minutes later, steam the oven again. Resist opening the door for 15 minutes. Then open the door to allow the steam to escape. If necessary, turn for even browning.

12. Bake for a total time of 20–25 minutes or until a deep golden caramel brown colour.

13. Remove the loaf from the oven and immediately glaze with hot apricot glaze. Return to the oven for 1 minute.
14. Remove again and cool on a wire rack.

Apricot Glaze

1. Mix the apricot jam and water together in a saucepan, bring to boil and then simmer for 1–2 minutes, stirring constantly.
2. Apply while the glaze is still hot.

RACHEL SCOTT BREAD

To become an excellent baker requires a depth of passion and feeling, and Rachel Scott definitely has what it takes. She was always passionate about art, passionate about architecture, and once she discovered great food and in particular great bread, she developed an intense interest, knowing 'that bread is my thing'.

Rachel worked in London at the Pont de la Tour bakery and travelled extensively in Europe, indulging in wonderful foods and quality primary produce before returning to her home in Amberley, in New Zealand's South Island, after seven years away. In 1995 she set up a small bakery on her parents' property where she set about developing and refining her own distinct style of bread, which won instant acclaim from customers.

Rachel is committed to a process that allows the bread to be made in a slow natural rhythm. Her loaves are easily digestible and have a hand produced rustic quality with chewy resilient texture and plenty of complex flavour. Her reputation for excellent bread has spread by word of mouth, and although her winemaking neighbours in the surrounding Waipara wine district are her greatest fans, her breads can be bought in gourmet and specialist food stores around the country.

Walnut and Honey Baton

Organic walnuts are grown commercially in New Zealand's South Island and Rachel uses them in her bread. Be sure to use fresh sweet walnuts as any rancidity will ruin this loaf. It is super for serving with cheese at the end of a meal.

Day one: the ferment

1. In a mixing bowl, mix all the ingredients together to form a dough, then place on the bench and knead until fully developed. This should take 8–10 minutes.
2. Place in a lightly oiled container and cover with plastic wrap and leave overnight to ferment, at least 12–16 hours.

Day two: the dough

1. Sieve the flour and salt onto your work surface. Make a well and add the yeast, oil, honey, fermented dough and water, mixing well until it forms a mass.
2. Mix or knead the dough by hand using the technique shown in the All About Bread Section. Continue kneading until the ingredients are well combined and the dough is fully developed. This final kneading should take approximately 10–15 minutes (check if you have fully developed the dough by using the stretch test).
3. Add the walnuts and gently knead into the dough, ensuring that they are well incorporated. This should take 2–3 minutes.
4. Lightly oil a bowl large enough to allow the dough to almost double in bulk. Put the dough in the bowl and cover with plastic. Leave in a warmish place (23–25°C/73–77°F) for 45 minutes. By this time the dough should have started to gas and nearly doubled in size.
5. Gently knock back the dough in the bowl. This will deflate it slightly, but will develop more strength. Cover again and leave for another 30 minutes – the dough should be fully fermented.
6. Tip the dough out onto a lightly floured bench and, using a dough scraper, cut the dough into 2 pieces. Gently mould the dough piece into a round ball. Do not aggressively punch it down, or squeeze all the gas from within. Pick each piece up and gently tuck the edges underneath, pulling the surface tight around the mass.
7. Uncover the dough and mould each dough piece into a vienna or baton shape. To achieve this flatten the dough piece out then tightly roll the dough towards you as you would for a swiss roll. Apply pressure with your hands as you roll – the tighter the roll the better – taper each end of the moulded loaf. Lay the first loaf on the proofing cloth, but before laying the second loaf down pleat the cloth so that the loaves cannot touch as they rise.
8. Final proof for approximately 1–1½ hours or until almost doubled in size. Cover with plastic to prevent skinning and chilling of the dough. Use the indentation test to tell when the dough is three-quarter-proofed.
9. The oven should be preheated to 230°C (445°F), with a baking stone in place. Gently tip one loaf out onto a peel lightly dusted with semolina. Lightly dust the loaf with flour.

FERMENTED DOUGH
100 g (¾ cup) strong flour
good pinch of salt
¼ teaspoon dried active yeast
60 ml (5 tablespoons) water

DOUGH
500 g (4 cups) strong flour
10 g (2 teaspoons) sea salt
¾ teaspoon dried active yeast
25 g (1½ tablespoons) walnut oil
40 g (2 tablespoons) honey
fermented dough from above
290 ml (1½ cups) water
80 g (¾ cup) walnuts, lightly toasted and roughly chopped

Finished Dough Temperature:
  24–26°C (75–79°F)

10. Using a razor blade or sharp knife, cut one 45° diagonal cut in the top.

11. Just before you load the bread into the oven, spray water into the oven cavity with a spray gun. Close the door quickly so you don't lose any of the steam.

12. With the peel and loaf in one hand, open the oven with the other, and gently 'flick' the loaf off the peel and onto the baking stone. Close the oven door again immediately.

13. Repeat this for the second loaf, but be careful not to spray water directly onto the first loaf of bread. Close the door again and wait two minutes before opening the door slightly and spraying more water into the oven. Two minutes later, steam the oven again. Resist opening the door for another 20 minutes.

14. After the first 20 minutes, turn the heat down to 200°C (390°F), and check the loaves for even baking. If necessary, turn for even browning.

15. After a total of 30–35 minutes the loaves will be ready to come out of the oven. Check for correct baking by tapping the bottom of each loaf – it should sound hollow.

16. Cool on a wire rack.

Normandy Cider Boule

The cider brings a slight hint of nutty sweetness to this unusual bread. It is a dense rough texture and has a crusty finish. Serve it with cheese and fruit paste, or use it for simple sandwiches.

Day one: the ferment

1. In a mixing bowl, mix all the ingredients together to form a dough, place on the bench and knead until fully developed. This should take 8–10 minutes.

2. Place in a lightly oiled container and cover with plastic wrap and leave overnight to ferment, at least 12–16 hours.

Day two: the dough

1. Sieve the flours and salt onto your work surface. Make a well and add the yeast, fermented dough and cider, mixing well until it forms a mass.

2. Mix or knead the dough by hand using the technique shown in the All About Bread Section. Continue kneading until the ingredients are well combined and the dough is fully developed. This final kneading should take approximately 10–15 minutes (check if you have fully developed the dough by using the stretch test).

3. Lightly oil a bowl large enough to allow the dough to almost double in bulk. Put the dough in the bowl and cover with plastic. Leave in a warmish place (23–25°C/73–77°F) for 30 minutes.

4. Gently knock back the dough in the bowl. This will deflate it slightly, but will develop more strength, cover again and leave for another 30 minutes. By this time the dough should have started to gas and nearly doubled in size.

5. Tip the dough out onto a lightly floured bench and, using a dough scraper, cut the dough into 2 pieces. Gently mould the dough piece into a round ball. Do not aggressively punch it down, or squeeze all the gas from within. Pick each piece up and gently tuck the edges underneath, pulling the surface tight around the mass.

6. Lay the pieces back on the floured bench and cover with a proofing cloth (or tea-towel). Give an intermediate proof of 10–15 minutes. While you wait, lightly dust two cane-proofing baskets with flour, or alternatively line two round bowls with clean tea-towels and then dust with flour.

7. Uncover the dough and mould each piece of dough into a boule shape. For the boule, shape each piece into a ball by cupping your hands around and moving in a circular motion, pulling the skin tight over the dough. Don't overdo it though, or the skin will rip and this will spoil the appearance of the finished product. The final shape will look like a smooth ball, but with a rough, scrunched-up bottom.

8. Place the moulded boules smooth-side down in the floured cane proofing basket or prepared bowl.

9. Final proof for approximately 60 minutes in a warm, draft-free place. Cover with plastic to prevent skinning and chilling of the dough. Use the indentation test to tell when the dough is three-quarters proofed.

FERMENTED DOUGH
100 g (³/₄ cup) strong flour
good pinch of salt
¹/₄ teaspoon dried active yeast
60 ml (5 tablespoons) water

DOUGH
200 g (1¹/₂ cups) strong flour
150 g (1¹/₄ cups) wholemeal flour
150 g (¹/₄ cup) rye flour
10 g (2 teaspoons) salt
³/₄ teaspoon dried active yeast
fermented dough from above
315 ml (1¹/₂ cups + 2 tablespoons) full flavoured cider

Finished Dough Temperature:
24–26°C (75–79°F)

10. The oven should be preheated to 230°C (445°F), with a baking stone in place. Gently tip the dough piece out onto a peel lightly dusted with semolina (so that the top of the dough piece has now become the bottom). Using a razor blade or sharp knife, slash 90° cuts in the top of the first boule in a decorative pattern. Repeat for the second loaf.

11. Just before you load the first dough piece into the oven, spray water into the oven cavity with a spray bottle. Close the door quickly so you don't lose any of the steam.

12. With the peel and loaf in one hand, open the oven with the other, and gently 'flick' the boule off the peel and onto the baking stone. Quickly repeat with the second dough piece. Spray the oven again with water, quickly closing the oven door. Wait for a further 2 minutes and spray the oven again, quickly closing the door, resist opening the door.

13. Bake for 30–35 minutes, then check the loaves for even baking. If necessary, turn for even browning. Tap the bottom and listen for a hollow sound.

14. Cool on a wire rack.

REMBRANDT'S PATISSERIE

*R*embrandt's Patisserie in the busy affluent suburb of Remuera in Auckland sparkles with glass cases and mirrors that show off Peter Rood's fine chocolate and patisserie work. Peter is one of a handful of chocolatiers in New Zealand who make handmade European-style chocolates using the finest imported chocolate. His dainty morsels sit beside fine patisserie work that has earned him several gold medals.

Like many bakers, Peter grew up to his trade, and is a fifth generation baker. In fact, there are presently 35 bakers in his family, who have fanned out across the world to ply their craft. Peter opened his patisserie in 1997 and designed the kitchen, with its specialist areas for baking and chocolate work, himself. He is on a planned growth curve with plenty of room for expansion, and is currently training an apprentice.

Easter and Christmas are the busiest times at Rembrandt's for there is a real demand for his superb chocolate eggs, novelties and cakes. This is a true specialty bakery with rows of mouthwatering chocolates, neat patisserie and delectable cakes and gateaux.

Gevulde Koeken

Halfway between a cake and a biscuit, these little almond rounds are found all over Europe. The strong almond flavour makes them a delight to eat, and they will keep for a week or two if stored in an airtight tin.

Biscuit Dough

1. Lightly cream the butter and sugar in a mixing bowl fitted with a beater or beat in a bowl with a wooden spoon (do not over cream the butter and sugar).
2. Add the egg and lemon juice and mix until combined.
3. Lastly add the sieved flour, salt and baking soda, and mix until the paste comes clean off the bowl. Be careful not to overmix or the pastry will become too elastic and doughy.
4. Transfer to a bowl. Cover and refrigerate for 30 minutes or overnight.
5. On a lightly floured workbench roll the pastry out into a sheet about 3–4 mm (¼ inch) thick. Using a 7 cm (3 inch) crinkled round pastry cutter, cut 12 round discs out and place on a lightly greased or baking paper lined baking tray, ensuring that there is enough space between each biscuit – approximately 2 cm (¾ inch).
6. Using the same biscuit dough at the same thickness, cut a further 12 round discs, this time using an 8 cm (3¼ inch) crinkled round pastry cutter. Set aside.
7. Place the almond filling (see recipe below) into a piping bag fitted with a plain piping tube. Pipe a thin layer of almond filling onto the 7 cm (3 inch) discs (approximately 25 g (1 oz) per biscuit).
8. Lay the 8 cm discs on top of the biscuit base and almond filling and gently press the edges down to seal. Using a fork dipped in flour can assist in sealing the edges down by gently applying pressure to the top biscuit dough.
9. Using a pastry brush lightly egg wash (using the two beaten egg yolks) the top of the biscuit dough.
10. Lightly press one whole blanched almond in the centre of each biscuit, and glaze again using the same egg wash.
11. Place directly into a preheated oven set at 205°C (400°F) and bake for 12–14 minutes until golden brown.
12. Allow to cool slightly; remove using a palette knife and place on a wire cooling rack.

Almond Filling

1. Mix all ingredients together to form a spreadable filling. This almond filling should not be firm, because it is to be piped through a piping bag.

Note: this almond filling will keep in the refrigerator for 2 weeks if stored in an airtight container.

DOUGH
150 g (⅓ cup + 2 tablespoons) butter
125 g (¾ cup) caster sugar
25 g (½) egg
5 ml (1 teaspoon) lemon juice
250 g (2 cups) plain flour
good pinch of salt
good pinch of baking soda
2 egg yolks, beaten
12 whole blanched almonds

FILLING
130 g (½ cup) ground almonds
130 g (½ cup + 2 tablespoons) granulated sugar
75 g (1½) eggs (variable)
1–2 drops almond essence (optional)

Almond Filling
Biscuit Dough

Weihnachsstollen

Traditionally baked at Christmas, this fruity, spicy bread is somewhat reminiscent of a brioche dough. The interior reveals a rich almond paste and the stollen has a shelf life of up to two weeks. For a perfect Christmas gift, wrap in cellophane and tie with a Christmas bow and ribbon.

FRUIT PREPARATION

150 g (1 cup) sultanas

95 g (³/₄ cup) currants

40 g (¹/₄ cup) mixed peel

40 g (¹/₄ cup) chopped red cherries

150 g (1³/₄ cups) split or flaked almonds

40 g (¹/₄ cup + 2 tablespoons) chopped walnuts

40 ml (5 tablespoons) rum

100 g (³/₄ cup) strong flour (for later use)

FERMENT

165 g (1¹/₄ cups + 1 tablespoon) strong flour

10 g (2 teaspoons) dried active yeast

135 ml (¹/₂ cup + 1¹/₂ tablespoons) water

Finished Dough Temperature:
   29°C (85°F)

DOUGH

200 g (1¹/₂ cups) strong flour

60 g (¹/₄ cup + ¹/₂ tablespoon) granulated sugar

5 g (1 teaspoon) salt

80 g (¹/₃ cup) softened butter

2–3 drops vanilla essence

2–3 drops lemon essence

5 g (1 teaspoon) nutmeg

5 g (1 teaspoon) mixed spice

50 g (1) egg

icing sugar for dusting

ALMOND PASTE

75 g (²/₃ cup) ground almonds

75 g (¹/₃ cup + 1 tablespoon) granulated sugar

15 g (¹/₄) egg (variable)

1–2 drops almond essence (optional)

Day one: the fruit preparation

1.   Place the sultanas and currants in a mixing bowl. Cover with warm water and soak for 1 hour.

2.   Drain well in a sieve.

3.   Add the mixed peel, red cherries, split almonds, walnuts and rum and mix together.

4.   Cover with plastic wrap and stand for 24 hours.

Day two: the ferment

1.   Mix all the flour, yeast and water to form a well-developed dough. This should take 5–8 minutes kneading by hand.

2.   Lightly oil a bowl and place the developed dough into it. Cover with plastic wrap.

3.   Leave in warm place to ferment for 25 minutes or until double in size.

Day two: the dough

1.   Place all the ingredients in a mixing bowl fitted with a beater.

2.   Cream together for 5–10 minutes on medium speed. Scrape the sides of the bowl down.

3.   Add the ferment and mix in until clear and well combined. Scrape down the sides of the bowl.

4.   Place the 100 g of flour into the soaked fruit and evenly toss the fruit until it is well coated.

5.   Add the fruit to the ferment/batter mixture and mix the dough until clear and well combined. **Note:** the dough will be very tacky and soft, so use plenty of dusting flour to stop the dough from sticking to everything.

6.   Divide the dough in half and gently mould into an oblong shape, 18 cm (7 inches) in length.

7.   Give an intermediate proof of 5–10 minutes with the seam facing upwards. Cover with plastic or a clean tea towel.

8.   Flatten slightly and make an impression with a rolling pin slightly off centre.

9.   Place a rope of almond paste (see recipe opposite) into the impression. Fold the short side over the almond rope and seal the two edges firmly.

10.   Place onto a lightly greased or baking paper lined baking tray.

11.   Proof in a warm place for 20–30 minutes. Do not give excessive proof time as the dough may collapse during the baking cycle.

12.   Place directly into a preheated oven set at 200°C (390°F) for 20–30 minutes.

13.   When baked remove from the oven and place onto a wire rack. Using a pastry brush, brush liberally with melted butter while still hot.

14. Allow to cool slightly and then place in the refrigerator to set the butter. Remove after 30 minutes.
15. Just before serving dust heavily with icing sugar.

Almond Paste

1. Mix all the ingredients together to form a firm paste, more egg can be added if required.
2. Divide the mix in half and roll into a sausage shape.
3. Wrap in plastic wrap until required.

Note: this almond paste will keep in the refrigerator for two weeks if stored in an airtight container.

Oma's Dutch Apple Tart

This is a traditional Dutch recipe for a delicious apple tart. 'Oma' is the Dutch word for grandmother and this tart reflects the love of baking and passion that the Dutch have for family occasions. Serve with whipped cream for a real dessert treat.

PASTRY

300 g (1½ cups) butter

150 g (¾ cup) caster sugar

25 g (½) egg

5 ml (1 teaspoon) lemon juice

450 g (3⅓ cups) plain flour

5 g (1 teaspoon) salt

FILLING

5 Granny Smith apples, peeled, cored and sliced

100 g (½ cup) sultanas

50 g (3 tablespoons) apricot jam

100 g (2 cups) white sponge or cake crumbs

cold custard (see recipe below)

½ tablespoon lemon juice

5 g (1 teaspoon) cinnamon

CUSTARD

75 ml (⅓ cup) milk

10 g (2 teaspoons) sugar

25 ml (2 tablespoons) milk

10 g (2 teaspoons) custard powder

GLAZE

300 g (1 cup + 1 tablespoon) apricot jam

150 g (½ cup) water

Tart Dough

1. Lightly cream the butter and sugar in a mixing bowl fitted with a beater or beat in a bowl with a wooden spoon (do not over cream the butter and sugar).
2. Add the egg and lemon juice and mix until combined.
3. Lastly add the flour and salt, and mix until the paste comes clean off the bowl. Be careful not to overmix or the pastry will become too elastic and doughy.
4. Transfer to a bowl. Cover and refrigerate for 30 minutes or overnight.
5. On a lightly floured workbench roll the pastry out into a sheet about 4 mm (¼ inch) thick, and big enough to cover a 23 cm (9 inch) greased, deep, loose bottomed tart tin.
6. Use the rolling pin to pick the pastry up and lay it over the tin. Gently press the pastry into the tin so that it fills all the contours. Be careful not to stretch the pastry or it will tear, or shrink back in the oven. Return it to the fridge for another 30 minutes, or more if the pastry still feels soft. Reserve the scraps for the trellis top.
7. Add the prepared apple filling (see recipe below), ensuring that the tart is full to 1 cm (½ inch) from the top.
8. On a lightly floured workbench roll out the remaining pastry to approximately 3 mm in thickness and at least 25 cm (10 inches) in width. Repeat if necessary.
9. Cut the dough into 5–10 mm (½ inch) strips and lay each strip over the top of the tart to give an attractive lattice effect. Trim off any excess from the edges.
10. Place directly into a preheated oven set at 195°C (380°C) and bake for 40 minutes or until golden brown.
11. Allow to cool for 45 minutes before removing from the tin. Leave the base on the tart as this makes it easier to handle. Place on a wire cooling rack.
12. Using a pastry brush glaze the lattice top with apricot glaze (see recipe opposite).

Apple Filling

1. Once you have prepared the apples place them in a bowl of cold water with lemon juice in it. This prevents the apples from going brown while you are preparing the rest of the filling. Drain and dry well before combining with the other ingredients.
2. Mix the remaining ingredients with the apples.
3. Place in a bowl until required, but this filling should not be kept for days.

Custard

1. In a saucepan place the first amount of milk and sugar. Stir and bring to the boil.
2. Mix the second amount of milk with the custard powder in a bowl.
3. Add the boiled milk to the custard mix, then pour into the saucepan and return to a medium heat to thicken.
4. Cool before use.

Apricot Glaze

1.   Mix the apricot jam and water together in a saucepan.
2.   Bring to the boil, but do not boil too long as this will evaporate the water.
3.   Once boiled pass through a sieve to remove any lumps or coarse apricot pulp.
4.   Use while hot. You may need to warm the glaze from time to time.

Note: the consistency of the glaze can be adjusted with water.

Baileys Chocolate Truffles

These moreish truffles will be a favourite with young and old. Take care to read the notes on chocolate before starting as chocolate work is a very precise art. Imported chocolate can be purchased from specialty food stores and kitchen shops.

250 g (½ lb) fine milk chocolate
250 g (½ lb) white chocolate
200 ml (1 cup) fresh cream
50 g (4 tablespoons) unsalted butter
25 g (1½ tablespoons) liquid glucose
25 ml (2 tablespoons) Baileys Irish Cream
icing sugar – to powder hands
300 g (1¼ cups) melted tempered milk or white chocolate – for rolling truffles in

1. Break both types of chocolate into small pieces and set aside.
2. Place the fresh cream, butter and glucose in a heavy bottomed saucepan and heat until 90°C (195°C) or just below boiling point.
3. Remove from the heat and add the broken chocolate, stirring until the chocolate has melted.
4. Pour the truffle mix into a baking tin lined with greaseproof paper (the size of the tin is not important, however, a 20 cm (8 inch) square tin is recommended).
5. Leave to set for approximately 8 hours in a cool place (not the refrigerator).
6. Cut into 2 cm (1 inch) squares with a sharp knife. Remove any greaseproof paper at this stage.
7. Using the icing sugar, powder the palms of your hands and roll the squares into even, round balls.
8. Place the balls onto a sheet of greaseproof paper and leave to set for a further 8 hours in a cool place.
9. Using the melted tempered milk or white chocolate (see notes on tempering chocolate below), cover your hands with chocolate and roll the balls in the chocolate, ensuring that you obtain an even, thin covering of chocolate around the balls. Alternatively, place the balls onto a chocolate dipping fork and dip into the melted chocolate. Tap to remove excess chocolate. Repeat until all the truffles have been covered in chocolate.
10. Place the truffles back onto the greaseproof paper to set.
11. Store in a cool dark place. Always serve truffles at room temperature.

Tempering Chocolate Coverture

This is an important procedure if you are using chocolate coverture.

1. Half fill a saucepan with cold water, bring to the boil, turn off the heat and remove the saucepan from the heat.
2. Break the chocolate into small pieces and place in a stainless steel bowl that will fit inside the saucepan of water. Place the bowl of chocolate in the hot water. Never allow any water to come into contact with the chocolate as this will cause the chocolate to thicken.
3. Stir the chocolate with a clean wooden spoon until it has reached 40°C (105°F) and the chocolate has melted. You may need to remove the bowl from the water from time to time to avoid overheating the chocolate.
4. Tip two-thirds of the chocolate onto a marble slab or cold, clean work surface and using two palette knives rotate the chocolate until the chocolate has cooled to 27°C (80°F).
5. Place the cooled chocolate with the other third and mix thoroughly until well combined.

6. Place the bowl back onto the warm water and warm the chocolate coverture to exactly 30°C (85°F). Always use at this temperature and you will achieve a nice sheen on the chocolate once it has set.

Melting Chocolate Compound

You can use chocolate compounds which do not need to be tempered but the quality is inferior. Chocolate compounds only require melting and usually have a higher melting point.

1. Half fill a saucepan with cold water, bring to the boil, turn off the heat and remove the saucepan from the heat.
2. Break the chocolate into small pieces and place in a stainless steel bowl that will fit inside the saucepan of water. Place the bowl of chocolate in the hot water. Never allow any water to come into contact with the chocolate as this will cause the chocolate to thicken.
3. Stir the chocolate with a clean wooden spoon until it has reached 40°C (105°F) and the chocolate has melted. You may need to remove the bowl from the water from time to time to avoid overheating the chocolate.
4. Use chocolate compound at 40°C (105°F) to achieve a nice sheen once the chocolate has set.

KAY THOMPSON & MICHELLE WILSON
ROCKET KITCHEN

*T*he 'ultimate food with attitude' is how Kay Thompson and Michelle Wilson (below) describe the endless stream of food that comes from their busy kitchens. Kay moved from her position as head pastry chef at Pandoro Bakery to bake wholesale cakes in a small private hotel in Remuera. Her technical expertise needed business guidance so Michelle, who has the passion for driving the business, joined her in 1994 and the Rocket Kitchen was born in 1996.

It has been a very creative bakery, with a superb range of cakes and, latterly, savoury items, all baked with top notch ingredients. Aimed at the wholesale market, their primary showcase is a very busy retail operation on Ponsonby Road, Auckland, and a catering kitchen which is attracting discerning clients. The main bakery is in Panmure, where they test bake and develop new lines and bake for their wholesale customers. Rocket Kitchen produces thoroughly modern food, beautifully presented and full of flavour.

Kay and Michelle have an excellent business plan with a goal to expand into frozen lines, to recognise the skills of their employees, and to build on their success.

Wild One (Raspberry Mud Cake)

Very aptly named, the Wild One will become an all-time favourite. The combination of chocolate and raspberries is almost unequalled and the presentation is stunning, too. The chocolate shards require a fair amount of skill, but they are well worth mastering.

1. Place the hot water in a saucepan and bring to the boil.
2. Remove from the heat and add the butter, then set aside until just melted but still hot.
3. Combine the sugar, cocoa powder and chocolate in a mixing bowl fitted with a whisk.
4. Add the hot butter and water to the chocolate mixture. Whisk on medium speed until smooth.
5. Mix in the mashed raspberries and raspberry essence.
6. Add the eggs one at a time while mixing. Scrape down the sides of the mixing bowl.
7. Sieve the flour and add to the mixture. Whisk on low speed until the mixture is smooth.
8. Pour into a 23 cm (9 inch) round loose base cake tin which has the sides and bottom lined with baking paper.
9. Place directly into a preheated oven set at 150°C (300°F) and bake for 1½ hours or until a cake skewer comes out clean.
10. Once cool remove from the cake tin and take off the baking paper. Allow to cool completely on a cooling rack.
11. Place a sheet of baking paper underneath the cooling rack, then slowly pour the ganache (see recipe below) over the cake, starting at the centre and moving towards the outside, ensuring that the cake is completely covered (you may need to use a palette knife).
12. Give the cooling rack a shake to allow the ganache to settle evenly on the cake.
13. Once the ganache has finished dripping, carefully lift the covered cake off the cooling rack and place onto a serving plate.
14. Using a wide-bladed, pointed knife pierce the top of the cake where you want to place the white chocolate shards (see opposite), then carefully insert the shards into the holes.
15. Before the ganache is completely set, place the dark chocolate shards around the outside of the cake.
16. Tie a wide ribbon around the outside of the dark chocolate shards.

Chocolate Ganache
1. Place the cream in a saucepan and bring to the boil.
2. Remove from the heat and add the chocolate buttons.
3. Stir using a wooden spoon until the buttons have melted.
4. Leave to rest in the saucepan to thicken to pouring consistency – this should take approximately 45 minutes.
5. Use as directed.

CAKE
435 ml (2 cups) hot water
325 g (1½ cups + 1½ tablespoons) softened butter
235 g (1 cup + 3 tablespoons) granulated sugar
40 g (½ cup) cocoa powder
400 g (14 oz) dark chocolate pieces
140 g (½ cup) mashed raspberries
5 ml (1 teaspoon) raspberry essence (optional)
175 g (3½) eggs
285 g (2 cups + 4 tablespoons) self rising flour

GANACHE
300 ml (1½ cups) fresh cream
500 g (1 lb 1½ oz) dark chocolate buttons

SHARDS
375 g (13 oz) dark chocolate
375 g (13 oz) white chocolate buttons

Creating the Chocolate Shards

1. Half fill a saucepan with cold water, bring to the boil, and remove the saucepan from the heat.

2. Break the dark and white chocolate buttons into small pieces and place in separate stainless steel bowls that will fit inside the saucepan of water (one bowl at a time). Place the bowl of dark chocolate in the hot water. Never allow any water to come into contact with the chocolate as this will cause the chocolate to thicken.

3. Stir the chocolate with a clean wooden spoon until it has reached 40°C (105°F) and melted. You may need to remove the bowl from the water from time to time to avoid overheating the chocolate.

4. Use chocolate compound at 40°C (105°F) to achieve a nice sheen once the chocolate has set.

5. Repeat for white chocolate.

6. When both chocolates have melted, spread a thin layer (2 mm/$^1/_8$ inch) of each onto a large sheet of baking paper using a palette knife.

7. Allow to nearly set, then using a sharp knife cut into shards. For the dark chocolate shards keep them straight and for the white chocolate shards cut them in a wave-type pattern.

8. Wait until the cut chocolate shards have completely set then carefully remove them from the baking paper by sliding a palette knife under each shard. You may need to have a few extra shards to allow for breakage.

Lime and White Chocolate Cheesecake

In this rich baked cheesecake the lime cuts through the sweetness of the chocolate, giving it a refreshing zing. If you haven't got a springform tin, be sure to bake the cake in a loose bottomed tin. The raspberries make this a spectacular dessert cake.

Base

1. Place the digestive biscuits in a plastic bag and using a rolling pin crush the biscuits until even crumbs are formed.
2. Place the butter in a bowl and melt in a microwave.
3. Mix the melted butter and crushed biscuits together.
4. Press into a 23 cm (9 inch) round loose base springform cake tin which has the sides lined with baking paper. Chill.

Filling

1. Place the cream cheese and sugar in a mixing bowl fitted with a beater. Beat until light and fluffy, scraping down the sides from time to time.
2. Place the cream and chocolate in a bowl and microwave on high for 4 minutes. Stir until the mixture becomes smooth.
3. Mix the lime zest and juice with the cream cheese until smooth.
4. Then add the eggs slowly, mixing until smooth.
5. Lastly add the cream and chocolate and gently mix in until smooth.
6. Remove the crushed biscuit base-lined tin from the refrigerator and pour in the mixture. Smooth out the top if required.
7. Place directly into a preheated oven set at 120°C (250°F) and bake for 1 hour or until the mixture has just set.
8. Remove from the oven and cool.
9. Loosen the springform tin and remove the cheesecake. Carefully remove the baking paper.
10. Decorate with fresh raspberries, mint leaves and zested lemon and lime rind which has been poached in a simple sugar syrup (see recipe below).
11. Serve sliced with a raspberry coulis (see recipe below), fresh raspberries and freshly whipped cream.

Raspberry Coulis

1. Place the raspberries in a saucepan and bring to the boil, stirring to break up.
2. Rub the cooked raspberries through a fine sieve to remove all the seeds.
3. Add enough simple sugar syrup to obtain a smooth, but not too sweet, taste.
4. Finally add a few drops of lemon juice. Cool before serving.

BASE
250 g (9 oz) digestive biscuits (1 packet)
100 g ($^1/_2$ cup) melted butter

FILLING
750 g ($3^3/_4$ cups) cream cheese
220 g (1 cup + 2 tablespoons) caster sugar
150 ml ($^3/_4$ cup) fresh cream
150 g ($^2/_3$ cup) white chocolate
2 limes (zest and juice)
175 g ($3^1/_2$) eggs

COULIS
250 g (2 cups) fresh raspberries
simple sugar syrup (1 part sugar to 1 part water, boil until sugar dissolves)
lemon juice

Orange and Pinenut Polenta Cake

This is quite a chunky cake, with a great flavour that comes from the yoghurt and orange. Choose a fine polenta or cornmeal, and use whichever fruits you like to decorate the top.

CAKE

450 g (2¼ cups) plain yoghurt

130 g (¾ cup) polenta (or coarse cornmeal)

zest of one orange (zested on the large grate of the grater)

200 g (1 cup) softened butter

320 g (1½ cups + 2 tablespoons) caster sugar

½ teaspoon baking soda

300 g (2¼ cups) self rising flour

275 g (5½) eggs

45 g (⅓ cup) roasted pinenuts

75 g (¾ cup) raisins

TOPPING

250 g (1¼ cups) granulated sugar

150 ml (¾ cup) water

1 cinnamon stick

5 star anise

lemon rind strips (made by peeling 1 lemon with a potato peeler)

3 glacé pineapple rings (cut into 8 pieces)

5 dried apricot halves

2 tablespoons crystallised ginger

2 dried figs (cut into quarters)

1. Place the yoghurt, polenta and orange zest in a bowl, mix together and stand for 2 hours, covered.
2. In a mixing bowl fitted with a beater, cream the butter and sugar until light and fluffy.
3. Add the egg over 5 small additions, beating well between each to avoid curdling.
4. Sieve the flour and baking soda and mix in the roasted pinenuts and raisins.
5. Fold the dry ingredient mix into the creamed mixture. Once three-quarters mixed add the yoghurt and continue to mix until the batter is smooth. Do not overmix at this stage.
6. Place into a 20 cm (8 inch) round cake tin lined with baking paper on the bottom and sides.
7. Place directly into a preheated oven set at 150°C (300°F) and bake for 1 hour or until a cake skewer comes out clean.
8. Cool before tipping onto a cooling rack. Remove the baking paper.
9. Decorate the tops with poached glacé fruits (see recipe below).

Poached Glacé Fruits

1. Place the sugar, water, cinnamon stick, star anise and lemon rind in a saucepan, heat on low until all the sugar has dissolved, then bring to the boil.
2. Reduce the heat to allow the sugar syrup to simmer.
3. Add the fruits and poach for 5 minutes.
4. Drain well and arrange on top of the cake.

ANDREW FEARNSIDE AND ANDREW KLEINE

WILD WHEAT

In the first year of business at their wholesale bakery in Auckland, Andrew Fearnside and Andrew Kleine established a reputation for excellent breads and chefs throughout the city were quick to order specialty breads and rolls for their restaurants. The pair had originally worked together as chefs at Papillon, a popular restaurant of the late eighties in Auckland's Herne Bay. They then separately left for overseas and gained experience in a variety of kitchens in London.

Andrew Fearnside worked in the Conran-owned Pont de la Tour bakery in London and a six-month job turned into 18 months as he fell under the spell of the creativity of baking. Back in Auckland he spent three years baking at Pandoro's retail shop in Parnell. Andrew Kleine worked as a pastry chef at such prestigious London restaurants as the Ivy and Caprice, and on his return baked for Antonio Crisci in the kitchen of Non Solo Pizza.

The pair realised that there was a gap in the market for niche baking, and they set out to identify customers' needs and to provide the exact product that they sought. Their sourdoughs are outstanding and they modestly claim that they were lucky to bake exceptional products in their first year. They had imagined they would supplement their breads with patisserie but such is the demand from chefs, retail outlets and other customers that the pair work 15 to 16 hour days to fill orders.

Potato Sourdough

This bread is a very fine example of a sourdough that is moist and flavourful without any notable sourness on the palate. With its crusty exterior and soft open interior it is a super bread that will appeal to everyone. Great with smoked salmon.

Day one: the potato preparation

1. Place the potatoes and salt in a saucepan and cover with water. Bring to the boil and cook until soft.
2. Remove from the heat and drain well.
3. Place in a bowl, cover with plastic wrap and leave overnight at room temperature.
4. Before you require the potatoes, mash them well to produce a smooth texture.

Day two: the dough

1. Sieve the strong flour and milk powder onto your work surface. Make a well and add the sourdough starter, mashed potato, wholemeal flour and water, mixing well until it forms a mass.
2. Mix or knead the dough by hand using the technique shown in the All About Bread Section. Continue kneading until the ingredients are well combined – approximately 5 minutes (the dough is not fully developed at this stage).
3. Put the dough into a bowl, and cover with plastic. Leave the dough for 20 minutes to rest.
4. Add the salt.
5. Continue to knead the dough by hand. Every couple of minutes you should stop and check the gluten development and temperature of the dough. This final kneading should take about 10 to 15 minutes (check if you have fully developed the dough by using the stretch test).
6. Lightly oil a bowl large enough to allow the dough to double in bulk. Put the dough in the bowl and cover with plastic, leave in a warm place for 1¹⁄₂ hours, then place the bowl in the refrigerator for 10–12 hours. By this time the dough should have started to gas and ferment.
7. Tip the dough out onto a lightly floured bench and, using a dough scraper, cut the dough into 2 pieces. Be gentle with the dough, do not aggressively punch it down, or squeeze all the gas from within. Pick each piece up and gently tuck the edges underneath, pulling the surface tight around the mass. Lay the pieces back on the floured bench and cover with a proofing cloth (or tea-towel). Give an intermediate proof of 10 minutes. While you wait, generously dust a proofing cloth or tea-towel with flour, ensuring the cloth or tea-towel is sitting on a baking tray.
8. Uncover the dough and mould each dough piece into a vienna or baton shape. To achieve this flatten the dough piece out then tightly roll the dough towards you as you would for a swiss roll. Apply pressure with your hands as you roll – the tighter the roll the better – taper each end of the moulded loaf. Lay the first loaf on the proofing cloth seam-side down. Before laying the second loaf down

POTATOES
100 g (1 medium) potato, peeled and cut in half – ensure you use the floury type, not the waxy type
¹⁄₄ teaspoon salt
cold water

DOUGH
380 g (3 cups) strong flour
5 g (1 teaspoon) milk powder
125 g (³⁄₄ cup) rye sourdough starter (see Pane Acido recipe, however use rye flour on the last three feeds instead of white flour)
mashed potato from the day before
25 g (3 tablespoons) wholemeal flour
250 ml (1 cup + 2 tablespoons) cold water
8 g (1¹⁄₂ teaspoons) salt

Finished Dough Temperature:
24°C (75°F)

pleat the cloth so that the loaves cannot touch as they rise. Dust the top of the loaves with flour.

9. Loosely cover the dough pieces with plastic to prevent the dough from forming a skin. Place directly in the refrigerator for a further 10–12 hours (overnight).

Day three

1. Remove from the refrigerator and leave at room temperature approximately 5 hours or until almost doubled in size. Ensure the dough pieces are still covered with plastic. Use the indentation test to tell when the dough is three-quarter proofed.

2. The oven should be preheated to 250°C (480°F), with a baking stone in place. Gently tip one loaf out onto a peel lightly dusted with semolina – the dough is very soft at this stage so be careful. Using a sieve lightly dust the dough pieces with flour.

3. Using a razor blade or sharp knife, cut two 45° diagonal cuts in the top.

4. Just before you load the bread into the oven, spray water into the oven cavity with a spray gun. Close the door quickly so you don't lose any of the steam that has been created.

5. With the peel and loaf in one hand, open the oven with the other, and gently 'flick' the loaf off the peel and onto the baking stone. Close the oven door again immediately.

6. Repeat this for the second, but be careful not to spray water directly onto the first loaf of bread. Close the door again and wait two minutes before opening the door slightly and spraying more water into the oven. Two minutes later, steam the oven again. Resist opening the door until required, as this will allow the steam to escape.

7. Bake for 5 minutes, turn the heat down to 220°C (430°F) and bake for 20 minutes. Check the loaves for even baking. If necessary, turn for even browning.

8. Bake for a further 15–20 minutes with the oven door slightly ajar to allow the moisture to escape (this will assist in the development of a crisp crust). Check for correct baking by tapping the bottom of each loaf – it should sound hollow.

9. Cool on a wire rack.

SOURCES

The following shops and establishments stock specialist baking/cooking equipment and ingredients:

AUSTRALIA

ACCOUTREMENT

611 Military Road
Mosman, Sydney
Phone   (02) 9969 1031
Fax   (02) 9969 7929

AMANO

12 Station Street
Cottesloe, Perth
Phone   (08) 9384 0378
Fax   (08) 9385 0379

BLACK PEARL EPICURE

36 Baxter Street
Fortitude Valley, Brisbane 4006
Phone   (07) 3257 2144
Fax   (07) 3257 2044

EXECUTIVE CHEF

132 Merivale Street
South Brisbane
Phone   (07) 3255 2955
Fax   (07) 3844 1688
Website   www.execchef.com

SCULLERYMADE COOKWARE SPECIALIST

1400 High Street
Malvern, Melbourne 3144
Phone   (03) 9509 4003
Fax   (03) 9509 4120

THE VITAL INGREDIENT

206 Clarendon Street
South Melbourne 3205
Phone   (03) 9696 3511
Fax   (03) 9696 5549

NEW ZEALAND

THE EPICUREAN WORKSHOP

6 Morrow Street
Newmarket
Auckland
Phone   (09) 524 0906
Fax   (09) 524 2017
Call Free   0800 555 151
Website   www.epicurean.co.nz

MILLY'S SPECIALTY COOKSHOP

273 Ponsonby Road
Ponsonby
Auckland
Phone   (09) 376 1550
Fax   (09) 360 1520
Call Free   0800 200 123
Fax Free   0800 200 246
Website   www.millys.co.nz

MOORE WILSON

Cnr Tory and College Streets
Wellington
Phone   (04) 384 9906
Fax   (04) 382 9263

BIBLIOGRAPHY

Reinhart, Peter *Crust & Crumb*. California: Ten Speed Press, 1998.

Ortiz, Joe *The Village Baker*. California: Ten Speed Press, 1993.

Field, Carol *The Italian Baker*. New York: Harper and Row, 1985.

Silverton, Nancy *Breads from the La Brea Bakery*. New York: Villard Books, 1996.

Connelly, Paul and Pittam, Malcolm *Practical Bakery*. London: Hodder & Stoughton, 1997.

Gisslen, Wayne *Professional Baking*. New York: John Wiley & Sons, Inc., 1985

Hanneman, L.J. *Patisserie*. London: Heinemann Professional Publishing Ltd, 1980.

Hanneman, L.J. *Bakery: Bread & Fermented Goods*. London: Heinemann Professional Publishing Ltd, 1980.

Roux, Michel and Albert *Patisserie*. London: Macdonald & Co (Publishers) Ltd, 1986.

Galli, Franco *The Il Fornaio Baking Book*. San Francisco: Chronicle Books, 1993.

For more information on New Zealand baking in general visit the New Zealand Baking Society of Employers Inc. website, **www.nzbakers.org.nz**

INDEX OF INGREDIENTS, EQUIPMENT AND BASIC TECHNIQUES

INDEX OF RECIPES